INTERACTION IN INFORMATION SYSTEMS:
A REVIEW OF RESEARCH FROM DOCUMENT RETRIEVAL TO KNOWLEDGE-BASED SYSTEMS

British Library Cataloguing in Publication Data

Belkin, Nicholas J.
   Interaction in information systems : a review of research from
   document retrieval to knowledge-based systems. — (Library and
   information research reports, ISSN 0263-1709; 35)
   1. Electronic data processing — Research
   I. Title   II. Vickery A.   III. British Library   IV. Series
   001.5′072   QA76.27

   ISBN 0-7123-3050-X

INTERACTION IN INFORMATION SYSTEMS:
A REVIEW OF RESEARCH FROM DOCUMENT RETRIEVAL TO KNOWLEDGE-BASED SYSTEMS

NICHOLAS J BELKIN

ALINA VICKERY

Library and Information Research Report 35

Abstract

The report is a review of research connected with the interaction of users with information systems. This includes the interaction of users with skilled intermediaries carrying out searches on their behalf. The report arose from a proposed programme of research to collect and study data from all stages of the search process from the initial expression of an information need to evaluation of the search results. Its main focus is on computerized bibliographic systems but it includes a chapter on question-answering and expert systems.

Library and Information Research Reports are published by the British Library and distributed by Publications Sales Unit, British Library Lending Division, Boston Spa, Wetherby, West Yorkshire LS23 7BQ. In the USA and Canada they are distributed by Longwood Publishing Group Inc, 51 Washington Street, Dover, New Hampshire 03820, USA.

ISBN 0 7123 3050 X
ISSN 0263 1709

Typeset by Type Out, London SW16, 01-677 1788, and printed in Great Britain at the University Press, Cambridge

Contents

List of figures and tables *Page*

Grateful acknowledgement is made to Academic Press for permission
to reproduce Figures 7.1 and 7.2.

1 Introduction

1.1 Information retrieval interaction

In recent years, research in information retrieval (IR) has begun to experience a shift in emphasis from the study of document or text representations and associated search techniques, to study of the users of IR systems, characteristics of the questions or problems which they bring to them, and interactions of users with intermediaries and with other aspects of the IR mechanism, including evaluation of its success. In general, one might characterize this shift as an explicit recognition of the integrated nature of the information system as a whole, and especially of the importance of understanding and dealing with the entire information search process, even if emphasis in any study is to be placed on only one aspect. This shift has lagged behind, but is roughly coincident with, the increasing importance of interactive systems for IR, which we feel have been a major impetus to this wider understanding of IR.

This book is a review of research relevant to the study, understanding and improvement of what we have called 'IR interaction', or, more generally, interaction in information systems. By the term 'IR interaction' we mean to characterize the following situation.

> A person, with some problem or goal, decides that her or his state of knowledge is insufficient or inadequate for accomplishing the goal. She or he therefore has recourse to some knowledge resource or database, which may be able to provide information appropriate to the person's situation. The person's access to this resource is through some intermediary mechanism whose role is to help the user to obtain an appropriate response.

This is the very general information system context; with our term we aim to stress especially the interactive nature of the situation, and to emphasize that it is an integrated, dynamic whole aimed at retrieving information for helping the user to manage a problem. In addition, since we are mainly concerned with document or reference retrieval systems, we will tend to concentrate on work which has focussed directly on such systems, when it is available, and to interpret work on other types of systems in terms of its potential relevance to this main interest.

This situation can be characterized as a sequence of activities or states, as in Figure 1.1, a representation of the search process. This general

1

representation, from recognition of problem to, at least, satisfaction of 'need', we consider as the macrosystem for IR searching. Each step in the macrosystem can be considered as a system in its own right, a microsystem. We see the microsystems and the macrosystem of Figure 1.1 as being essentially dynamic systems, and believe that strong interactions exist among the microsystems. Thus, although it may be possible to study a microsystem on its own, this representation of the search process seems to indicate that at the very least it is appropriate to study the microsystems within the context of the macrosystem.

In Figure 1.1, the left column represents the stages of the search process, and the right column the general type of data which is appropriate for study of the particular stage, or microsystem. Notice that we do not attempt to account for every eventuality in this representation, but rather only to indicate a general framework, in which our partitioning is only one possibility, and the data mentioned are only examples of what could be investigated. The point of representing the search process or IR interaction in this way is to begin to indicate what kinds of research might be relevant to its understanding.

1.2 Aims and background of this review

The intention of this book is to review research relevant to the study and understanding of the IR interaction, as indicated in Figure 1.1, in whatever disciplines it may occur. From Figure 1.1, it is obvious that many disciplines are potentially relevant to this problem, and that indeed there will be many in which work has been done explicitly on aspects of it. For instance, logic and linguistics have studied questions, sociolinguistics and philosophy have studied conversation, artificial intelligence (AI) and ergonomics have investigated human-computer interaction, and so on. What we wish to do here is to provide an overview of what theories and methods have been used to study the various categories of data relevant to the microsystems of the IR interaction, to give some indication of how they might be relevant to or used in the study of IR interaction as a whole, and, finally, to give a summary of the state of theory and research in IR interaction overall. This book should, therefore, serve as an introduction to the IR interaction situation; as an indication of what disciplines might bear upon its study; and as a state of the art review of research in the problem area. We hope, therefore, that it will be of use to students beginning the study of information system interaction, primarily in the information science context, but also in the cognate disciplines, as well as to researchers in the field, and information system professionals.

Microsystem	Data type
1 User has problem or goal which needs to be resolved	User's situation User's goals
2 User's information behaviour arises from recognition of inadequate (anomalous) state of knowledge	User's characteristics User's knowledge
3 User seeks to resolve anomaly by searching for information in system	User's problem statement User's expectations
4 Presearch interaction (with e.g. human or computer intermediary)	User's question Intermediary's characteristics User/intermediary interaction
5 Presearch formulation of search strategy and query	User/intermediary interaction System's characteristics User's query
6 Searching activity	User/intermediary/ system interaction
7 Initial evaluation of results	User/intermediary assessment
8 Reformulation of problem/question/ query/strategy	User/intermediary interaction
9 Evaluation of retrieved text(s) (if any) by user	User satisfaction
10 Use of information	User satisfaction User's goals

Figure 1.1 Representation of the search process in IR interaction

These were not the original intentions of this work. When we began this review, it was to be a relatively brief preliminary literature review to a further project — to construct a large database of records of IR interactions, which could be used by many different researchers, from different points of view, and studying different microsystems. In the course of the review, however, it became apparent that there was just too much research being done for us to be able to comply with the formal constraints with which we had begun. It also became clear that our model for organizing the review also gave us a structure that could lead to something more generally useful than our original intention. And finally, we became progressively less enamoured of the database idea, as the costs and problems of such a resource became more evident. We hope that this rather mixed genesis for our review will not affect its potential usefulness for the general academic, professional and research community concerned with information system interaction, for whom we think the end product most appropriate.

1.3 Structure and presentation

This work as a whole is in two volumes: review and bibliography. The reason for this arrangement is that the volume of literature relevant to our topics was so great, that we could not hope to review it all adequately. We therefore decided to base our review proper on a selection of the literature, at the same time attempting to collect a more comprehensive list of references which would be representative of the broad spectrum of research in at least some of the areas covered. Volume 1, this review, is self-contained, in that all items directly cited and discussed are included in the list of references for that volume. Volume 2, the bibliography, is published separately as British Library Research and Development Report 5846 (microfiche). We feel that even without the context of the review it is nevertheless of substantial value, especially with its KWOC index to the over 1,500 references which we have identified as relevant to research on IR interaction.

The text of the review is structured more or less according to the sequence of microsystems in Figure 1.1. Thus, Chapter 2 deals with investigations into why people might engage in information-seeking behaviour. Some factors which are discussed are: the user's cognitive state; the user's goals and beliefs; human needs relevant to the situation; social and other systems of which the user is a part; problems facing the user; and the uses to which the information will be put. Chapter 3 concentrates on the analysis of questions, and in particular on question types; question processes; the logic of questions; questions in problem-solving; and questions in IR. Chapter 4 deals with the study of human conversation, concentrating on linguistic aspects of the topic. Interaction between people, primarily in the context of the search negotiation, is outlined in Chapter 5. Chapter 6 deals with techniques and theories of human-computer interaction, surveying interface designs and design criteria for interactive systems. Chapter 7, on search strategy, covers the interactive mechanism of searching in the computer systems itself, human search techniques, and those areas of cognitive studies and AI which may contribute to further development of IR. Chapter 8 is a review of question-answering and expert systems, and Chapter 9 discusses methods and theories employed in the wide field of evaluation of IR interaction.

For logistic reasons, and for reasons of personal preference and expertise, we organized our work in this review by each of us being primarily responsible for separate chapters. Thus, A V has written Chapters 3, 5, 7 and 8, and N J B Chapters 2, 4, 6 and 9; This has inevitably led to some disparity in style among the chapters and to some overlap; we hope that this approach has allowed us to devote sufficient energy to each of the topics so that the level of detail will compensate for this problem.

We would like to take this opportunity to thank the British Library Research and Development Department for its support of this work, and especially for its patience with us as the work became progressively grander, and later. We would also like to express our debt to our colleagues, R N Oddy and Tefko Saracevic, whose interest in the study of interaction and of questions instigated this work, and to Nathalie Mitev, who did much of the searching, locating and organizing which was necessary for this project.

2 Precursors to information-seeking behaviour: 'information need'

2.1 Introduction

This study as a whole reviews theories and methods proposed for the investigation of the various elements of the information search process, in whatever disciplinary context they may be found. An obvious place to begin such a review is to consider what has been said about the circumstances which lead people to engage in information-seeking behaviour. This topic is relevant for several reasons: first, because the enquirer's question to the mechanism will be based on them; second, because much of the intermediary's (or mechanism's) interaction with the enquirer will be devoted to understanding the question in terms of these circumstances; and, finally, because evaluation of the success or failure of the IR interaction will be made on the basis of these circumstances. So it seems reasonable to suppose that an understanding of the reasons for the enquirer's having engaged in information-seeking behaviour will be necessary for any general study of IR interaction.

The problem of what it is that leads people to look for information is difficult for a number of reasons. One is that investigators normally have access to the situation only after the enquirer has actually begun looking for information; that is, has already decided that he or she 'needs' information. This means that other alternatives have been considered and rejected (at least subconsciously), and that the situation, for the enquirer, has been constrained by this choice. This is a practical or empirical problem, which is serious but in principle soluble. Less tractable is the issue of why people look for information at all; that is, what is the status of the concept or category of *information need*? By this, we mean to ask, is there such a thing as a need for information, which can be considered on its own, as a human need, or is information-seeking behaviour contingent upon the desire to satisfy other types of needs, or to resolve situations which are not in themselves information-dependent?

What we have seen in our review of the literature is a progression of sorts, over time, from an idea of undifferentiated information need, to a more complex concept of information being necessary to solve problems, to a perhaps even more complex concept of human needs leading to situations whose resolution may be helped by the acquisition of information. This view has been gained primarily by reference to other reviews of the field of 'user studies', which often include comments upon the concept of information need, although rarely treating this topic alone. There are a good number of such reviews, many of them of high quality. Those that have been most important to us, in terms of discussion of the problem of the circumstances which lead to information behaviour, are (in chronological order): Paisley (1968); Allen (1969); Brittain (1970); King and Palmour (1974); Martyn (1974); Windel (1980); Plagemann and Windel (1981). These publications have offered, as well as reviews of the literature of user studies, some organizing framework for, and/or comments upon, the concept of information need, and are thus valuable in and of themselves in the development of the 'information need' concept, as well as being reviews of the literature in which this concept may have been discussed. The concept of information need has also been investigated in a context rather different from that of library and information science; that is, communication research. Although there has been some connection between this work and library and information science, notably in public library research, by and large the communication studies work has had little effect on information system user studies, and *vice versa*. We have attempted to incorporate some results of this work in our review. A final potential source for this chapter is the discipline of human needs studies, which is largely, although not exclusively, based on psychology. We attempt, in this chapter, to draw on work from all these fields, in order to get an interdisciplinary perspective on the general topic of factors which lead to information-seeking behaviour.

2.2 Information need

The traditional view of the issue of information-seeking behaviour in library and information science is that of undifferentiated information *need*. That is, it is assumed that the 'user' arrives at the 'information system' with a 'need' for some (more or less) well-specified information. The system's task is then taken to be to provide the information which the user has asked for, in just this sense. Information need is thus seen as a category of need in itself, the underlying assumption being that human beings 'need' information in much the same sense that they need food or shelter. We say underlying, because the assumption is almost never explicitly stated, but is evident in that only the need itself, and its specification, are considered important. This is the sense of information need which underlies the 'user studies' of the 1950s and 1960s, and a substantial proportion of those of the early 1970s.

These user studies were primarily concerned with the issue of improving the performance of existing information systems in two general ways. The first was to evaluate the extent to which the services of the system were being used by the population they were supposed to serve. This type of study, the 'information use' study, still enjoys wide popularity, and seems at least to be a reasonable monitoring tool. But it does not address the question of whether the services which the system provides are actually the services which the potential users 'need'. The second type of study, the 'user needs' study, was intended to address this question.

User needs, in this context, were usually defined by asking users what sorts of information services they would like, in addition to those being offered. The assumption here, of course, is that the users know what it is that they need, and are indeed even able to specify the appropriate delivery mechanism. Thus, this type of information need study is perhaps more appropriately called a 'potential information services' study, and was primarily concerned with identifying such character- istics of groups of people. Both these general approaches equated information use with use of information services.

The question of information need as a specific category arose in these studies only within the context of requests put to the system. These requests were seen as demands upon the system, which the services provided by the system should be able to satisfy, within the terms of the request itself. There is, of course, a substantial early literature on the well-known reluctance of users to say what it is that they want or need, but it is almost always assumed in this literature that, in principle, they *know* what they need or want, in terms of information, and that, once they are persuaded to specify this need, the system's task is accomplished by providing that information (or at least a reference to a potentially relevant source). Information *use*, outside the context of use of information services, is, with important exceptions discussed later, hardly considered at all, for expressed information need is taken as a sufficient category in itself.

Thus, in this early literature, one sees hardly any reference to the use to which the information gained via the system is eventually put, or, more generally, the function which it performs in the user's life. The general outlook is that these factors, even when noticed at all, are outside the purview of the information system; that is, what the person does with the information is that person's own business. This attitude or standpoint has its roots in liberal philosophies of librarianship, and is, in a sense, admirable, in that it stems from the idea of unrestricted access to information and the principle of anti-censorship. Unfortun-

8

ately, when applied strictly, and as an underlying theme to the idea of information behaviour, it made it difficult to consider the concept of information need outside the context of the information system.

Of course, we rather overstate the case when we say that no-one ever considered the impact of information on the life of the user. In the next section we discuss some of the significant exceptions, and there was always a school of thought which had education or 'improvement' of the user or public as a major justification for library services. Nevertheless, until well into the 1970s, these viewpoints played relatively minor roles in most empirical studies of information behaviour. Even in the context of industrial and research organizations, where the justification for information services was often made on the pragmatic grounds of promoting innovation and reducing superfluous work, the need for information was rarely related to that environment, which was usually seen as external to the information service.

What are the consequences of this view of information need? All the reviews cited above have made the point that user studies in this early period have been largely ineffectual in developing any generalizable system design principles. They all cite a number of reasons for this characteristic, some of which are not relevant to our discussion here, such as methodological inadequacies and incommensurability of situation-specific studies, but others of which derive directly from the concept of information need which underlies the studies. A recurring theme is that, until the 1970s, there are almost no studies of *why* people engage in information-seeking behaviour, and only a few which even attempt to relate the concepts of information need and information use. This situation is taken, by most of the authors and by us, to lead directly to the two consequences stated above, since there is no framework within which information behaviour in the various circumstances of the studies can be interpreted, nor is there any context in terms of which the user's activities can be explained that is more general than the information system of which he or she is a part. Therefore, we conclude that an undifferentiated concept of information need as a given is insufficient for the purpose of research on information behaviour. Since the mid to late 1960s, however, some alternatives to this conceptualization have been proposed, which may offer some guidance for effective research on IR interaction.

2.3 The user as a member of social systems

One major alternative approach to the question of information behaviour is the idea of considering the 'user' of information systems as a part of a complex of other systems, all of which affect that person's

9

information behaviour. The first major proponents of this view in library and information science were Paisley (1968) and Allen (1969). Allen, indeed, managed to operationalize a part of this view within large-scale empirical studies of information behaviour (e.g. Allen, 1966).

The major intellectual influence on this school of thought was the work of Talcott Parsons who proposed a system-theoretic sociology. The point of this school is that human behaviour is influenced by a large number of social systems; that is, that a human being is a member of a number of different systems, and that consideration of human behaviour in any one of these systems cannot be divorced from the influence of the other systems upon that behaviour. Thus, information behaviour (and perhaps information need) is dependent not only upon the information system of which the user is a part, but also upon the user's cultural system, political system, membership group, reference group, invisible college, formal organization, working team, legal/economic system, and, of course, her or his own psychological system (Paisley, 1968). Thus, in order to understand information behaviour, it is necessary to interpret it not only within the context of the information system, but also within the context of all the other social systems of which the user is a part. This is an interesting, even compelling ground plan, which has subsequently been modified and/or elaborated by many people, including Allen (1969) and Bock (1971). This point of view is certainly an advance on the undifferentiated information need concept, for it is an explicit formulation of the thesis that there are circumstances external to the information 'need' presented to the information system which led to the person's information-seeking behaviour. In empirical terms, however, it has not led to many great advances, beyond considering the effect of the work place on a person's information behaviour.

Allen's studies, especially Allen (1966), are good examples of this approach in action. This work is based on the concept that information is sought and used for a particular purpose, and information behaviour is interpreted and evaluated in terms of how successful it is in helping the person to accomplish that purpose; the purpose in this case is to solve a particular technical or scientific problem. Thus, even before beginning the empirical study, Allen has assumed that there is a reason for the users' information behaviour: solving a problem. He then goes on, as do most other people who have followed the same theoretical structure, to examine the actual information behaviour of a group of people in terms of how it affected problem solution, but generally without asking what, in the problem, led to the information-seeking behaviour itself. It is assumed that the fact that a problem is set perforce means that the persons will engage in information-seeking behaviour of one sort or another, the research problem being then to see what patterns of information behaviour lead to successful problem solution. Thus, although this approach represents an advance on the undifferentiated information need concept, it does not offer a great deal, other than a theoretical framework which demonstrates that external factors are important, in terms of understanding why someone engages in information-seeking behaviour. We now know that we must recognize that the information will be used for some purpose, and that we must consider this use, but beyond this realization we obtain little guidance. It is of interest to note, also, that there is precious little empirical work which even attempts to take into account, in interpreting information behaviour, any of the systems beyond the work place and invisible college.

This approach to information behaviour was then followed, within information science, by one which put more stress on the *use* to which information would be put. Good examples of this point of view are the reviews by King and Palmour (1974) and Martyn (1974). This work extends, in at least some ways, the social systems approach, by being much more explicit about the role of the use of information in investigating information behaviour. Their model is one of communication, and their point of view is admirably summed up in the following quotations.

The ultimate value of any information communication system should be thought of in terms of the uses that are made of the information and the subsequent impact of the information on the users' scientific and technical activities. The way in which information affects the conduct of these activities is probably the most important function of a system. ... Although this is the critical function of user behaviour, it is rarely measured, let alone even considered in many user studies. (King and Palmour, 1974.)

Our proper preoccupation is, after all, with the interrelationship of people and ideas. (Martyn, 1974.)

A key innovation in the King and Palmour review is a revision of a communication model of the scientific information system due originally to Lin and Garvey (1972), which connects the previous beginning and end points of the system, information needs and information uses respectively, with one another by a component called 'user behaviour', which interacts with each. This new component represents the centre of study for King and Palmour, and it is important for us in that it demonstrates that 'needs' and 'uses' are interdependent, influencing one another in a complex way which determines many aspects of the user's behaviour. This approach thus indicates that the purposes for which information is sought (its uses) need to be identified in order to evaluate and understand information behaviour.

Warner *et al* (1973) and Dervin *et al* (1976, 1977) have also considered the uses of information to be the significant variable, but in their work use has been investigated especially beyond the context of the information system. They have been primarily concerned with the information behaviour of urban residents, and have established a paradigm in which information systems *per se* were not significant at all, but only identification of factors which led or did not lead to information behaviour, including, importantly, consideration of every-day problems. They then identified how these problems were resolved, and finally looked to see what use of information systems and resources resulted. Thus, this work began from a non-institutional setting, considering first everyday problems of people, then discovering how these problems were resolved, and only finally investigating the explicit use and source of information in their resolution. Use of information is here seen as *potential* use, in terms of problems for which information may be relevant, rather than the actual use of some information in some context, at least initially.

The success of this type of communication research in identifying at least some characteristics affecting information behaviour leads us to conclude that it has some special relevance for the study of IR interaction. Its focus on everyday life apart from information institutions is important, for it tells us that information behaviour derives from concrete problems from all aspects of life, most of which have little or nothing to do with information systems. They also demonstrate that a significant component for analysis of information behaviour is what is going to be done with the information (indeed, Dervin stresses that information as a concept is only interpretable in terms of its use); that is, the question of problem resolution. In this sense, it is similar to the approaches from library and information science discussed in this section, but it departs radically from them in that its first research priority is identifying categories of problems which lead to information behaviour, whereas the other work typically begins with an established problem type. The implication of this research for the study of information interaction seems to be that, in order to interpret and evaluate the success of information behaviour, it is necessary to find out something about the nature of the user's situation which led her or him to engage in that behaviour. Of course, they make the point that there are many situations which one might reasonably suppose would result in information behaviour, but which do not, and also many forms of information behaviour which are not traditionally recognized as such (that is, which are not institutionally based). From the point of view of this study, this is an interesting result, but one which little can be done about, since the interactions with which we are concerned are primarily limited to the institutional setting.

So, overall, these sociologically based studies have demonstrated that there are factors outside the information system which need to be studied in order to interpret information behaviour, and that these factors have to do with the person's social situation, with the problems which the person faces, and with the uses to which the person intends to put any information gained through the information-seeking behaviour. We thus begin to see strong arguments against the sufficiency of the concept of undifferentiated information need, with some suggestions as to how these theoretical arguments can be put into practice.

2.4 Cognitive/individual views of information behaviour

At about the same time as these sociological approaches toward information behaviour were gaining prominence, a somewhat different, psychological approach to information behaviour was being introduced in library and information science. The first inklings of this seem to be in the work of Taylor (1968), whose research on question negotiation in reference interviews can now be seen as seminal in a number of fields of information science. From our point of view in this chapter, Taylor's work is significant in that it postulated that the user engaged in information behaviour only after having recognized some internal, inexpressible but significant psychological state which eventually led to an expressed request or command for information. Thus, what the system got from the user was something which somehow depended upon the user's internal 'visceral' need, but which was so 'compromised' by various translations (internal and external), that extensive negotiation with the librarian was necessary in order even to come close to that original need. Indeed, Taylor's thesis was that the first-stage need was in principle inexpressible. Although this framework postulated information need at some level as an absolute category, it did so in a context outside that of the usual interpretation of the information system, and indeed outside the contexts of use of services or of information, implying rather some internal, psychological basis for this category.

Although Taylor did not explicitly investigate this level of need, his work marked a departure from considering social or other external aspects of information behaviour to looking at the internal, cognitive justifications for information behaviour. Since his initial work, others have developed this viewpoint, and looked explicitly at this type of precursor to information behaviour. Below, we discuss two examples of this trend.

Wersig (1971, 1979), from a rather different starting point from that of Taylor, developed this idea further with the concept of the 'problematic situation'. Wersig was concerned with developing a sound theoretical structure for information science, within a communication paradigm and based upon an operational concept of information. In order to accomplish this goal, he discussed *why* people engaged in information-seeking behaviour, and what information-seeking behaviour meant in such a context, within the framework of individual communication situations. Thus, he began with the idea of effect of information. His concept of information, based upon the idea of reduction of uncertainty, need not concern us here; the means by which he proposed to make it operational are, however, of direct significance to us. This was done by constructing a cybernetic model of human behaviour (based on Stachowiak, 1965), in which a person's actions are based upon internal models of, *inter alia,* her or his environment, knowledge, situation and goals, the last two expressed primarily as events with associated certainty values.

A 'problematic situation', then, is the situation of an individual whose internal models of environment, knowledge, actions, etc. are insufficient for that individual to attain the appropriate goals; that is, whose model of the situation is such that it may require input from external resources in order to attain the degrees of certainty required for reasonable action. Thus, Wersig suggests an explicit account of the precursors to information-seeking behaviour, based on models of the knowledge, beliefs, goals, environment and situation of the individual, stating that information-seeking behaviour occurs when these internal models are insufficient for the individual to act in accordance, especially, with his or her goals. Thus, the problematic situation, an explicitly internal, psychological and individual concept, obviously related to Taylor's 'visceral need', provides an account of information behaviour which relates the individual's knowledge and goals to the effect and use of information.

Belkin (1977, 1980), concerned with developing an information concept which could be used as the basis for design of IR systems, suggested a concept similar to the 'visceral need' and 'problematic situation': the 'anomalous state of knowledge' (ASK). This was an attempt to provide a framework in which the reasons for a person's seeking information could be explicitly represented and used for IR. Belkin's major thesis was that people, when they do engage in information-seeking behaviour, do so because their states of knowledge concerning some particular situation or topic are recognized by them as somehow being 'insufficient' or 'inadequate' for that situation; that is, that there are *anomalies* (gaps, uncertainties, lack of relations or concepts, etc.) in their conceptual state of knowledge concerning the topic, which they perceive as needing to be resolved in order to achieve their goals. Since what was needed to resolve these anomalies would not, in principle, be specifiable by the person, Belkin's major concern became means for representing ASKs, and using them as the basis for IR, rather than queries put to a system, which are specifications of what is needed to resolve them. This was done by asking people to talk about the problems that they were concerned with, what they intended to do and what they perceived as problems or difficulties, and using these narrative texts as the basis for a representation of the user's conceptual state of knowledge of the topic, which would isolate or indicate its anomalous characteristics. The texts were analysed by a basically statistical algorithm, which was then displayed as a network of concepts (word stems) and relations, with strength of association between concepts being indicated by distance from one another, as well as by arcs. Some typical anomalous characteristics were nodes with a large number of weakly associated concepts, and clusters of strongly associated concepts which were distant from or unconnected to other such clusters. The intention in this research was to use these structural characteristics to define search strategies for texts which would respond directly to them (Belkin, Oddy and Brooks, 1982).

The work of Belkin and his colleagues attempts to relate the reasons for information-seeking behaviour directly to strategies for reacting to those reasons, via the mediating conceptual state of knowledge. These reasons were seen as explicitly cognitive and related directly to goals or problems confronting the individual. The major thrust of this work is the attempt explicitly and usefully to represent these precursors to information-seeking behaviour, and in this sense the work is unique. The question of use or effect of information is implicit in their research, in that the strategies for response are based on the idea of effective change in state of knowledge, in terms of the goals of the individual.

We see, then, in this cognitively oriented work on information behaviour, a progression of sorts from Taylor's concept of the 'visceral need' as an unanalysable, unrepresentable and independent category, to the attempts by Wersig to interpret cognitive reasons for information behaviour in terms of the individual's goals and problems and by Belkin actually to represent such cognitive structures. It is perhaps significant that for both Wersig and Belkin, the problem which the user faced was the determinative factor in producing the psychological state which leads to information behaviour. Thus, this explicitly cognitive, internal and individual-based view of information behaviour becomes directly related to problems which the user is attempting to resolve. This may, perhaps, relate this work to that of, e.g., Dervin, and certainly to the rather wider view of problem management discussed in the next section.

A major implication of this cognitively oriented work is that there is really no such thing as an information *need* in the abstract, but rather circumstances which lead to information behaviour. This idea has been forcefully proposed from a rather less cognitively oriented starting point by Wilson (1981) who argues that there are, indeed, categories of human needs, which relate to a systems schema rather similar to Paisley's (1968), but that a need for information is not one of them. Rather, information need (if the term is to be used at all) is a secondary category, in that information is typically required only as a *means* toward satisfying some more basic, primary need (such as role reassurance). Wilson's approach is of special interest because he demonstrates that there are many categories of need for which information might be appropriate, which are not cognitive or strictly problem-oriented (at least in the sense of decision-making type of problems). The need to maintain status, which might be satisfied by knowing more about some topic than one's subordinates, is a typical example.

Wilson's proposals are obviously related to the more general topic of human needs research, for they imply that, in order to understand information behaviour, one must understand (or at least take account of) the needs which led to it. Thus, one would like to have a catalogue, or, better, a classification of human needs, which one could then investigate in various situations, in order to see how they might result in information behaviour, and whether different needs might require different types of information responses for their successful resolution. Unfortunately, our rather cursory look at the literature of this field, (e.g. Lederer, 1980), seems to indicate that, although some categories of human need are well established (e.g. food, shelter), others, which are perhaps more relevant to the issue of information behaviour (e.g. reassurance, identity, work) are highly problematic, indeed controversial. That is, it is not clear whether they are primary or secondary needs (in the sense above), nor are their implications in regard to further behaviour clear. Thus, it seems that, at this point in time at least, human needs research offers relatively little guidance for the study of information behaviour, in the sense suggested by Wilson. Its two most direct contributions appear to be: first, corroboration of Wilson's thesis that need for information is not a category of primary human need; and, second, that the human needs which might give rise to information behaviour form a highly complex, interactive group of cognitive, affective, social and political factors which need to be studied both in terms of their individual characteristics and of their interactions, especially in the natural setting.

The lessons of the suggestions from both cognitive and need-oriented research in information behaviour for the study of information inter-action seem plain. First, it now appears to be quite certain that an undifferentiated concept of information need as a human need is insufficient for the study of information behaviour. Second, the study of individual information behaviour will require some sort of represent-ation of the psychological state of the user, in terms not just of knowledge (or lack of it) but also beliefs, aspirations, goals, and so on. Third, the problems, in a wide sense, which people face affect their psychological states, just as their internal states can be interpreted as problematic in themselves. And, finally, in order fully to represent and understand these states, needs, related to systems of which the person is a part, must be considered.

These points all tend to reinforce the results of the sociological approach to information behaviour, and to extend them, insofar as they take account of the user's internal state as it interacts with external factors (the user's model of the world), offer some ideas about the analysis and representation of such states, and some suggestions as to how such states relate to information and information behaviour. This trend has been most recently explicated in the idea of problem management.

2.5 Information, behaviour and problem management

In a publication called, significantly, *Information and behaviour* (Wersig *et al*, 1982), it has been suggested that the best way to view information behaviour is as an aspect of human behaviour in general, in particular in terms of information as supportive of problem management. The argument is complex, but in essence it suggests that information relates to human behaviour explicitly within the realm of problem management, where problem is taken in a very wide sense, approximately that of contradiction between aspirations (goals, needs) and resources or capabilities, at levels ranging from internal individual states to social conflict. In this sense, much of human behaviour is

17

concerned with problem management, and the role of information is to be supportive in the appropriate management of such problems.

This view has been used by the authors of the report to provide a framework in which to integrate information behaviour and the role of information provision across the entire spectrum of levels, from individual to political. These ideas have been implemented within the information system context by a functional analysis of the general information provision mechanism, which has been used to suggest a distributed architecture for such systems (Belkin, Seeger and Wersig, 1983). The functions which the group identified included, importantly for the study of information interaction, identification of the user's state in the problem treatment process; the type of user and the user's intentions; the type of problem the user faces; and description of the problem in terms of topic, structure and environment. These functions are seen as essential, and interdependent, in being able to respond reasonably to the user. Existence and necessity of these functions were confirmed through analysis of real-life information interactions (Belkin and Windel, 1984), and through a simulation of such a system using humans for each function (Belkin, Hennings and Seeger, 1984).

From our point of view, this work is significant in that it appears to demonstrate that the integrative framework of problem treatment is useful, and that, therefore, the underlying idea of information behaviour might be appropriate for the study of information interaction. Since it also demonstrates that the problem- and intention-related functions occur and are important in real information interactions (including online interviews), it suggests that such data must be available for a full description of information interaction. It also seems that this underlying idea, drawing as it does on cognitive, affective and social system influences, tends to integrate within one model the results of the different approaches to information behaviour discussed above. That they can be integrated argues, in our view, for the appropriateness of these results, and especially, for the importance of taking them into account in the study of IR interaction.

2.6 Summary and conclusions

First, it is clear that information 'need' is too simplistic a concept to be tenable in serious research in information interaction. Rather, the results of research in information behaviour since the mid 1960s have consistently argued (in some cases demonstrated) that information behaviour is related to some problem situation in the relationship between the user and the user's world or model of the world. Furthermore, this research has suggested that significant factors in

18

understanding information behaviour will include the user's cognitive state, the user's goals and beliefs, the human needs relevant to the situation, the social and other systems of which the user is a part, the problems which the user faces, and the uses to which the information will be put. Unfortunately, most of the research offers little guidance for what sorts of information about these factors ought to be collected and analysed, nor for methods for doing so.

Perhaps the major implication of this research for the study of information interaction is that data will be necessary which will provide at least minimal information on problems, goals, state of knowledge, intended uses and general standing in the social system of the user. Some of the work, especially Belkin, Oddy and Brooks (1982), Dervin (1976, 1977, 1980) and Wilson and Streatfield (e.g. 1977), offers some concrete suggestions for categories of data and their collection, but much more research needs to be done before this issue is clarified.

3 Question analysis

3.1 Introduction

In English as well as in all other languages, there are a number of diverse linguistic phenomena which can be brought together under the general heading of questions. All questions have in common the fact that a person utters them with the intention of inducing a linguistic response from the hearer. 'The grammar of questions (interrogative sentences) is explored by linguists. In addition to grammar there is also the logic of questions. Humans have developed systems for asking valid questions, giving answers, correcting invalid questions, and the like. We should expect that these systems will be made explicit and refined' (Harrah, 1973). Discussions of questions and the study of their logic date at least from Aristotle, but a serious and thorough study of questions originated within the last 20 years.

Questioning is an activity which can have various kinds of linguistic expression and can even be fulfilled without using any language. Questions cannot be distinguished from other locutions on the basis of grammatical criteria alone. For example they can be classified according to the subject that they cover, such as medical, architectural, archaeological, or according to their meaning, in which the requested person has to express a judgment, perhaps a moral one, or to make a decision, e.g. on a course of action. From the point of view of their meaning, questions have sometimes been considered as more fundamental than statements. For example, R G Collingwood (1939) claimed that to understand a statement which is an answer to a question, it is necessary to know the question. David Harrah and N D Belnap classified questions as 'true' and 'false' according to their presuppositions. Questions, then, stand in relation to certain statements as answers and to certain as presuppositions. The linguistic, psychological (cognitive psychology and developmental psychology), and social aspects of question-asking in verbal discourse are discussed by Kearsley in his review on questions and question-asking (Kearsley, 1976). Kearsley draws together research from the above-mentioned fields of knowledge. His paper consists of five sections. The first section reviews linguistic knowledge regarding the forms of questions and leads up to a taxonomy of question forms. The next three sections summarize data on question-asking in verbal discourse by children and adults. The last section suggests areas of future research, attempting to place the study of question-asking in the mainstream of research in cognitive psychology, psycholinguistics and AI.

3.2 Question forms

This section considers the different types of questions on the basis of structural characteristics or form. Question form is based mostly on syntactic criteria while question function is based on semantic characteristics. It is sometimes not possible to draw an exact correspondence between question form and syntax, and question function and semantics, owing to certain difficulties in distinguishing the syntactic from the semantic features of questions. Kearsley presents a taxonomy of question forms:

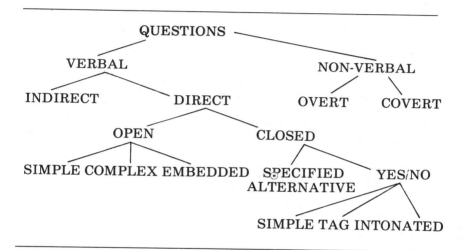

Figure 3.1   A taxonomy of question forms

A distinction is made between verbal and non-verbal questions. Non-verbal questions may be overt or covert; overt questions are gestures, facial expressions, etc., and covert questions are internally directed questions, which we ask and answer ourselves. Verbal questions divide into direct and indirect questions. Direct questions are indicated in a verbal discourse by certain intonation patterns. They can be subdivided into two major groups, open questions and closed questions. Open questions usually have a falling intonation and are formed by the use of wh-constructions (Who? Why? Whom? etc.) and hence are also called wh-questions. Closed questions have a rising intonation pattern and two subgroups: specified-alternative questions which provide alternatives acceptable in answer (e.g.: Do you want coffee, tea, or hot chocolate?), and yes/no questions which require confirmation or denial of the assertion of the question. The yes/no questions have three subforms: simple yes/no questions formed by an auxiliary verb, e.g.: Is that dog dead?; tag-type yes/no questions which involve inverted auxiliaries at the end of the question, e.g.: That dog is dead, isn't it?; and intonated declaratives, created by raised intonation, e.g.: That dog is dead?

This taxonomy of question forms may be useful for a descriptive analysis. However, a purely structural analysis neglects important functional differences between question types and should be supplemented by analysis of question functions.

3.3 Question functions

The functional intent of each question is to elicit a verbal response from the addressee. But questions may serve over and above the elicitation of verbal responses. Figure 3.2 gives a classification of question functions developed by Kearsley. While the categories of the structural hierarchy of question forms presented in Figure 3.1 are exclusive of each other, the categories in Figure 3.2 are not. This means that a particular question may have two or more of the purposes simultaneously.

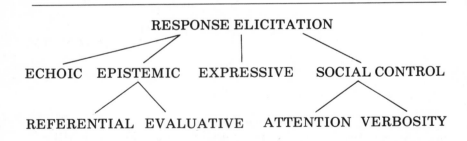

Figure 3.2 A taxonomy of question functions

Maybe a short explanation of terms will be useful here. Echoic questions are those which ask for the repetition of an utterance, or confirmation that the utterance has been interpreted as intended, e.g.: What? Pardon? or sometimes a paraphrase of an original question (as distinguished from a literal repetition).

Epistemic questions serve the purpose of acquiring information. These have been subdivided in Figure 3.2 into referential and evaluative questions. Referential questions intend to elicit contextual information about situations, events, actions, purposes, relationships and properties. Evaluative questions are asked not for information but to establish the addressee's knowledge of the answer. They are used in various test situations (examinations, interviews, discussions). All epistemic questions can make use of the wh form of questions. Table 3.1 lists each kind of wh-word and modes of wh-questions compiled by Kearsley from Robinson and Rackstraw (1972).

An expressive question is independent of its information content. Particular syntactic patterns (and their intonation patterns) convey different expressive statements. Disjunctive form of a yes/no question usually expresses impatience, e.g. Are you coming or aren't you?, while the question: Aren't you coming? uses the negative form of the auxiliary verb and indicates surprise or disbelief. The question: You are coming, aren't you? with the tag form of the auxiliary expresses a state of doubt.

The social control purposes of questions are also independent of the information content. The metamessage of attention questions is 'listen to me' or 'think about this'. Questions with the characteristic of verbosity are asked only for the sake of politeness or to sustain conversation. These questions are asked in situations in which the interrogator may not be interested in an answer and may even not listen to one. They may serve to avoid embarrassing silences in conversations and maintain interaction between speakers.

The functional categories are not exclusive of each other; some questions are intended to serve only one purpose, others two or more purposes. The use of different purposes depends on various situational variables (e.g. number of people involved in the discourse, degree of intimacy, peer pressures) and on individual variables (age, education, sex, etc.). Kearsley suggests a need for systematic observation on how these individual and situational variables influence the use of questions.

There are simple and complex relationships between formal and functional categories. The two taxonomic schemes which classify questions on the basis of either form or function are useful for organising and suggesting empirical studies about questions and may be helpful for discussing question processes.

Table 3.1   Modes of wh-questions

Wh-Question	Mode	Example	Answer
Who (Whom)	1. Unique person specification 2. Role specification	Who is that?	John The man
Where	1. Geographical/common knowledge 2. Relative location 3. Shared private knowledge	Where does he live?	In Canada Two miles south Near your parents
When	1. Objective date 2. Relative time 3. Personal age 4. Shared private knowledge	When were you there?	In 1975 Last year When I was 20 Before we met
How	1. Evaluative (ascriptive) 2. Evaluative (nonascriptive) 3. Explanation of procedure 4. Justification	How are you? How many are there? How do you play this? How come I always lose?	

Why	1. Justification of reasons 2. Puzzlement 3. Information 4. Explanation	Why did you do that? Why doesn't it work? Why do you ask? Why did it happen?
What	1. Specification of objects, activity, definition	What kind is that? What do you mean? What is he doing?
Which	1. Specification of objects, attributes	Which book do you want?
Whose	1. Specification of ownership	Whose car is it?

Esther Horne (1980) also suggests that questions can perform several functions. These functions are performed during any communicative act of the individual. Occurring together or singly these functions can be described as communication interfaces between individuals, information transfer agents, linguistic probes, or as data acquisition facilitators. These functions are examined by utilizing two models. One model exhibits the cognitive behaviour of the individual and the other is an enquiry process model which illustrates how questioning behaviour relates to the psychological model. The psychological model is adapted by Horne from the NEED-DRIVE-GOAL relationship as expressed by Fuller who states that need can generate a drive state. In the model presented by Horne, the particular cues arise from the condition of the knowledge state of the subject and are cognitive and not physiological. The interactions between the cues and the drive maintain the stability of organization towards a goal.

The goal of the drive state, enquiry, is to change or maintain the knowledge state by means of data transformation. The enquiry process model is composed of two sub-systems: questioning and answering. The questioning sub-system exists cognitively, the answering sub-system is identified as a data system which is intrinsic to the event world. When the goal in the psychological model is met, the loop is closed. The knowledge state has gone from state [1] to state [2]. Sometimes the closing of the loop may initiate further enquiry and the process becomes iterative. Formulation of questions is the crucial factor in the cycle.

Horne analysed by means of categorization two data collections consisting of questions. She utilized concepts from Robinson and Rackshaw, Belnap and Steel, and White. Four patterns of question formulation emerged from the linguistic analysis: open mode (use of interrogatives); closed mode (use of binary logic and/or Boolean logic); modal (use of modal verbs); and conditional (use of 'if' conditional clause). The two data collections gave similar results, suggesting that there exists a consistent behaviour pattern in question formulation.

3.4 Question processes

Three levels of question process are here discussed: question selection, question formation and question-asking. Question selection is concerned with the cognitive problem of how a particular question arises; question formation investigates the generative rules by which a question, once decided upon, is formulated linguistically; and question-asking studies how a question is part of and maintains conversation and discourse. All three processes occur together and cannot be treated independently, so question processes will be discussed together.

The process of question selection involves the following functions: (a) how the cognitive context determines exactly what is to be asked about and (b) how the choice is made between asking an open- or closed-form question. This area of question process is dealt with in cognitive psychology and psycholinguistics. The cognitive context is discussed by Berlyne (1960, 1965). He postulates that according to the definition of information theory, there can be no information without prior uncertainty. The amount of information in an event is defined as a function of the probability of that event, and a probability cannot be assigned to an event unless it is an element of a 'sample space' or 'ensemble' of alternative events, any one of which might have occurred and each of which has its relative frequency or probability. If a sample space can be specified, it will be possible to assign an uncertainty value to it. The mathematical truth that information implies prior uncertainty corresponds to the biological and psychological truth that the role of information in animal life is contingent on conflict, the behavioural equivalent of uncertainty. Information is valuable to an animal only when it prevents or relieves conflict. We expect animals to seek information when they suffer for lack of it. How does this state of affairs arise? There may be lacunae in available information, in the sense of questions that have no answers. Or an organism may be beset by contradictory items of information that point to mutually incompatible responses. Additional information is then required to determine which of the discrepant items is to have precedence or how the inconsistency between them may be resolved. Finally an organism may suffer from congestion or information overload.

Berlyne relates a problem to a condition of an organism and states that a problem implies a condition of high drive. He postulates that it is such a drive which causes the organism to be curious, engage in exploration, and ask questions. Berlyne distinguishes three classes of epistemic response to a problem situation. The first consists of epistemic observation, i.e. responses which place the person in contact with external situations that will nourish the learning process. The second class consists of epistemic thinking whose function is not to call up remembered material (for handling the current problem), but to put the individual in permanent possession of new knowledge. The third class is consultation, behaviour which exposes an individual to verbal stimuli issuing from other individuals. Drive-inducing stimuli are required both to propel a quest for knowledge and to control its course.

Some quests for knowledge start with an explicit question, either put to the subject by another person or formulated by himself as a consequence of his own thoughts or observations. A questioner is driven to put the question (an epistemic response) under the pressure of his subjective uncertainty or conceptual conflict. The listener can either respond to the question with an immediate answer or the question will arouse a set of alternative, competing responses in him, and he will be placed in a condition of conceptual conflict paralleling that of the questioner. It is difficult to ignore a question without at least attempting to make some sort of reply. And it has often happened in the history of science, in mathematics, in philosophy, or even in art that the mere recognition of an unanswered question has driven a person to the intellectual labour from which an innovation sprang. Questions serve the purpose of reducing subjective uncertainty and conceptual conflict.

Various theories of attitude formation in social psychology are closely related to this statement. The common consistency theories (Abelson *et al*, 1968) present an idea that people operate under a strong need for internal consistency among their beliefs. The consistency tendency provides a convenient tool for mapping the structure and functioning of human thought processes. There is a strong tendency to conserve both the connectedness and the internal consistency of the conceptual system. Receipt of any new information, and especially new and discrepant information, produces considerable conceptual activity, involving a great deal of readjustment, until the information is absorbed by the system with the least loss in internal consistency and the greatest gain in connectedness. Each individual attempts to maintain a system of consistent beliefs, to avoid 'imbalances' and to reduce 'dissonances'. Dissonance is defined in terms of logical contradiction. When a dissonance is present, there is a drive toward its elimination. Dissonance can be reduced in various ways, e.g. by changing evaluations of conflicting elements, by reducing the importance attached to them or by seeking social support from other persons who share them.

The ideas of Berlyne and those of the cognitive consistency theorists suggest how questions arise. They do not explain how a particular question is selected in relation to the specific context of occurrence. In order to explain the generation of a particular question, a theory is needed which relates the context to the conceptual structure of the individual. Kearsley (1976) attempts such a theoretical formulation in relation to referential questions.

The essential notion is that question-asking involves filling in the 'gaps' in a cognitive model, where a cognitive model is defined as that sub-portion of an individual's entire conceptual structure which currently conveys the meaning of events or objects in the immediate environment. *Filling in the 'gaps' involves specifying the concepts and relations in six basic reference frames: space, time, properties, causes, procedures, and roles.*

Kearsley suggests that wh-questions attempt to select subsets of relations for a reference frame relevant to the current context, while disjunctive and yes/no questions (closed forms) are intended to specify particular concepts within the selected reference frame. His theory is intended to predict the content and form of questions to be asked, given the details of a specific context and the conceptual structure of a particular individual. The actual syntax of question formation is beyond the scope of his theory.

Katz and Postal (1964) developed a thorough consideration of the transformational rules for question formation. They believe that questions are derived from an underlying phrase structure by the application of transformation rules of deletion and transformation. They use two semantic markers: a Q morpheme which indicates that the phrase is a question (indicates the condition: 'I request that you answer...') and a wh morpheme which specifies the element that is 'questioned'. The wh morpheme is considered to operate as a scope marker for the Q morpheme. Chafe (1972) has provided a generative semantics account of question formation.

Not much empirical work related to the processes of question formation has been done. Wright (1972) showed that fewer errors were made in answering questions about a sentence when both the sentence and the question were in the same mode (active/passive). Fillenbaum (1968, 1971) described psycholinguistic studies in which he has investigated whether phrasing of a question may reveal presumptions of its answer and consequently the constraints that the question imposes upon the expected answer. He demonstrated differences in processing times between compatible and incompatible answers as well as differences in recall for expected and unexpected answers to yes/no questions. Subjects exposed to these experiments took less time to process compatible answers than incompatible answers; they also performed better on compatible items. The principal virtue of a multiple assessment approach was that it allowed him to isolate and independently identify (a) effects at the time of initial processing (understanding and storage), as well as (b) memory and retrieval effects.

Question-asking must be viewed as part of an interactive and social discourse and not just as a process inherent in the generation of a single question. Question-asking has to be considered as a social activity as well as a cognitive one and therefore has to be approached also from a *sociolinguistic* perspective. Mishler (1975) considers question-asking as a mode of exerting authority or control over others. He suggests that the actual interrogative unit is not just question and answer, but question(Q), response(R), and confirmation(C). He identifies three modes by which questions may serve to connect dialogue units and thus produce a type of discourse that is both question-initiated and question-sustained. These are referred to as 'chaining', in which the conversation is extended through successive questions by the initial questioner; 'arching', in which the response-utterance contains a question; and 'embedding', in which there are two responses to a question. Chaining is used by the questioner to maintain control of the discourse; arching is used to regain control when asked a question; and embedding reflects a more equal power structure. Chaining and its different patterns could reflect role relationship between speakers. Mishler, who studied children's discourse in elementary schools, collected evidence that teachers use chaining and arching to maintain control over pupils and that children use these patterns to exert authority over each other. Mishler focussed also on the length of discourse, and on variations in length and in rates of successive questioning as a function of differences between questioners and respondents in terms of age and sex. He suggests that through the act of questioning one speaker defines the way in which the other is to continue with the conversation and thus defines their relationship to each other along a dimension of power and authority. He underlines the fact that the control function of questioning may be obscured by the assumed equivalence of the terms 'to ask' and 'to question'. Although often considered synonyms, they differ in their respective ranges of connotative meanings. According to Webster's *New international dictionary* (2nd edition) the synonyms for 'ask' are: need, entreat, beseech, petition, implore. 'All of them suggest that the questioner is in a subordinate or subservient situation vis-à-vis the answerer.' However, the synonyms for 'question' include: challenge, demand, dispute, call into question, examine, charge, accuse, and doubt. 'Here the questioner is clearly in a superordinate or dominant position vis-à-vis the answerer.' A question may mean either 'ask' or 'question'. There are other sparse references in the literature to qualitative and quantitative differences in question-asking/answering patterns, especially between different social classes.

There is little and partial knowledge about the three levels of question process and there has been little theoretical and empirical work done to test the existing ideas about question formation and selection. There is even less understanding of how these different levels interact and occur together in an interactive discourse.

3.5 Descriptive analyses of question types

The data which originate from the developmental studies of language are probably the unique source of descriptive analysis of questions in actual verbal discourse. Piaget (1926) suggested that question-asking behaviour reflects the stage of cognitive development reached by the child. Changes in the content of questions over age should reflect cognitive growth of the child. Continuation of this study was made by E A Davis (1932) and by Meyer and Shane (1973) who classified children's questions using the categories derived by Piaget. However, we do not feel this work is sufficiently relevant to discuss in detail.

In the work described earlier, Kearsley suggests that the study of questions and question-asking has not yet begun in earnest. He also implies that insofar as question-asking is one of the major modes by which knowledge is acquired by humans, it should be of vital interest to those who are concerned with the representation and reorganization of knowledge. With respect to cognitive psychology, questions provide an indication of how an individual's knowledge system is organized and how it is reorganized as new knowledge is acquired. Thus questions are a behavioural reflection of change in conceptual structure. Questions play an important role in problem-solving, concept formation, verbal learning, etc. In psycholinguistics, question-asking provides a convenient medium in which syntax and semantics may be related. Psycholinguistics seeks to explain how the psychological context specifies both the content and the form of the question — which occur concurrently with the generation of the linguistic expression of the question (correct word order, tense, etc.). Furthermore, an understanding of question-asking is necessary if computer programs for natural language understanding are to be extended from isolated sentences to connected discourse and conversation. The representation of knowledge is currently of interest to the entire spectrum of workers in AI (Michie, 1976). As more work is done with large knowledge-based programs, it will be highly desirable to allow the program to modify and build its knowledge via self-directed question-asking.

3.6 The logic of questions

Logicians try to reveal the logical structure of questions, the logical relations between questions and between questions and answers. For this purpose they propose to represent the questions and the answers in some formalized language with a clear logical syntax. Their semantic interpretation of the language defines such notions as truth and falsity, entailment, validity and presupposition.

During the last 20 years there have been investigations which have utilized to some extent the techniques of symbolic logic. In 1936, there appeared in the *Actes du Congrès International de Philosophie Scientifique* a paper by E Sperantia entitled: 'Remarques sur les propositions interrogatives: projet d'une logique du problème.' Earlier material of the same nature can be found in the *Elements of logic* and *Elements of rhetoric* of Richard Whateley.

The term 'logic of questions' or erotetic logic was first used by Prior and Prior in 1955 and should be thought of in analogy to the logic of statements. Erotetic logic is part of logic; it does not include the proof theory but rather two other parts, grammar (syntax) and semantics. The approach is to imagine a questioner and a respondent in possession of a common language sufficient for purposes of scientific communication, and then to ask how this language could be enriched so that it could be used to ask and answer questions in an orderly, fruitful way. This suggests a twofold task. On the object-language level one would like to create a carefully designed apparatus permitting asking and answering of questions. On the meta-language level one would need to elaborate a set of concepts useful for categorizing, evaluating, and relating questions to answers (Belnap, 1976). The aim of question analysis is to understand the meaning of a question, but there is still a need to come to an agreement between the query system and the user as to what counts as an answer to the question, regardless of how, or if, any answer is produced.

The notion of a direct answer to a question is basic in the logical analysis. A direct answer is a piece of language that completely, but without redundancy, answers the question. A direct question may be true or false. A question is an abstract thing, and the notation for it is an interrogative. An elementary question has two parts, a subject and a request. The subject presents a set of alternatives, and the request identifies how many of the true alternatives are desired in the answer and what sort of claims for completeness and distinctness are to be made. Questions whose subjects present an explicit, finite list of alternatives are called whether-questions. Questions whose subjects present a set of alternatives that is possibly infinite are called which-questions.

The request can be parsed into three components. The first, selection-size-specification, is a quantifier-like indication of the number of true alternatives requested, e.g. at least one, all, 5%. The second component of a request is a completeness-claim-specification, which indicates whether the questioner wishes the answer to include a claim concerning the degree to which the selection-size-specification is met. Finally, the distinctness-claim-specification is that component of the request that asks for an answer to address the issue of whether the alternatives are really distinct as opposed to being nominally distinct, for example, '7' as opposed to 'VII'. It is not the case that all types of questions require all components of the request.

Whether and which questions are elementary questions. The kind of questions we deal with are asked not so much to relieve a vaguely defined mental anxiety as to seek some definite piece of information. It is very hard to predict in advance just what kind of answer would satisfy the questioner. Sometimes we think that he does not really know himself what he wants, but receiving a reply, he will tell if the answer relieves his anxiety. Maybe, he will also ask a clearer question.

Where there is a question and its direct answers and we intuitively are aware of this, we may, for logical purposes, identify the question with the set of its direct answers, and then explicate many of the basic notions of question logic in terms of the set theoretic relations between sets of answers (Stahl, 1956; Hamblin, 1971; Harrah, 1963). It has been proved that no system can be complete, i.e. given any reasonable system for expressing questions, we can construct new questions not expressible by that system (Harrah, 1973). 'The upshot is that we must choose between having completeness in our realm of questions and having completeness in our system of expressions. Some compromise is necessary.' It is still not known whether there is such a thing as the best compromise and whether we can even anticipate where to start to look for it. 'This is what makes the logic of questions interesting' (Harrah, 1973).

One way of exploring this problem is to choose some types of questions which are important in natural languages, and develop an analysis of these within the formalism of set theory. The next step is to develop a system of expressions which will be reasonably complete for the types of questions chosen in the first place. This is the practice presently accepted among the scholars in the field of question logic. With some variations they have all concentrated on what may be called questions of standard enquiry, or standard questions. The term 'standard' refers to a situation in which the questioner knows exactly what his problem is and how to express it effectively. He knows the set of possible alternatives, he knows that one of these is true but he does not know which one. He wants to know which it is and he believes that the respondent will be able to help him. This is an ideal situation and as Harrah expresses it: 'One need only ask such questions as: Does the questioner always want (need) the answer? Does the questioner always believe that the respondent will help him? Must the questioner also believe that he will receive help if and only if he asks the question? Can he merely believe these things, or must he know them? Wouldn't a "reasonable degree of confidence" suffice?' In view of these doubts it is best to regard the notion of standard as very approximate.

Three scholars who have been working in the logic of standard questions are Harrah (1961), Aqvist (1965) and Belnap (1976). Harrah and Belnap differ from Aqvist in two main ways (Bell, 1975). They consider that classical first-order logic is sufficiently powerful to represent the structure of questions, whereas Aqvist thinks it is necessary to employ a modal logic which combines epistemic logic as well as imperative logic. Second, Belnap and Harrah believe that a clue to a correct logical analysis is the relation of question to answer. 'The foundation of any logic of questions must lie in the specification of question-answer relationship' (Belnap, p 13). In contrast, Aqvist's opinion is that 'logical relations among questions can be studied without our having to specify in advance any question-answer relationship' (Aqvist, p 11).

Harrah represents every question as a proposition of a certain form, so that, for him, the logic of questions is merely part of standard logic. 'The usual definitions of consistency, satisfiability, validity and entailment can then be applied to questions and sets of questions. Thus one question may entail another, or be inconsistent or consistent with it, and so on' (Bell, p 195).

The idea of Belnap is that every question, whether a sentence or a wh-question, presents a set of alternative propositions, but also makes a request about the selection from the set that a direct answer should make. He thinks that this request consists of two components: (1) the request first specifies how many of the presented alternatives are to be selected; (2) the request then specifies that exactly one of these be selected and that the selection exhausts the set of true alternatives. Thus for Belnap, as he himself puts it, a direct answer is required to tell the truth, the whole truth and nothing but the truth; but not all questions require the whole truth, and just how much of the truth is required is determined by the second component of the request. Belnap uses the notion of a request only in the informal analysis of questions. Aqvist differs from Belnap in wanting to represent questions directly as requests, or in general as commands, in the formalization itself, and so makes use of devices of so-called imperative logic. Bell formulates it as follows: Aqvist sees questions in their 'standard' use — in a question the questioner articulates what he already knows about a certain topic, and requests his audience to increase his knowledge.

After consideration of the above-mentioned notions, Bell asks himself what a question really is from the logical point of view.

If we say that a question is a proposition, we go against our intuitions that questions are not themselves the sort of things that can be asserted, or believed. Maybe we should go against our intuitions, and accept the consequence that questions are true or false; Harrah and Belnap think that we should. On the other hand if we distinguish questions as commands of some sort, we run into difficulties over unasked questions.

Aqvist's theory of epistemic requests has been applied by Lang (1970) in a field study of question and answer behaviour in natural language, while Orgass (1970) and Kubinski (1970) developed Belnap's theory of linguistic requests in the field of computer science.

Harrah (1963) constructs a model of a rational procedure for asking questions and giving answers applicable in situations where an individual wants to 'acquire information, explore meanings, and evaluate the quality of the sender as an information source'. The word 'model' is used in the sense of 'theory'. The situation analysed in the model is one in which a message affects the receiver. One speaks about 'impact' which a message may have on the receiver when one uses an empirical interpretation; with a normative interpretation one considers how the receiver evaluates or ought to evaluate the message. When a receiver obtains the message he does not evaluate the message by itself, but in the light of all his background knowledge. The receiver can also assess the value of messages in terms of how completely they answer his question, how early in the message sequence the crucial one occurs, etc. The evaluation of messages is done on the one function, the information function. In the model, the receiver can plot profiles which express, for example, the amount of information over time, or message adequacy against message number. A communication sequence is a sequence of communication events, different types of sequence being defined by different relationships among the messages and the receivers of those messages. A sequence of communication events with one message receiver but different messages could be taken as a standard model of static communication situations, such as of a person reading a book. A different model is that of an interview situation, in which the receiver's knowledge and interest may grow during the course of the communication interaction. Other instances include situations of education or persuasion. The result of the analysis of message effect depends on assumptions regarding the receiver, his questions (including language), his knowledge, the information contents of answers, the respondent and his knowledge.

The conditions of the model are given as follows:

1. The questioner is responsible for his questions. He will be penalized if he asks questions which are defective.

2. The model explicates 'question' in such a way that every question is effectively recognizable as being a question. There can be no doubt in the respondent when he is being questioned.

3. The theory explicates 'question' in such a way that for every question there is a reply which answers the question in some reasonable sense.

4. The theory distinguishes between replies which are complete as answers and those which are incomplete. Both the questioner and the respondent should be able to determine, for any given question, what replies count as complete-and-just-sufficient answers to that question. Just-sufficient answer means that the respondent must know how to put together something which the questioner will accept as an answer. This requirement is indispensable. It would be absurd to demand criteria for true or correct answers.

5. The theory explicates various relations of relevance among questions.

6. The theory explicates 'answer' in such a way that answers can be language implied by statements.

Which of the existing information theories will the Harrah model satisfy? Two major types of information theory have been developed. The first is the theory of selective information, initiated by Shannon, developed to give measures of the capacity of a communication channel to transmit information; it construes information as a statistical concept, and its central concept is *average information*. Roughly, the average information in the messages being considered is the average surprise-value of the messages, the average surprise of the receiver at the receiving of the messages. The degree of average surprise is computed from empirical probabilities, the relative frequencies of occurrence of different messages.

The model cannot deal with selective information functions, because this theory is concerned with large sets of messages and is not intended to assign information values to individual messages.

The second available theory is the theory of semantic information, created by Keremy, Carnap, and Bar-Hillel. This theory was developed to provide a measure of the 'logical strength' of individual statements, so that one might measure the 'degree of daring' of a hypothesis or the 'weight' of a piece of evidence. The amount of semantic information is determined logically rather than empirically. This theory of information is also not suitable for the model. Information is not defined in the model. A partial characterization of information is given by way of a set of axioms.

Mackay discusses how questions and commands can be analysed in informational terms similar to those for the analysis of indicative sentences. The object of a question is to evoke communicative activity. A question is a purported indication of inadequacy in its originator's state of readiness, calculated to elicit some organizing work to remedy the inadequacy. It is as if the questioner uncovered and held out the incomplete part of his organizing system to the receiver for his attention. Questions work only because human beings are motivated to adjust one another's states of readiness. What makes an utterance a question cannot always be pinned down either to a peculiarity of its logical form or to the fact that it has elicited information.

3.7 Questions in problem-solving

A person facing a problem must first recognize that a problem exists and then specify it as a well-defined problem-statement. A well-defined problem-statement gives a set of possible solutions to the problem.

The process of passing through various stages in a problem-solving situation can be compared to a process of learning (Kochen and Badre, 1974). The progress of learning has been traditionally measured by the quality of questions a learner can answer. The improvement in performance of a learner can equally be assessed by the teacher observing the depth of the questions the learner asks.

The study of improvement in the quality of questions posed by the learner can be looked upon as 'adopting an approach that stresses the formation, revision and use of internal representation in the learning process. The representation is akin to a model: it is a set of interpreted sentences or hypotheses in an internal language that enables the learner to recognize, formulate, and cope with an ever-increasing variety of traps and opportunities in his environment'. The representation approach stresses the formation of shifts in a set of logically connected hypotheses. Kochen explores the nature of improvement in the quality of questions during problem formulation and the relation of problem formulation to the overall problem-solving. The assumption presented is that the questions the learner asks are evidence of his having formed and used an internal representation, and that shifts in his representation are revealed by shifts in the vocabulary of his questions. Major improvements in the solution of problems that require such shifts should therefore be correlated with improvements in the quality of questions.

As long as the learner is locked into one representation, he selects hypotheses from a fixed set of possible hypotheses on the basis of answers to his questions and his own observations. A shift in his representation can provide him with a new set of alternatives, which may produce a leap rather than steady or no progress in problem solution.

3.8   Problem formulation and problem solution

When a person faces a problem, he must first clarify it to himself. The state of problem formulation is ascertained when the subject asks a question or a sequence of questions containing a well-defined statement of the relevant problem.

Problem solution may have two phases. The first is an act of unplanned information gathering or random sampling. (Kochen presents an experiment with seven cups and a dime hidden under one of them; the subject may pick any cup at random and ask if it conceals a dime.) The second phase is solving, *per se,* a more systematic question-asking or search which is based on a specific hypothesis (about how the dimes are arranged).

A representation of the problem is useful in both the problem formulation and the problem-solving stages. A representation enables us to interpret the incoming information as knowledge, to structure this knowledge, and to analyse a problem statement into sub-problem statements and relate these to one another. Successful problem solution (solving in the second stage) is exemplified by two properties. First the problem statement is structured into a logically connected sequence of sub-problem statements so that the solution to the whole problem is a consequence of the solutions to the sub-problems in this sequence. Second, the problem statement is a special instance of a more general class of problem statements to which a unifying pattern of finding solutions applies (Polya, 1962; Gagne, 1970).

3.9 Representations

A representation can be viewed as specified by an internal language and a structured set of sentences within it. To specify an internal language is to specify a vocabulary that denotes constants, variables, predicates, quantifiers, functions, and rules for forming well-formed propositions, as in predicate calculus; this specifies a (generally infinite) set of possible well-formed strings. To specify a structured set of sentences is to specify certain of these well-formed strings as axioms, others as hypotheses and theorems; to specify also special rules of inference, certain well-formed strings as questions, and a set of logical connections among the questions. Altogether, such a structure is not only a set of formal strings but an associated system of interpretation, in the sense of model theory. Thus, with each well-formed string is associated an interpretation in a universe of discourse, an interpretation comparable with the corresponding state in the external environment.

3.10 The quality of questions in problem formulation

How a learner represents the task environment to himself is revealed by the questions he asks. If he is uncomfortable with the irrelevance or imprecision of his representation, he will tend to ask 'groping' questions (groping-tentative). Later, during problem solution, when the learner has a more relevant and precise representation, he will tend to ask specific and generic, yet precise and relevant, questions.

Three aspects of representation, three qualities of a question in problem formulation, are of interest for this study: relevance, precision, specificity. A question is specific if it yields information about a single noun-object such that the information cannot be generalized to any other noun-object or element in a class of noun-objects; otherwise it is unspecific or generic. A question is relevant if it reveals information about the experimental problem state; if it does not, it is irrelevant. If the predicate of a question can be sharply defined, it is a precise question; otherwise it is fuzzy.

During problem formulation, greater priority is given to relevance than to precision. An irrelevant but precise question is likely to elicit less information than a relevant but imprecise question. On the other hand, greater priority is given to precision than to specificity. By these criteria, a precise but specific question during problem formulation is informationally more useful (of higher quality) than a generic but imprecise one. And of two questions equally precise and specific, the one that is more relevant to the representation of the problem the experimenter has in mind will be more useful, for without achieving relevance problem formulation could never succeed. And of two questions both relevant and specific, the one which is more precise is of higher quality, for the interpretation of its answer will be less ambiguous and more distinctive than that of an imprecise one. With two questions that are equally relevant and precise but that differ in degree of specificity, the quality of the generic question should be greater because it has more potential for reducing uncertainty.

Suppose we encode the quality, q, of a question as a three-bit number, s, p, r. Here s denotes degree of specificity, which is 1 if the question is generic, and 0 if specific; p denotes the degree of precision, 1 if the question is precise and 0 if not; and r denotes relevance, 1 if the question is relevant and 0 if not. This encoding partitions the set of all questions into eight possible classes.

3.11 The quality of questions in problem-solving

The criteria for quality of questions during problem-solving are different from those described above (for problem formulation). In the first stage of problem-solving, in the so-called problem formulation stage, a subject is trying to understand his task. He terminates this stage when he realizes that his task is to discover some pattern (for example, that by which the dimes are distributed — in the described example). All stages beyond this first one belong to the problem solution stage. The quality of a question in problem solution depends on the other questions the subject is asking, and on the representation on which it is based. Suppose that a particular representation admits a number N of possible hypotheses about the pattern for distributing 'dimes'. If a hypothesis corresponding to the actual pattern is in the representation, then it is among the N; if not, and the subject eventually learns the actual pattern, then a shift to another representation that includes the valid hypothesis must have occurred.

A certain question may fail to eliminate any hypotheses in a given representation, no matter what the answer, because it does not apply to this representation. The ideal question is one that eliminates all but one of a set of hypotheses from which we, the observers, consider the subject capable of choosing. If it did, it would be a perfect question early in the sequence, but we would recognize it as such only later, after the subject had asked more questions that reflected how he had eliminated all but one hypothesis. A question which elicits a contradiction as its answer is good because it eliminates a hypothesis. Likewise, a question that brings out the incompleteness of a representation is good.

In brief, a question is good during problem solution to the extent to which it comes close to being one of the ideal questions just mentioned.

The results obtained from Kochen's study indicated that there was a relation between asking good questions during problem formulation and subsequent problem solution. The finding that improvement in the quality of questions during problem formulation is accompanied by improved performance in problem solution is in line with demonstrations in AI research (Amarel, 1971) that the way a problem is formulated is highly related to the efficiency with which it will be solved. That is, the process of finding a solution depends on the choice of an appropriate representation during the initial part of the problem-coping process. This finding suggests that it may be possible systematically to predict problem solution from a learner's vocabulary during problem formulation.

In one experiment, a series of problems were presented. The results showed that, on the whole, problem solution improved from one problem to the next. Improvement from run one, to two, to three was constant. But from run three to four, a slight decrement appeared. The most likely explanation of such a trend is that while the first three problems (arrays, runs) were similar, the fourth and fifth introduced new elements into the situation, changes in the problem state that required shifts in representation. As the subject began the fourth problem, he had not yet experienced, and therefore not learned to expect, such changes. This delayed the required shift and therefore caused a slight decrement in performance. The trend from the fourth to the fifth problem indicates that the subjects may have begun to anticipate changes in the problem state and meet them with needed shifts in representation.

Had we found good problem solution without good questions during problem formulation, this could have been due to (a) shifts of representation that existed but were not expressed verbally in the form of questions; (b) problem solution on our task being governed predominantly by perceptual or rote-memory processes but not by cognitive maps or internal representations (as might also be the case for a person with a lot of experience with tasks of this kind); or (c) defects in our method of measuring the quality of questions.

Had we found good questions without good problem solution, this might have been due to (a) inability to utilize good representations; (b) inability to register, maintain, or retrieve relevant memories long enough, if memory plays an important role; (c) inability to form coherent questions (as in aphasia or other disturbances of linguistic performance); or (d), again, defects in our method of measuring the quality of questions.

It is therefore not trivial or obvious that the quality of questions during problem formulation is correlated with problem solution, because this lends credence to the psychological reality of the 'internal representations' that we take for granted in fellow humans.

3.12 Questions in IR

An IR system consists of a store of documents (or their representations) to which requests may be directed and from which answers may be derived. Thus, we have a collection of documents and a query, and the system has to assign an answer to the query. A relationship between the query and the resulting set of documents retrieved must exist. In other words, an IR system consists of a set of queries S, a set of documents X, and a relation R (relevance) between these two sets. An answer A consists of a subset of X. Most operating IR systems treat the process of IR as a matching procedure between the query and the documents in the file (store).

Saracevic has described the study of problems arising in question analysis. He classified them and suggested possible theoretical and experimental studies that may lead to new approaches. Question analysis is considered as a set of procedures in IR that: (1) provide assistance to users (or their representatives) in *formulation* of a question and (2) accomplish *transformation* of a question into language, logic and form acceptable to the requirements of the IR system. The significance of question analysis lies in this, that IR systems exist to answer questions, i.e. they are 'driven' by users and controlled by questions; how question analysis is performed greatly affects retrieval performance.

The performance of an IR system is affected by internal factors over which the system has considerable control (such as acquisition, indexing, file organization), external factors over which a system has virtually no control (e.g. existence of given information, nature of information problems of users) and interactive factors over which a system has some degree of control — question analysis is such a factor. IR systems devote considerable attention and effort to internal factors, but relatively little attention to interactive factors. There is a need to increase the probabilities for fruitful interaction involving question analysis. Question analysis is still largely a matter of educated intuition and art rather than of systematic procedures. This is a very complex problem area in need of research, experimentation and then investment.

3.13 Problems in question analysis

Problems in question analysis may be divided into:

1. semantic, i.e. difficulties in (i) expressing a question and (ii) establishing a common language with the file;

2. syntactic, i.e. difficulties in establishing strategies for system interrogation.

For help in semantic problems, thesauri, dictionaries, aids in profile construction etc., were developed. To help with syntactic problems we have search statistics, diagrams, trail prompting etc., but question analysis is still a major problem in IR. It is believed that additional question analysis procedures are needed to retrieve from the system what one wants and on a scale one can handle. The idea is not to build new systems, nor to make drastic changes in existing systems, but to add new routines and procedures as options for those who desire help in overcoming semantic and syntactic problems in question analysis. 'To achieve this some new procedures have to be developed, maybe some old concepts and experiments should be pulled out of the dust and reexamined, and maybe information science should look into other areas for help.' Saracevic suggested areas that we have in fact looked at in our review.

The logic of questions and answers, erotetic logic as treated by Belnap and Steel, is an attempt 'to create a formal language that can be used to ask and answer questions in an orderly fruitful way .... The logic of questions and answers is particularly relevant to computer usage, where retrieval of information depends on the formulation of the questions that are asked.' Saracevic notes that these authors discuss question grammar and different types of question. Further potentially useful theoretical work may be found in the work of Belnap and Anderson on the system of axioms that captures the notion of relevance. In information science is the work of Goffman on dynamics of communication and on principles and methods of partitioning a population of information-conveying objects (e.g. documents) into equivalence classes. Saracevic suggested a number of promising experiments to be conducted in question analysis. The experiments should start from the premise that they would utilize records and vocabulary tools as a database. Three areas of experimentation were outlined.

1. *Display* to the enquirer of a semantic road map (or maps) of terms (or other elements) from which a question can be constructed for initial entry to the system; these road maps (originally suggested by Doyle) could be constructed from a thesaurus or from a vocabulary used in records. (Doyle's work on semantic road maps will be discussed in the section on search strategy.)

2. *Clustering* of records to show relations that are there but are not presently obtainable; the clusters could be in terms of intercommunication classes (as suggested by Goffman) or using other measures (e.g. Salton); the clusters could be constructed independently of questions on the file and reused with updates, or they could be done on initial larger outputs obtained for a question in the usual search way; elements other than index terms could be used for clustering (e.g. authors, co-authors, citation — output from one file could be entered for clustering in a citation index).

3. *Adjustment* of questions and/or outputs on the basis of feedback (e.g. Salton's relevance feedback), on the basis of ranking, or on the basis of variations in thresholds for clusters; adjustment could be done on the basis of 'walking' through different paths of the road maps of terms or clusters.

In 1980, Saracevic prepared a research proposal for work on the classification and structure of questions in IR. He noted that most investigations in IR have dealt with problems of representation, organization and storage of information and only a few have addressed problems of question analysis and formulation of search strategy. Even fewer dealt with questions themselves.

Because the procedures associated with question asking and handling are still not systematic, still less so algorithmic processes, the effectiveness of providing and obtaining answers may, and often indeed does, vary greatly, even for the same question and file, depending on who did the question handling and how it was done. In general, questions and question handling may be investigated in relation to:

1. question aspects: nature and structure of questions; lexical and linguistic aspects;

44

2. behavioural aspects: handling of analysis, transformations etc.;

3. system aspects: design and deployment of appropriate tools and/or procedures within the IR system for effective question handling.

Saracevic's proposal is directed towards question aspects and towards semantic problems in particular. Its goal is to investigate the categorization of questions into types. He uses the following working definitions as a framework for the classification of questions:

INFORMATION PROBLEM:
    An unknown in the work or life of a potential user of an IR system.

INFORMATION NEED:
    A motivating force in question asking. A desire to be furnished with personal knowledge, level and motivation of a user or group of users.

QUESTION:
    A verbalized representation (oral or graphic) of information need. An interrogative statement.

REQUEST:
    A question as transmitted to a retrieval system in expectation of a response. The request and the question do not necessarily adequately represent the information need and information problem.

QUESTION ANALYSIS:
    Procedures in retrieval which:
    (a)provide assistance to users in the formulation of a question;
    (b) provide for semantic, syntactic and pragmatic elaboration and/or clarification of a question.

SEARCH STRATEGY:
    Procedures in retrieval which:
    (a)accomplish transformation of a natural-language question into a query (vocabulary, form, logic) acceptable to a given retrieval system;
    (b) establish or modify the search tactics which further the effectiveness of output and efficiency of searching.

SEARCH:
    Physical manipulation of files to obtain answers.

ANSWER:
A string of words or items (including a document) that have the potential of being a relevant response to a question and/or pertinent to an information need. In this respect:
RELEVANCE is the property that assigns an answer to a question and
PERTINENCE is the property that assigns an answer to information need.

In a pilot study carried out in 1979, and reported (preliminary work) in 1980, Saracevic devised a classification of questions based on the following properties:

1. searchability of words and questions;
2. grammatical status;
3. thesaural status;
4. specificity of meaning.

Searchability refers to words which can or cannot be searched in an IR system. In the pilot study a word lacked this property if it could be considered a candidate for a stopword list. Those which were excluded from the stopword list were then analysed for their thesaural state and specificity of meaning. Words with low searchability such as 'performance' or 'contemporary' would need to be rephrased.

Grammatical status refers to two aspects:

1. type of words and phrases in a question, and type of syntactic constructs;

2. frequency distribution of words (phrases) within one or many questions (or information problem statements).

The first aspect was studied in the pilot study by classifying the words and phrases into types of speech and then showing distribution. It was observed that phrase constructs have special significance in the formulation of terms for searching.

The frequency of distribution of words in questions was to be studied using the Zipf-Mandelbrot transition region between the high- and low-frequency words of any given text (which has been suggested as yielding content-bearing words of the text). By analysing a representative body of questions in a subject field such as engineering, terms may be automatically extracted to represent topics in the subject field. Thus it is possible to construct automatically a 'dictionary' or a 'thesaurus' so that any input question may be categorized by consulting the dictionary.

Thesaural status refers to the position of a question word within an established thesaurus in IR. In the pilot study words and relations between words were checked against four thesauri (ERIC, TEST, Psychology and LC Subject Headings). Thesaural road maps will be explored in the study as well as thesauri.

Specificity of meaning refers to the possible variations in the meaning(s) of a word in a question. In the pilot study specificity was considered in three ways:

1. Terms with four or fewer meanings as listed in the Webster *Third international unabridged dictionary* were considered as highly specific.

2. The ratio of highly specific terms to the total number of searchable terms in a question was derived.

3. The ratios ranged from 0 to 0.50. Those at the low end of the range were considered questions of low specificity, in the middle of the range as medium, and at the high end as highly specific questions. In addition an independent (not numerical) intellectual classification was performed. The results of the two classifications were in high agreement.

Additional properties of questions to be investigated include:

1. factual status, the degree to which 'facts' are presented in a question and/or requested in the answers;

2. complexity, the number of related concepts in a question (e.g. simple or multi-concept questions);

3. concreteness, the degree to which a topic of the question is concrete (well-defined topics);

4. exhaustivity, the degree to which the terms stated in a question need further elaboration and/or classification.

The following types of model were suggested to be explored:

1. Functional models, representing the elements, sequence of events and interactions in IR systems and other question-answering systems.

2. Logical models. This will involve the adaptation to the above functions of a formal logical structure as derived by Belnap and Steel in their effort to create a formal language that can be used to ask and answer questions in an orderly way. Their bibliography of the theory of questions and answers is subdivided into subjects: (i) logic and philosophy of language; (ii) linguistics, (iii) automatic question-answering and (iv) psychology and pedagogy; this exemplifies the type of work which has yet to be applied to the functions of IR systems.

3. Linguistic models, the adaptation of linguistic structures and models to the above functions (Eichman).

4. Behavioural models. Katz, Hitchingham attempted to provide explanation regarding behavioural aspects in reference and question analysis processes.

5. Communication models. These range from various adaptations of the Shannon-Weaver model to formal mathematically and philosophically based models, as well as relevance models.

It is intended that the study should accumulate a sample of at least 1,000 real questions (not search strategies) for analysis and classification.

A standardized and general protocol is needed to capture questions posed to IR systems in various subjects and locations so that they can be further studied and the results compared. The objectives of this protocol are to:

1. help formulate and record the question as well as possible;

2. obtain maximum amount of information on the background of the question.

The protocol will contain sections for recording the following classes of information:

1. the problem which resulted in the question;

2. statement of question;

3. state of knowledge of the user in relation to problem and question;

4. the uses to which potential answers will be put;

5. restrictions such as priorities in types of answers, number of answers;

6. examples of relevant answers, documents, passages.

The protocol will have also room for recording any possible dialogue between the user and question analyst and room for subsequent distinction between initial and final problem and/or question statements.

Belkin, Oddy and Brooks (1982) report on a design study based on the combination of the ASK hypothesis with the principle underlying the experiment retrieval system called THOMAS (Oddy, 1975, 1977). Oddy's work on IR systems based on relevance feedback without query specification and Belkin's assumptions on the knowledge structures underlying information needs are based on a cognitive viewpoint. De Mey (1977) suggests that 'interactions of humans with one another and with the surrounding world are always mediated by their states of knowledge about themselves and about that with which or whom they interact.' The cognitive view of the IR situation led the researchers to design some principles for an IR system in which they incorporated the THOMAS and ASK approaches. The experimental procedure employed by the project consisted of text analysis and production of structural representations and consequently evaluation of both the analysis and the representations.

4 Dialogue analysis

4.1 Introduction

Our model of the IR interaction situation has, as a central component, the interaction between user and intermediary. In the normal course of events, as information systems are now constituted, this interaction is usually a form of conversation or *dialogue* between the two human participants. We might think that, in the future, systems could be built in which the present human intermediary might be replaced, at least to some extent, by a machine which would simulate at least some of the functions that that person performs in the dialogue. But, in order for this to occur, we assume that it will first be necessary to understand just what does take place in the human-human dialogue. Thus, both from the point of view of understanding and improving IR interaction as it is presently performed, and from the point of view of building new interactive systems, it will be necessary to study the rather special sort of dialogue that takes place in information interaction.

What sort of dialogue is this? It is two-party, with an external database to which both parties have recourse. It is goal-oriented, with the goals of one of the parties (the user) being primary, and it assumes (or hopes) that the database will be able to help the user to attain the goal. The two parties each have special, distinct roles to play in attempting to attain the goal, and they engage in their interaction with one another and with the database until the user feels that the goal has been attained or decides to stop the interaction for some other reason. It will be noticed that the interaction as specified has some of the characteristics of normal conversation, and of certain types of restricted dialogue, such as interviews. In particular, it is a *cooperative* dialogue, which we may assume follows some sort of general rules for cooperation, which is sometimes successful, and sometimes not. We can understand what occurs in such dialogues on two interacting levels: the linguistic level and the level of non-linguistic characteristics of the partners. In this chapter, we will consider work which has been done in trying to study and understand dialogue from the point of view of analysis of linguistic behaviour; in the next chapter we consider the social context of such human-human interaction.

Conversation, discourse, dialogue, talk are phenomena which have attracted interest in a number of fields, for a variety of reasons. This interest has led to some tentative models and theories of the phenomena, and to some methods for investigating them. Indeed, it has been enough to produce two journals, *Text* and *Discourse*

Processes, devoted to the general topic. There are also available a number of reviews and texts on the topic, including Coulthard (1977), Rosenberg (1980), Belkin (1981), Stubbs (1983) and Brown and Yule (1983). In addition, there have been a number of monographs on various aspects of the analysis of spoken discourse which include substantial review components, as, for instance, Edmondson (1981) and Carlson (1982). This chapter has drawn heavily on these sources, and is not intended as a substitute for them. Rather, we would like here only briefly to characterize some of the theories and methods which have been suggested, on the basis of those which seem to us most likely to have relevance to the study of the dialogue component of the IR interaction. We choose examples from philosophy, linguistics, sociolinguistics, cognitive psychology, and AI and computational linguistics. We stress that these are only examples, and that they do not by any means exhaust the variety of approaches to the topic, but represent, at least to us, some characteristic approaches, which might be useful in information science (or which have been used). We conclude this section by mentioning some work in library and information science on the analysis of dialogue.

4.2   Philosophy of language

There are three philosophers who have greatly influenced the contemporary study of conversation and discourse: J L Austin (1962), with 'performatives', John Searle (1969), with the theory of 'speech acts', and Paul Grice (1975), with his lectures on 'conversational implicature'. For brevity's sake, because of its undoubted influence on all subsequent discourse analysis, and because of its emphasis on *conversation,* we will comment in detail only on the latter's work, although Austin's and Searle's ideas are fundamental to most discourse analysis.

Grice, in his William James lectures of 1967 at Harvard University, published in part as Grice (1975), suggested that there is a logic to discourse (that is, conversation), which follows from some natural rules for conversation. The problem he was concerned with was the alleged discrepancy between formal logic and the 'natural logic' of natural language. In particular, he meant to demonstrate that this discrepancy was only apparent, and arose from a misunderstanding of the 'nature and importance of the conditions governing conversation'. That is, he was concerned with providing a logical basis for explaining how people understand conversations in which sequences of statements do not seem to follow 'logically'. To this end, Grice first formulated a principle basic to a particular type of conversation, the Cooperative Principle (CP):

Make your conversational contribution such as is required, at the stage at which it occurs, by the accepted purpose or direction of the talk exchange in which you are engaged. (Grice, 1975, p 45.)

In accordance with the CP, Grice proposes four categories: Quantity, Quality, Relation and Manner, under each of which fall certain maxims and submaxims. His claim is that these maxims, together with the CP, are necessary, and understood to be necessary, in cooperative conversation. Briefly, the categories and their maxims are:

QUANTITY:

a. Make your contribution as informative as is required for the current purposes of the exchange.

b. Do not make your contribution more informative than is required.

QUALITY: Supermaxim — Try to make your contribution one that is true.

a. Do not say what you believe to be false.

b. Do not say that for which you lack adequate evidence.

RELATION: Be relevant.

MANNER: Supermaxim — Be perspicuous.

a. Avoid obscurity of expression.

b. Avoid ambiguity.

c. Be brief (avoid prolixity).

d. Be orderly.

A participant in a conversation, according to Grice, may fail to fulfil a maxim in various ways, including the following:

The participant:

a. may quietly and inconspicuously *violate* a maxim (seeking to misinform);

b. may *opt out* from a maxim and the CP;

c. may be faced by a *clash* between two maxims;

d. may *flout* a maxim.

It is the last case which concerns Grice, for it is this instance that gives rise to 'conversational implicature'; that is, that *exploits* a maxim for some communicative purpose.

For example, a flouting of the first maxim of quantity:

> A is writing a testimonial about a pupil who is a candidate for a philosophy job, and his letter reads as follows: 'Dear Sir, Mr. X's command of English is excellent, and his attendance at tutorials has been regular. Yours, etc.' (Gloss: A cannot be opting out, since if he wished to be uncooperative, why write at all? He cannot be unable, through ignorance, to say more, since the man is his pupil; moreover, he knows that more information than this is wanted. He must, therefore, be wishing to impart information that he is reluctant to write down. This supposition is tenable only on the assumption that he thinks Mr. X is no good at philosophy. This, then, is what he is implicating.) (Grice, 1975, p 52.)

Grice's lectures are of interest in many ways, but two are particularly of interest in our context. First, he has begun to codify the rules by which certain types of conversation (cooperative) are assumed to take place by participants in such conversations (at least in a particular cultural context). And, second, he demonstrates that conscious violations of the rules are regularly used by participants to further communication. It is of special interest to note that many such violations, if not all of them, are context-dependent (either linguistic or social context or both).

4.3 Logic and linguistics

Since the publication of Chomsky's thesis (Chomsky, 1957), much of theoretical linguistics (especially in the USA) has been concerned with the analysis and understanding of the syntax of single sentences, in the context of language *competence* (the ideal single sentence, by the ideal speaker), rather than language *performance* (language as actually spoken or used). The dominance of this paradigm in the USA lasted until well into the 1970s, and meant, essentially, that theoretical linguistics had little to contribute to the study of human dialogue, concerned as the latter study is with performance in the context of many sentences. This paradigm did not, however, have the same effect in Europe, where substantial schools concerned with the functions of language and with the structures of the whole texts developed and matured during this period.

By the early to mid 1970s, some fundamental problems in the generative/ structural account of language were becoming apparent. In order to solve them, some theoretical linguists in the USA and elsewhere began to shift their attention to issues of pragmatics, performance and inter-sentential structures. This trend, combined with the alternative tradition, meant that by the mid to late 1970s, there was a substantial effort within theoretical linguistics to develop linguistic theories which took account of, or explained, such phenomena as the context of whole texts or dialogues.

Gordon and Lakoff (1971) is an example of such work in the USA, much of which was heavily influenced by Grice (1975). They attempted, still within a generative framwork, to provide a formal structure which would specify the preconditions to implicative utterances in conversation, thus allowing an at least quasi-formal analytic procedure for determining the meaning of sentences in (conversational) context. In its essence, this work was an attempt to formalize and extend some aspects of Grice's maxims for conversational implicature. In order to do this, Gordon and Lakoff (and others) found it necessary to set up an at least semi-formal logical apparatus, by means of which they were able to specify a number of conditions which were minimally necessary in order for a hearer to understand not only the propositional meaning of an utterance, but also its communicative meaning.

Other linguists, notably Sperber and Wilson (1982) in Europe, have begun with Grice's basic ideas about implicature, and especially relevance, and developed them into linguistic theories of comprehension of utterances in discourse context. As yet none of this work is sufficient for practical or complete theoretical analysis of dialogue, primarily because it rarely deals with natural data, but also because of the early state of the theory. Nevertheless, in the fragments and suggestions which are available, it does seem to offer substantial promise for the development of a formal pragmatics of conversation. Interestingly, the connections of this originally linguistic work with logic become stronger the more it deals with the issue of dialogue.

In Europe, in the meantime, much work had gone on in the study of whole texts (text linguistics), some of which is potentially relevant to the study of dialogue. We say potentially, because although most such work postulates a speaker and a hearer, it seems to concentrate upon analysis of the text produced by the single speaker, even if from the point of view of the influence of an interpretation by the putative hearer. This means that although it has managed to build up theories of whole text structures (e.g. van Dijk, 1977), there has been little possibility of doing the same for conversational interaction, where speaker and hearer change roles. One exception to this is the work on 'dialogue games' by Carlson (1982).

Carlson suggests that one can consider dialogues from the point of view of game theory, following from earlier work by Hintikka (e.g. 1973) on game-theoretical semantics. Important characteristics of Carlson's work are that it is highly logic-oriented, that it begins with the study of conversational interaction and that it develops an at least semi-formal model for analysing, describing and explaining a particular sort of conversation: cooperative information exchange dialogues. His argument is complex and extended, and highly technical in part. In essence it says that, if the goals of a dialogue can be established, one can treat the ideal dialogue as a formal game in which the participants choose strategies, turn by turn, which will maximize payoffs to each in terms of the goals. Using this game-theoretical model, he is able to specify, formally, the sorts of contexts that are required and used by both participants in order to understand one another and to reach the goal, turn by turn. This general framework has then been applied by Carlson in this study to the analysis and explanation of a number of aspects of English discourse, including some real dialogue fragments. Although whole-scale analysis of real dialogue is something for the future, this is at least a specific example of a logico-linguistic approach to the study of dialogue which offers some hope for a formal theory about the linguistic characteristics of dialogue.

Thus, various trends in linguistics seem to us to be leading to at least the possibility of the development of formal linguistic theories for explaining why different utterances are used in dialogues, especially in terms of what the hearers have understood of previous utterances and how they have achieved that comprehension. That is, this work appears to be leading toward theories of conversational interaction based on theories of *meaning* in discourse. Furthermore, the emphasis on logic, and in at least some work on overall structure of the interaction, appears to be leading toward theories which will at least explain, in a formal sense, the relationships of the utterances of a dialogue to one another.

4.4 Sociolinguistics

The approaches we have considered to this point can, in principle, be applied to all sorts of texts, rather than being limited to dialogue. There is, however, a type of analysis of conversation as a specific sort of text, which is now associated with the 'ethnomethodological' schools of sociology and sociolinguistics. Much of this work has strong associations with proposals by E Goffman (e.g. 1974), but it is also heavily dependent upon proposals in the 1960s for an 'ethnography of speaking'. Labov, Sacks and Schegloff are important investigators in this field, and some of their work will be mentioned later, but we will characterize it on the basis of a polemical introduction to the general field by Hymes (1972).

Hymes makes the case for the importance of descriptive analyses of language in a variety of communities. In particular, he, and others of this school, are concerned with the attitudes and knowledge of members of the community, as manifest in the rules by which speakers associate particular modes of speaking, topics or message forms with particular settings and activities. Thus, they are concerned with communication behaviour in its social setting, particularly with language behaviour. Again, this means an emphasis on human groups, rather than on grammar *per se*, but language is still basic data. In particular, these people are concerned with language *function*; that is, with separating what is *said* from what is *done*, and investigating the latter and connecting it regularly with the former. This, of course, is strongly related to Austin's performatives and Searle's speech acts. The emphasis in this school is also highly empirical, indeed Hymes (1972) and Sacks (1972) each suggest that descriptive theory or descriptive analyses and taxonomies are a primary aim of this type of sociolinguistics. Hymes, in this paper, suggests a categorization of units for the study of linguistic behaviour in this context. It is an hierarchical analysis which specifies context and variables, and which states that a complete description of language function must investigate them all.

The highest order unit, the social unit of analysis, is called the *speech community*. He defines this as a community sharing rules for the conduct and interpretation of speech, and rules for the interpretation of at least one linguistic variety. The next order unit is the *speech situation*; that is, situations associated with (or marked by the absence of) speech. Examples are ceremonies, interviews, fishing trips, and so on. A *speech event* is an activity within a speech situation governed by particular norms for the use of speech. For instance, a party is a speech situation, and a conversation during the party a speech event. A *speech act* is the minimal term within an event, as, for instance, a joke within a conversation. He suggests that discourse may be viewed in terms of acts both syntagmatically and paradigmatically; that is, as sequences of acts, and as choices among classes of acts. Here, a potential conflict with speech act theory arises. *Speech styles* and *ways of speaking* are also suggested as categories for investigation, but are not as well defined. More specific is Hymes's tentative categorization of the components of speech.

These components number 16, which are:

> *message form* (the structure of the message); *message content* (e.g. topic); *setting* (physical circumstances); *scene* (psychological circumstances); *speaker*; *addressor*; *hearer*, or *receiver*, or *audience*; *addressee*; *purposes — outcomes*; *purposes — goals*; *key* (manner or tone of event); *channels* (medium of transmission); *forms of speech* (e.g. dialects); *norms of interaction*; *norms of interpretation*; and *genres*.

The four components *speaker, addressor, hearer* and *addressee* can be grouped together as *participants* and differentiated according to community and participant purposes.

These, Hymes claims, are the variables of interest in the study of speech in its social context.

Notice that Hymes has not, at least explicitly, suggested a theory of speaking, but rather a method for its investigation. Of course, there is a strong theoretical component in the specification of method and choice of problem, but the eventual statement of generalities follows from the data which are collected. These data and their analyses can be very interesting and fruitful indeed. Hymes's suggestions have been concerned with the study of language behaviour in general. His requirements are so difficult to meet, however, that there has been no full-scale attempt to cover a speech community in this way. Some people, however, have tried to use his schema, or something like it, in the study of conversation in particular. There have been three especially interesting approaches to this problem, one represented by work by Labov, the second by a school of sociolinguists taking their lead from Sacks, and now represented by Schegloff and others, the third by groups associated with, and drawing from, the English Language Research Unit in Birmingham, including Sinclair, Coulthard and Brazil in the UK, among others.

Labov's (1972) orientation has been to try to discover the rules governing the structure of conversation by deep analysis on all dimensions of some conversation. In order to do this, he has proposed some basic units of discourse, and has tried to discover how they are put together in conversation (of a particular sort) and how people manage to understand them. In his search for rules, Labov especially looked at 'questions' and 'answers', of all types. For example, in the sequence:

A: Are you going to work tomorrow?
B: I'm on jury duty.

his rule is: if A makes a request of B of the form Q(S1) and B responds with a statement S2 and there exist no rules of ellipsis which would expand S2 to include S1, then B is heard as asserting that there exists a proposition known to both A and B of the form 'if S2, then (E)S1', and from this proposition there is inferred an answer to the request (where (E) is an existential operator). This rule is invariant, and emphasizes the role of shared knowledge in conversation. Labov's units and rules are of great interest, especially because of his concern with questions and answers. We cannot summarize his work here, but would like to mention its embodiment in the book *Therapeutic discourse* (Labov and Fanshel, 1977) in which, by an extremely detailed analysis over a 10-year period of one 15-minute conversation between a psychiatric patient and her therapist, Labov and Fanshel manage to formulate a set of general rules for conversation.

Sacks's work, and that following his by Schegloff and his group (e.g. Sacks, Schegloff and Jefferson, 1974), is different in that he and his colleagues have been concerned with analysis of one aspect of conversation at a time; typically, with the organization of turn-taking and other sequential structures. The structure that Labov investigated was logical (in some sense); the structure that this school investigates is organizational. The methods also differ, as Schegloff looks at many conversations, rather than one, but the results are equally interesting. Jefferson (1972), for instance, notes a feature which she calls the *side sequence*, which is a special sort of interruption of a conversational turn, marked by a *questioning repeat*. That is, something is said by A, and B repeats it. This mechanism is part of a *misapprehension sequence*, which follows a regular pattern, which is certainly familiar to those who have worked on reference desks or as intermediaries.

The English Language Research Unit has followed a slightly different path, usually investigating conversation within specific speech situations, and looking at many aspects of dialogue within that context. Their work, as represented by, for example, Sinclair and Coulthard (1975), has been especially important in developing methods for collecting, categorizing and analysing the linguistic data, and relating it to the social aspects of the speech situation. Thus, conversations between teachers and pupils in the classroom are analysed in order to shed light on their relationships; at the same time, knowedge of their social roles informs the analysis of the linguistic data. Within this interactional and social framework, the basic unit of investigation for them is what is being *done* in the conversation.

These studies are examples of a specifically interactional approach to language, concerned with functions rather than with the words themselves.

4.5 Psychology

Cognitive psychology has offered a rather different approach to the study of discourse and conversation from those we have looked at so far. Much of the work in this field has been concerned with reading and understanding texts as discourse units, which is rather different from conversation, although certainly related to it. The relation holds especially in the role of shared knowledge, which has surfaced in both the philosophical and sociological approaches to conversation, although in rather different ways. Some cognitive psychologists have concerned themselves explicitly with conversation as communication, and we would like to discuss this approach on the basis of work by Erik Hollnagel (e.g. Hollnagel, 1978, 1979) who contributes to information science as well as to psychology.

Hollnagel's cognitive view is basically that the individual's knowledge (that is, model of the world) is an active mediator in the individual's interactions with the world. In the communication situation, this can be shown in the following diagram of communication between two parties.

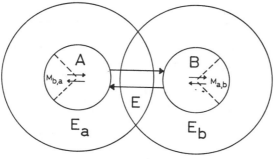

$$A \supset M_{b,a} \supset M_{a,b}^2 \qquad\qquad B \supset M_{a,b} \supset M_{b,a}^2$$

Figure 4.1   A cognitive model of two-party communication (Hollnagel 1978, p 7). Reproduced by permission of the author.

What Hollnagel is concerned to demonstrate in this scheme is the significance of the environment of each participant, of their shared environment, and of their explicitly non-shared environment (environment taken to include, for instance, knowledge). In this schema, one explicitly recognizes that for communication to take place, each of the parties must have a model of the other, which almost certainly does not correspond to the other's model of herself or himself. In Hollnagel's analysis, one of the functions of communication can be to try to influence the model that the other participant has of one, explicitly for the purpose of making the communication more effective (at least from the sender's point of view). Hollnagel summarizes the conditions necessary for human communication as:

a. The participants must have a common language or a common code.

b. The participants must have a common understanding of essential parts of the environment.

c. Each participant must have a model of the partner.

Hollnagel goes on to consider the third requirement in some detail, especially as it concerns the notions of *credibility* and *intention*. Credibility can be affective or cognitive; that is, based on trust or on knowledge, respectively. Although both are important in human to human communication, Hollnagel suggests that the former is not relevant to human-machine communication, and so concentrates upon describing the essentials of establishing cognitive credibility. One of the most important means to this end is that the partner is able to explain the structure of what he or she is attempting to communicate, and to explain why it is so. This explanation proves to the other partner that the sender does understand the subject matter. Another means to the end is by demonstrating, again usually by explanation, competence in the knowledge that is assumed to be shared by the participants. This type of communication Hollnagel calls *secondary communication*. That is, it is a sequence of questions and answers which are designed to increase credibility, and thus to corroborate the *primary communication,* the impartation of the information. Notice that secondary communication is concerned with affecting the model that one participant has of the other. Thus, in this sense, such models appear to be necessary for effective primary communication. In Hollnagel's model, the goal of primary communication is to extend the range of the shared environment, which cannot, however, be extended to include the models that the two parties have of one another.

Hollnagel also suggest that knowledge of purpose and intention by each party of the other is useful in dialogues which are aimed at a single goal (that is, where one party is primary). Thus, another function of secondary communication is to establish, in the model that A has of B, B's purposes and intentions in having engaged in the dialogue. The lack of such a model will seriously inhibit the successful conclusion of the dialogue in attainment of the goal. Hollnagel has suggested that one way to model purpose or intention is to understand the user's strategy in problem-solving. Since Hollnagel works at the OECD Research Reactor in Norway, the example of communication between human and machine at Three Mile Island is not inappropriate here. In that situation, one of the primary causes of the disaster was the unwillingness of the human operators to *believe* the information that the machines provided for them. This information was literally incredible: the suggestion is that perhaps it was of this status just because the machine lacked credibility, and that the cause of this was the lack of a model of the user.

Hollnagel's point of departure in his investigations is to understand, and subsequently model, effective primary communication among human beings (that is, communication of information for specific goals), in order to design effective human-machine communication systems. His emphasis, notice, is always on knowledge, and models of knowledge and participants, and especially on how these models mediate the process of information assimilation. This, then, is an abstract, cognitive view of communication, with some, but not much, bearing on and interest in language itself.

4.6 AI and computational linguistics

Computational linguistics and AI are fields which are specifically concerned with language; the former strictly so, the latter primarily in its attempt to simulate intelligent behaviour. We will not concern ourselves with the question of natural-language understanding systems, which has been a primary concern in these fields, but rather with investigations in other aspects of the human-machine interface in human-machine systems. A number of people have concerned themselves with this problem, especially with the following issues: how can dialogue structures be found and modelled in a human/machine environment? to what extent ought these interfaces to reflect human-human conversational modes? and how is the human-machine dialogue to be implemented? (see, e.g., Association of Computational Linguistics, 1980).

A number of workers in AI have been concerned with the issue of understanding and modelling dialogue. This has largely been within the context of building natural-language understanding systems, but forms a distinct school. Examples include work by Grosz (1977, 1978), Cohen *et al* (1981) and Sidner (1980).

The basic problem with which all this work has been concerned is the issue of how *automatically* to understand and respond to natural human discourse. Some of the reasons why this is problematic include such issues as anaphora resolution, deixis, shifts in topic, partial utterances, and so on, which cannot be adequately interpreted by current linguistic theory. One approach in attempting to resolve the specific issues has been to consider the discourse as a dialogue, and to try to understand how the (often putative, sometimes real) hearer manages to understand the speaker's utterances. Especially important for much of this work is that it is concerned with systems which aim to answer questions put by the user. Thus, this work has investigated aspects of human dialogue, in a strictly dialogue-oriented context.

One aspect of this general approach (of which Cohen *et al*, 1981, is a good example) has noticed that speakers have overall *plans,* according to which they produce specific utterances, and that hearers interpret the utterances, and respond effectively to them, according to their own perceptions of the other's plan. Thus, the implication is that, in successful cooperative dialogue, it is at least necessary for the hearer to know the speaker's plan. Cohen *et al* (1981), for instance, have investigated some real (although brief) human-human information dialogues, in order to discover how this sort of knowledge affects responses, and how the appropriate plans are modified. This work has not yet resulted in any computerized system, but it certainly seems to have demonstrated that this sort of knowledge is necessary to successful information dialogues.

A problem in more extended dialogues is to know what the speaker is referring to when an utterance may, in principle, have a number of possible referents. Sperber and Wilson (1982) use the logico-linguistic concept of relevance to approach this problem. Grosz (1977) introduced the idea of *focus* to model and predict this aspect of dialogue. The basic idea is that as a dialogue progresses, its focus, that is, what is being talked about, shifts, and that in order to understand and respond appropriately, each participant must know what the current focus is, that is, what ought to be paid attention to, out of all possible relevant knowledge. Of special interest to us is that, in order to investigate this issue, Grosz collected and analysed a number of real dialogues (in constrained settings), which are similar in many respects to dialogue in the information interaction.

The analysis of these dialogues allowed Grosz to specify some overall structural characteristics which indicated potential change of focus, and also some specific utterances, or utterance types, associated with focus shifts. Since her work was explicitly concerned with human-computer interaction, she used her results to structure the access to the knowledge base used by a computer natural-language understanding system. And, although the dialogues she analysed were between two people, they were constrained so that they could be considered as human-computer dialogues. Nevertheless, the results appear to offer significant insight into how the topic of a conversation at any one time is identified by the parties, and into at least some methods for identifying when the topic has changed.

Another aspect of dialogue studies in AI is that which has to do with the interface between human and machine. Hayes (Hayes and Reddy, 1979; Hayes, 1980) is representative of the school that says that, in order for human-machine communication to be effective, it will be necessary for the systems to incorporate a number of aspects of human dialogue structure. He calls these the 'non-literal aspects of communication', arising from:

non-grammatical utterance recognition;

contextually determined interpretation;

robust communication procedures;

channel sharing.

The first two points are relatively clear, but the last two require some clarification. By robust communication procedures, he means such things as error correction, back-tracking, asking for clarification, etc. By channel sharing he means turn-taking, in the sense of Sacks, Schegloff and Jefferson (1974). Hayes's contention is that these aspects of dialogue have not been taken into account in most human-machine interfaces, and when they have been considered the results have been:

a. naive, e.g. half-duplex mode, brooking no interruptions; or

b. straightforwardly imitative of superficial aspects of non-literal communications, e.g. 'Hi there, I'm your friendly computer system'.

In particular, Hayes suggests that many aspects of non-literal communication can now be incorporated in human-machine systems in ways that are not possible in human-human communication, but which are appropriate to the human-machine environment, and are responsive to dialogue functions. This is largely due to developments in the technology of interaction, and he points to hardware which allows simultaneous presentation of a variety of information, with provision for highly robust means of interaction. Thus, systems can be designed which indicate, on the screen, what the machine considers to be the current focus of attention, or where the machine is having problems in understanding. Similarly, many options can be presented simultaneously for choice by the user (as in a menu system), if clarification is necessary (cf. side sequences). He suggests that, because of technology which allows multiple output to the screen while the machine is still accepting (and echoing) input, turn-taking in the human sense may not be necessary at all.

The point here is that Hayes (and others, e.g. Shneiderman, 1980a; Hiltz *et al*, 1980) are suggesting that the modes of communication possible between human and machine are such that human dialogue structure should not be mimicked, since it is no longer directly appropriate, but rather that new structures should be devised which respond to the communication needs and functions represented by human dialogue structure. Unfortunately, it seems to us, and to others (e.g. Schegloff, 1980; Wynn, 1980), especially sociologists, that AI's understanding of these needs and functions is perhaps not too well informed, and often biased by the attractiveness of the technology.

4.7 Dialogue and the IR interaction

We have presented examples of five different approaches to the analysis and modelling of conversation, or dialogue: philosophical; linguistic; interactional; cognitive; and computational. Because each of these is grounded in a particular intellectual framework and in a particular problem structure, each is necessarily context dependent, and therefore not applicable directly and *in toto* to some other situation (e.g. the IR context). We would like to point out, briefly, how each of these approaches responds to the IR context, and how each might inform the study of dialogue in this context.

Recall again the IR context. It is a formal, goal-oriented communication system, with (normally) two participants, one of whom, the user, instigates the communication and evaluates its success, while the other, the intermediary, functions as expert in the organization and manipulation of the database. Each participant has specific tasks to perform if the entire communication is to be as successful as possible, but there are certain barriers to their accomplishment. In particular, it is difficult for the user to indicate to the intermediary what is necessary to resolve the problem, and socio-cultural factors mitigate against the straightforward achievement of the goals.

The philosophical approach, especially as exemplified by Grice (1975), stresses the cooperative nature of conversation, and suggests methods by which one might formally analyse and understand what is meant in conversation, rather than merely what is said. In addition, Austin (1962) and Searle (1969), and their school, have proposed schemas by which one might be able formally to decide about the functions of (or acts performed by) particular utterances. Thus, this work responds directly to the cooperative and goal-directed nature of IR interaction.

The linguistic/logical approach, as in Gordon and Lakoff (1971) or Wilson and Sperber (1981), offers theories, and potentially methods, for understanding and identifying the meaning of specific utterances or linguistic structures within the dialogue as a whole. Thus, the substantive topic of the dialogue, a major consideration from the IR point of view, is describable. Other work, as in, for instance, Carlson (1982), or the text linguistic school, offers suggestions as to how the entire structure of dialogues can be identified or characterized, and the utterances embedded within them understood, in semantic and pragmatic terms. Thus, the whole interaction can be considered in a formal sense, which might lead to ways to model or simulate such dialogues.

The interactional approach, with its stress upon the speech situation, offers theories and methods to take account of the roles of the participants in the conversation, and of the social relationships of the participants with one another, and the relationships of these factors with the utterances performed by the participants. It also points out ways for interpreting the actual exchanges between participants, including pauses and other non-linguistic conversational phenomena, a strong characteristic of normal IR interaction. And, especially importantly, it offers methods for collection, analysis and interpretation of conversational data in natural, but well-defined settings.

The cognitive approach to conversation concentrates upon the interaction between the states of knowledge of the participants, how they mediate in the understanding that each party has of the other, and the ways in which the parties elaborate their models of one another. For IR interaction, where the parties have distinct roles and specific knowledge of quite different topics, yet require understanding of one another in order to achieve their mutual goal, this is an especially vital issue.

The approach of computational linguistics or AI to the study of conversation is especially important to IR interaction because of its emphasis on computability and formal procedures, and because at least one of its aims is to produce systems which interact with people in real settings. One of the goals of the analysis of conversation for IR interaction is precisely to build such systems, and thus this work is directly relevant.

Thus, each of the approaches that we have surveyed can be seen to be, in one respect or another, relevant to the study of dialogue in IR interaction. Of course, each is also limited by its own specific preoccupations, and thus none seems to be applicable to this situation to the exclusion of the others. On the other hand, all the various approaches have two common characteristics: the emphasis which they all place on the importance of *shared knowledge* to effective communication in the dialogue; and the insistence of all that it is the *functions* that take place, rather than the surface of the dialogue, which are of significance in discourse analysis. It is this kernel of agreement among the various approaches which allows them to communicate with one another, and which may serve as a basis for developing a unified approach to the study of dialogue in the IR interaction setting. Indeed, there are already some examples of such research in library and information science, which, although perhaps not attaining complete integration of all approaches, do indicate some trends for the future.

One of the first investigations in library and information science of the dialogue components of information interaction was the Syracuse University Presearch Interview Project (Cochrane, 1981). The goal of this project was to discover if there were any systematic relations between characteristics of the presearch interview between reference librarian and user, and satisfaction with the interview. To this end, the project collected videotapes of a large number of such interviews and subjected these data to extensive analysis from a number of points of view. The coding and analysis of the verbal interaction is of most interest from our point of view here, since it amounted to a quasi-functional dialogue analysis.

Their method was to transcribe the interview, and then to identify the general *tasks* and specific *events* which were performed by the two parties (but especially by the intermediary), according to a pre-established classification and coding scheme. The tasks were essentially broad functions associated with information interaction, and included the following categories:

User Description; System Description; Database Selection; Tutorial Activity; Clarification of Request; Request Negotiation; Vocabulary Construction for Search; Search Strategy Formulation;

which were specified on the basis of previous studies, both by them and others. The events were essentially subdivisions or specifications of each task. Each utterance was also coded by one or more variables, which were descriptive identifiers of the utterance (laugh, question, etc.). The whole transcription and coding scheme, including instructions to coders, is specified in Crouch and Lucia (1980). Having categorized the date, the group then sought to characterize the interview according to which tasks and events were performed, and at what general point in the interview they took place. Specifically, they coded whether a task took place as the first event, in the first, second or final third of the interview, or as the last event. Although they were able to distinguish between some events associated with intermediaries and those associated with users, this characteristic was subsumed in the general data categorization. The end results were thus specific overall characterizations of each of the interviews according to which tasks and events were performed, and approximately when in the interview they occurred. Via the variables, there was also some attempt to relate particular kinds of utterances with tasks.

This study had inconclusive results in terms of its goals. It seems likely that this may have been due to the way data were categorized and subsequently grouped, but this remains unclear. Nevertheless, the coding scheme was reliably carried out by trained coders, and thus this can be seen as an example of successful functional analysis of dialogue, at least to some extent. That is, it was possible to characterize the utterances according to a classification of functions. The qualification is made because the verbal *interaction* between the participants was more or less ignored (in this aspect of the overall project), and dialogue features such as turn-taking could not be accounted for. So, for instance, features of the dialogue which might have influenced satisfaction with it, such as the extent to which the participants responded directly to one another, could not be investigated.

But despite the limits imposed by its theoretical framework and analytical techniques, and its lack of explicit reference to other dialogue analysis work, this project did at least show that the analysis of the verbal information interaction, especially by functions performed, is possible, within a schema directly derived from the context and goals of that interaction. In this sense, it at least intuitively responded to the results of general work in discourse analysis. We will refer to the study again in the next chapter.

Belkin and his colleagues (e.g. Brooks and Belkin, 1983; Belkin, 1984) are involved in a research programme whose explicit aim is to investigate characteristics of the dialogue aspects of information interaction. Their goals are varied, according to the specific project, but the overall assumption is that study of the functional and linguistic characteristics of this dialogue will lead to principles both for the design of human-machine systems and for the successful conduct of human-human information reactions. Their work is based upon a specification of the functions which an ideal information provision mechanism ought to perform, which was developed, at least in part, from the observation of information interactions (Belkin, Seeger and Wersig, 1983). The basic method of this group is to audio-tape interactions between intermediary (advisor) and user (advisee) in various sorts of information interactions, trancribe and partition these data into utterances according to one general schema, and then code the utterances of both parties according to various criteria, including information interaction function performed, knowledge needed to perform an utterance, types of internal model each utterance is aimed to elaborate, and so on. The functions which the group has so far identified include:

Problem Mode; Problem State; Problem Description; User Model; Dialogue Mode; Retrieval Strategies; Response Generation; Explanation;

which are to some extent related to the tasks used by the Syracuse group. They differ, however, in that the interactive tasks are more heavily emphasized, and that the theoretical foundations are perhaps more strongly established.

This work, which draws directly upon sociolinguistics for its data gathering, segmentation and to some extent analytic techniques, has led to some preliminary results which seem to justify its preconceptions. Because the data retain all sequential and temporal information, it is possible to relate sequences of utterances to one another. This has been used by the group to attempt to identify interactional characteristics of successful and unsuccessful dialogues, for instance, whether both parties perform similar functions at the same time (i.e. support one another), and whether specific sequences of functions lead to successful or unsuccessful interaction (Belkin, 1984; Price, 1983). They have also been able to make some preliminary

68

correlations of type of knowledge used by the intermediary with functions performed (Brooks and Belkin, 1983).

These projects thus represent a principled investigation of dialogue in the information interaction, which draws upon techniques and theories from several other disciplines concerned with dialogue analysis, but which is also specific to the information interaction situation. Although it is certainly far too early strictly to evaluate this work, the results which it has offered seem to speak in favour of the idea that emphases on *functions, knowledge, interaction* and *context* can serve as a means for successfully applying some techniques and theories of dialogue analysis in general to the study of dialogue in the information interaction.

5 Human-human interaction

5.1 Introduction

Interaction between people occurs in every kind of context, and has been widely studied by psychologists, sociologists and linguists. A helpful summary of the perspective developed on social interaction has been provided by Sherif and Sherif (1969), and their presentation is followed here.

Social interaction is affected by factors relating to:

the participating individuals;

the occasion for the communication;

the environment in which the interaction occurs;

the attitudes of the participants to each other, to the communication event, and to the environment.

As regards the participating individuals, their age, sex, educational level, occupation, status and so on can all affect their interaction. Differences between the participants in any of these characteristics can be relevant. The prevailing relations between them can affect interaction — are they strangers, casual acquaintances, regular colleagues? The occasion for the communication will influence information transfer. Is it idle interest, information urgently needed to complete a pressing task, another link in a slowly developing depth study, or an item to be remembered because it might prove useful later? The environment can be an equally important factor: the encounter can be on the ground of either participant, or on common ground; other people may be present or not; the physical conditions of communication may be good or bad; access of an enquirer to a source may be simple and informal, or a struggle with bureaucracy. Lastly, we come to attitudes — particularly those of the enquirer. How does he or she regard the source or the intermediary supplying information? Do their characteristics affect the enquirer positively or negatively? Is he or she at ease or not? Eagerly interested in the information sought, or is the search a necessary but distasteful chore? Past experiences, motive and moods affect each participant's behaviour relative to the other, to the requirement for information, and to the communication location.

The interaction that is of particular interest in this review is the interview between an enquirer and an information searcher. Studies of this interaction will now be examined in some detail.

5.1.1 *The place of the interview in the search process*

Negotiation in searching is not a single process but rather a series of complex interactions that may involve (1) a dyad consisting of a search analyst and a user interacting with each other, (2) the search analyst reacting with the computer system, (3) the search analyst or the user alone, reacting internally, or (4) reactions wholly within the computer system. Overall therefore, the negotiation process involves both human-human and human-machine interactions, each of them comprising many transactions, not all of which occur in all search processes. In addition, it is not yet clear how or indeed whether the negotiation process in online retrieval differs from the more traditional and more fully documented reference interview in the manual search for information. Nor is it yet clear what elements affect the user's ultimate satisfaction with the search, or how these factors may be separated, measured and related to the preceding elements of the search process (Auster, 1983).

Study of the search negotiation has a long history. By 1930 James Wyer in his manual on reference services was writing of the 'mind-reading' of the reference librarian 'who gives people what they do not know they want'. The first description of information-seeking behaviour based on an analytical investigation and not just personal impressions was written by Robert Taylor (1967). He considers the negotiation of reference questions as one of the most complex acts of human communication. 'In this act', he writes, 'one person tries to describe for another person not something he knows, but rather something he does not know'. Taylor tries to reconstruct the negotiation process between the library user and the reference librarian (or information specialist) as follows:

A. First of all there is a conscious or unconscious need for information not existing in the remembered experience of the enquirer.

B. At the second level there is a conscious mental description of an ill-defined area of indecision .... The enquirer may, at this stage, talk to someone else to sharpen his focus. He hopes and expects that a conversation with a colleague may clear some ambiguities of the question.

C. At the third stage, an enquirer can form a qualified and rational statement of his question. He is now able to describe his area of doubt in concrete terms, and he may or may not be thinking within the context or constraints of the system from which he wants to extract information.

D. At the fourth level the question is recast in anticipation of what the system can deliver. This is done usually by the searcher.

Taylor suggest that these four levels of question formation can be reformulated as shading into one another along a question spectrum:

Q1. The visceral need — the actual but unexpressed need for information.

Q2. The conscious need — the conscious, within-brain description of the need.

Q3. The formalized need — the formal statement of the need, still within the user's mind.

Q4. The compromised need — the question as presented to the information system. The information need is expressed as a query submitted to the reference librarian. Taylor calls it the 'compromised' need because the query asked may be modified by a reference negotiation between the user and the reference librarian.

It is the skill of the librarian to work with the enquirer back from the compromised to the formalized and even to the conscious need to develop an appropriate search strategy. Thus, by funnelling the request for information through a series of filters, the reference librarian helps the user in understanding his or her information need. The filters listed by Taylor are as follows:

1. subject definition;

2. objective and motivation;

3. personal characteristics of enquirer;

4. relationship of enquiry description to file organization (the relationship of the query to the way the information is organized);

5. anticipated or acceptable answers.

The request for information passes through the above-mentioned filters and the librarian selects significant data from each of the filters. This procedure helps the librarian in the completion of the search and in the ultimate provision of information.

These five general types of information necessary for the search definition are not mutually exclusive categories. It is also the structure of these filters, modified for the specific enquiry, that provides the compression of subject and time of an enquiry.

Recent models of the online search process clearly show the place of the search interview. Briggs (1976) while describing the entire set of interactions between the user and the analyst as the 'user interface', creates a model consisting of two major components: presearch and postsearch activities. These components involve interactive processes that reflected existing user interfaces as they occurred and were documented in actual searches.

All these models stress the importance of the online negotiation interview. Occurring in the early stages of the search process, it is the step that allows the searcher to determine exactly what the user's information needs are and allows the user to learn what the computer can and cannot do. During the interview the searcher must negotiate the information request and transform it into appropriate search statements that can be handled by the online system. Objectives, choice of terms, and search strategy must all be discussed and mutual agreement reached.

Meadow and Cochrane (1981) consider the presearch interview as a process consisting of certain usually occurring steps:

1. clarifying and negotiating the information need and search objectives. It is now that it is determined whether high recall, high precision, or retrieving some relevant items is most important to the user;

2. identifying relevant online databases;

3. formulating basic search logic and planning search strategies;

4. compiling the search terms, whether from thesauri or free text, and deciding their sequence;

5. making output choices, and placing limits on the ultimate form of the printouts;

6. conceptualizing the search as input to the retrieval system; search terms are arranged into concepts using such features as truncation and word proximity, concept groups are arranged in order of importance;

7. reviewing search results and considering alternative strategies with possible recycling of steps 1-6;

8. evaluating final results and determining user satisfaction.

The important role of the intermediary thus emerges. Francillon (1959) writes of the negotiation process that 'the first question often does not express the real intent of the requester. It is often necessary for the librarian to ask other questions.' Taylor (1968) states that 'reference librarians and information specialists have developed, both consciously and unconsciously, rather sophisticated methods of interrogating users'. In an instructional module for negotiating the reference query, Jahoda (1975) indicates that the librarian should use open questions in the initial negotiation stages, and closed questions at the final stages. Tessier, Atherton and Crouch (1977) suggest that during the interaction 'a user will provide an immense amount of information about his requirements, expectations and compromises'.

In her study of the behaviour of search analysts in presearch interviews, Cochrane (1981) listed tasks that other investigators had reported as taking place then, and developed a typology, already mentioned in Section 4.7:

1. descriptive and tutorial tasks;

2. request clarification tasks;

3. request negotiation tasks;

4. vocabulary construction tasks;

5. search strategy tasks;

6. other activities (e.g. administrative).

Parallels between manual and online searchers have been drawn by Knapp (1978), Hammer (1982) and others.

In reviewing these treatments of the online interview, it becomes obvious that it may sometimes include activities that take place at the terminal, if the user is present during the search.

5.2 The purpose of the interview

W A Katz (1978) underlines the responsibility of the librarian to understand the question put to him by the user as well as to be aware of possible motivations for asking a question indirectly or incompletely and to be sensitive to these reasons in negotiating a query. 'It is the librarian's responsibility, not the requestor's, to take steps to ensure that the query is fully understood before the search begins, and to conduct the reference interview with tact and sensitivity.' It is important to find out if clarification of the question by interview is necessary. Unnecessary questioning wastes the user's time and may confuse and frustrate him. Katz presents a 'checklist for identification of negotiable queries', which the reference librarian could use before starting an interview.

The librarian attempting to determine the user's motivation must be very careful not to give the impression of prying. The librarian must encourage the user to discuss the information request freely and feel comfortable about it. It is important that during the negotiation the user, not the librarian, should do most of the talking. If the librarian is to gain a fuller understanding of the information need, he or she must listen rather than dominate the discussion. As the user describes the information need, the librarian asks questions to clarify ambiguities, to encourage the client to continue talking, and to determine the amount of information desired, the level of answer which will be most useful, and any special limitations on the desired answer, such as language or time period. Genuine listening involves not only concentrating on what the user says, but also being alert to the user's tone of voice, facial expressions, and gestures. These nonverbal clues are a very good means of confirming the librarian's impressions of the user.

One of the reasons why the user may ask a question which does not express his or her need is underestimating the ability of the librarian and the library collection to provide a satisfactory answer. If the librarian is sure that he understands the question, he may demonstrate this during the interview. This would make the two persons involved in the dialogue into equal partners.

Katz in his chapter on negotiation techniques advocates the use of open and closed questions (as described by G B King, 1972) but also states that 'each librarian develops an individual approach to questioning clients during negotiation, and no one way of phrasing can be claimed as best for all librarians.' The authors agree with this statement and it has been proved by rich experience in online searching at the Central Information Service (University of London), where each of the employed search analysts has an individual interviewing style.

Somerville (1977) in a guide to the presearch interview divides its components into four groups: those common to all interviews; additional components if the user is unfamiliar with online searching; components if the user is present at the terminal during search; and components that can be omitted for frequent users.

The elements common to all interviews are:

1. the use of interpersonal communication and negotiation skills;

2. discussion of the subject with the user;

3. determination whether a computer search is the appropriate way to answer the question;

4. ensuring that the searcher understands the question;

5. determining the comprehensiveness of the question;

6. identifying limits to the search;

7. selecting databases and systems;

8. identifying additional sources;

9. identifying main concepts and developing search strategy;

10. identifying potential problems;

11. determining alternative strategies;

12. discussing confidentiality;

13. conducting post-search review.

5.3 Interview techniques

Geraldine King (1972) suggested that the reference interview is composed of two chronological segments: one in which the librarian encourages the user to discuss fully the request, followed by one in which the librarian asks questions to relate the request to materials available in the library (or in databases). She recognized that in the initial stage the librarian asks open-ended questions to encourage the user to discuss his or her information needs, and avoids closed questions until the final stage of the interview. The 'openness' versus 'closedness' of the questions, and other signs of encouragement from the librarian — silences, 'guggles', pauses between questions — she identified as especially important to successful negotiation.

Open questions, she suggested, were those prefaced by who? what? where? when? how?, and encourage the respondent to answer at length. Closed questions begin with words like is? do? can? will?, and call for shorter responses. King stressed the need for librarians to be good interviewers, and advocated greater use of open questions to elicit fuller responses.

Lynch's examination (1978) of reference interviews in public libraries tries to analyse eight questions:

1.   How often does a reference librarian interview the user who presents a reference query?

2.   Does this frequency vary according to the type of transaction involved?

3.   Are interviews more frequent when the librarian is less busy?

4.   When an interview does occur, what gross categories or levels of information are sought by the librarian?

5.   How often are the questions of the librarian open questions and how often are they closed questions?

6.   Does the reference librarian use the secondary questions (probes) used by other interviewers?

7.   How does a librarian discover that the query first presented is not the query the user wants answered?

8.   How many primary questions does the librarian ask the user in an interview?

The result of this study, carried out in four public libraries with 366 interviews recorded and 309 ultimately transcribed, revealed that open questions, i.e. those which allow flexibility in user response, were employed infrequently in the interview (8% of all questions asked); 90% were closed questions and 2% were considered to fall into an intermediate category. Primary questions (questions by which the librarian introduces some aspect of the user's search for information and asks for content new to the interview) were infrequently used in the interview; 52% of the interviews involved only one question. Another 37% had two or three questions.

Marylin White (1981) distinguishes four dimensions of the reference interview: structure, coherence, pace and length. 'A dimension is a quality of the interview. It is affected by decisions made during the interview'.

5.3.1   Structure

Structure refers to the content of the interview and how the interview is arranged. The structure reflects the librarian's goals for the interview. Goals are translated into tasks. Each task has its own information requirement, and requirements in turn affect the structure. During the interview the librarian may address any or all of the following topics:

1. the problem creating the original question;

2. the subject of the request;

3. the nature of the service to be provided, i.e. answer requirements;

4. situational constraints likely to affect selection or use of information, such as deadline;

5. personal variables that constitute long-term constraints, such as intelligence and attitude;

6. prior search history, i.e. what the user has already done to locate the information.

Two basic approaches can be followed in the reference process, and both have implications for the structure of the interview: systematic approach and heuristic problem-solving mode. In a systematic approach, the interview is a reasonably complete phase before the search, for example the interview preceding a later online search at which the user will not be present. In this situation, the librarian systematically covers all potentially relevant topics, perhaps gathering more information than actually is necessary to provide a basis for decisions during the later search without the user.

In a heuristic problem-solving mode, the interview is integrated more completely into the search phase. This approach combines personal interaction with trial lookup into sources, feedback from the sources, subsequent discussion with the user, additional search, and so on (a loop), until an acceptable solution is reached. In this situation, the interview may be segmented into relatively small parts, interspersed throughout the search process. With the user being on the spot, some interim relevance judgments can be made and fed into the negotiation system. This additional information can redirect the search at a different angle, usually resulting in a more successful yield.

5.3.2. Coherence

In some interviews, the structure may be readily apparent to the user because it has an external logical validity or because it matches his own perception of an appropriate approach. In other cases, an interview may be completely disjointed and reveal that the librarian has problems with determining goals, translating them into tasks, and identifying the informational requirements of those tasks. In still other interviews, the interview may appear to be disjointed to the user, but may indeed have a structure that matches the librarian's image of an appropriate approach and thus have an internal validity. Unless the user has tremendous confidence in the librarian's ability to succeed despite apparent difficulties, or excuses his perception of a lack of structure by his own inadequacies, he is likely to begin to curtail cooperation if the structure is not apparent, since he cannot comprehend what is happening.

The second situation described above (the actually disjointed interview) is the most serious one and can only be resolved by addressing the goal-related problems. The third situation (apparently disjointed) can be resolved by altering another dimension of the reference interview — its coherence. Coherence refers to the user's perception of the structure and is dependent on the systematic connection and integration of the parts of the interview.

The user's cooperation is closely related to his understanding of what is taking place and agreeing with it. He will understand the order and plan of the interview better if the reference librarian makes him aware of the context for individual questions or sequences of questions and thus allows him to see the relationships between and among the interview parts. The importance of context for comprehension is well known from research in psychology and linguistics.

White suggests that the reference librarian can transmit a plan or framework to the user through some combination of the following stratagems:

1. outlining the framework early in the interview:
   'Tell me about how you plan to use the information and then we can determine which databases to use and which subject terms would be appropriate.'

2. making transitional statements to reveal relationships between or among questions or to place them within a broader framework:
   'From what you have told me, I think I understand the topic you are working on, but let me ask you a few questions so I can determine what kinds of materials to check.'

3. summarizing the information exchange:
   'Now let me make sure I understand what you need. You want criticism — and particular form is not important — about Shelley's ode 'To a Skylark' that appeared over a 75-year span after its publication.'

The most effective approach is likely to include a combination of at least two approaches, although this has not been tested and may vary among types of interviews, searchers, and users. Summary statements integrate the bits of information solicited in questions or inferred during the interview. They may reveal misconceptions or identify missing information.

The final summary by the searcher describes the acceptable answer(s) and establishes guidelines for judging the relevance of information gathered during the search.

With this approach the user has ample opportunity to provide feedback and to alter the structure of the interview. With user's feedback, the librarian may alter the approach to give a rationale for a specific piece of information or specific strategy. The librarian as well as the user may ask questions about related subject areas rather than the specific topic, referring, for example, to inadequacies in the terminology.

Coherence is simply a perception, a perception by the user, not the librarian, which means that the librarian consciously has to make an effort to ensure that order readily perceptible to him becomes perceptible to the user.

5.3.3 Pace

Another dimension affected by procedures during the interview is its pace, which refers to the speed and efficiency of the question/response interchange. The librarian has a direct control over the pace of the interview by:

1. selecting the type of questions;

2. determining the sequencing of questions;

3. determining which information should serve as the basis for continued interaction;

4. determining the nature or method of providing feedback;

5. influencing the extent of digression tolerated or necessary within the interview.

The first decision, type of question, refers to the distinction between open and closed questions. Sequencing refers to the arrangement of types of questions. In sequencing decisions, the librarian has three general approaches:

1. the funnel sequence, moving from broad, open questions to closed, restrictive ones;

2. the reverse funnel sequence, moving from closed to open questions;

3. the tunnel sequence, using a series of the same type of questions, either open or closed.

Generally the funnel sequence is more effective if the respondent knows his topic or problem well and can express himself effectively. By using probing questions, i.e. follow-up questions on specific points, the librarian can expand or clarify any information gained through the open question. The inverted funnel allows the user to get involved slowly and is more likely to be effective when the user needs to be motivated or when he cannot supply relevant information at an early stage. The tunnel sequence inhibits the user from volunteering information, but may be useful near the end of the interview, when rapport between the interviewer and the interviewee has been established.

User and librarian are continually providing each other with feedback, sometimes in the form of verbal statement, at other times solely through nonverbal channels, such as posture, eye contact, gestures, or facial expressions.

The pace of the interview may vary. In a common model for the reference interview, the librarian establishes a leisurely pace initially, using techniques already mentioned to make the user feel comfortable and to establish role expectations. As both user and librarian become more involved in the problem and its solution, the librarian can turn to a faster pace, perhaps by asking closed questions. The final summary moderates the pace and allows both librarian and user to evaluate the outcome and modify it if necessary before the search.

5.3.4 Length

Every decision the librarian makes during the interview has implications for the use of time, and thus an effect on the length of the interview. Stringent time limitations, real and apparent, operate as constraints on both the librarian and user behaviour. A reference librarian can establish some control over length by varying other dimensions, particularly structure and pace. Compromising coherence is risky.

To shorten the interview, the librarian can modify the goals, his emphasis on them, the means of satisfying them and/or the sequence in which he addresses them. The librarian can also accept the user's request as an accurate assessment of information need. This decision allows him to avoid the area of problem definition and the resultant need for explanations, digressions, or indirect approaches, all of which are time-intensive. The librarian can also rely more on information activated within his own mind without verifying it with the user.

5.4 Attributes of the searcher

Gothberg (1974, 1976) explores the relationship between the 'immediacy' of a librarian's communication during the interview and user satisfaction. She defines immediacy in a communication process as a psychological closeness, such as warmth or sympathy. Her study is of methodological significance because it is one of the few to incorporate observations, and it assesses the relationship between quantified observations and a measure of user satisfaction.

In another investigation Fidel (1981), using the case study method, constructed a pattern model of searching styles which she labelled as either operationalist or conceptualist. In her view, operationalist searchers seemed to base their search formulations and interactions mainly on the manipulative power provided by systems. They 'understand' a request by translating it into search statements. They use a thesaurus as the main source for clarification and frequently as the only source, usually looking for terms submitted by the user. After they find the appropriate descriptors and know the categories to which they belong, they are ready to formulate the search. If they cannot find a descriptor corresponding to a user term, they do a free-text search using the original terms.

Conceptualist searchers, however, seem to formulate and modify their searches mainly by performing conceptual analysis of the user request. They 'understand' a request by fitting it into a conceptual structure (e.g.that of a faceted classification). In order to identify the different elements of the structure, they may need information not originally provided by the user, and they use all resources available to them (e.g. reference books) to acquire this information. They persistently search for descriptors to be incorporated into the initial search formulation — maybe using broader or related descriptors to represent one element in the conceptual structure if a specific one cannot be identified. During the formulation process they decide which elements of the structure are most important for the specific request, and investigate these thoroughly.

Fenichel (1980) examined the relationship between searching behaviour and searcher experience (with the ERIC database). She found that novices performed surprisingly well, although moderately experienced searchers performed the briefest and most cost-effective searches (measured as time per citation received).

5.5 User behaviour

Some users of online retrieval systems approach the system with a greater background knowledge of their query topic than others, because of a longer continuing involvement with the specific area of study. They seek to supplement already existing knowledge of literature in a subject. Saracevic (1970) has suggested that greater subject knowledge on the part of an assessor of search results leads to a more stringent assessment of relevance. One can also assume that greater subject knowledge allows more perceptive assessment of recall — the user can note an apparent lack of completeness in search results. Thus, knowledgable users demand more from the searcher, more from the search, and are more critical of the search interview.

One of the aims of a study by Hitchingham (1979a,b) was to analyse interaction between users and searchers with this factor in mind. She adopted a behavioural approach, using the Bales interaction process analysis schemes for observing the social and emotional behaviour of individuals in small groups. Her work was also influenced methodologically by a study by Carmon (1975). This had two goals: first, to collect descriptive and quantitative data concerning the reference process for computer-based literature searching, and, second, to develop a model of the user interface for a projected network project of system use. The study was conducted at two sites, the University of Georgia and UCLA. At the University of Georgia four intermediaries carried out searching; these were professional information specialists who were by job function involved almost exclusively with computerized literature searching; searchers at UCLA were more likely to have several other responsibilities in addition to computerized searching. User evaluation forms were issued, and a satisfaction measure was calculated. Transcribed interviews were coded at each institution. Slightly different, self-developed coding systems were used at each site.

In Hitchingham's study, the subjects were in-person users and searchers at three institutions providing MEDLINE searches. Here 11 searchers participated, all considered as being familiar with the database. The recorded interviews were divided at the time of transcription into interaction units according to Bales's methodology (1950). Transcribed interviews were coded by two experienced searchers at the Computer Search Service, MIT Libraries, after they had been made familiar with the Bales categories. This familiarization included an extended training session, after which the coders were able to demonstrate 82% agreement in test scoring. The analysed interviews provided data for scoring the volume of user information-giving and searcher question-asking, by counting the frequencies of events coded by category for user or searcher.

Interviews from 18 of the total 54 responding users were transcribed and analysed. Although online services had been available for several years, more than half (54%) of the recorded users were novice participants in an online interview. Slightly more than a third (34%) of the users indicated participation in one to five interviews; 10.3% of the users indicated they had been involved in six or more interviews (two users did not respond to this question). Approximately a third (34.9%) of the users were students; 22.2% of the respondents indicated faculty ranks (instructor, assistant professor, professor). Other medical personnel accounted for 18.3% of the MEDLINE users. Whatever their status, many of the MEDLINE users indicated that their primary reason for requesting a search was research.

The Bales categories into which the interviews were analysed consist either of positive social-emotional areas ('shows solidarity', 'shows tension release', 'agrees'); neutral areas ('gives suggestion', 'gives opinion', 'gives orientation', 'asks for orientation', 'asks for opinion', 'asks for suggestion'); or negative areas ('disagrees', 'shows tension', 'shows antagonism'). Not surprisingly, the investigator found that the information-giving activity by searchers was most striking, and that they showed higher levels of giving suggestions and opinions, while users were predominant in the agreement category.

This study, which analysed the interview situation and the user satisfaction in great detail, by itself provides a wealth of information on user-intermediary interaction. In general, the results provide no basis for suggesting that the presumed greater knowledgeability of faculty users (as evidenced by the higher degree levels attained by faculty, the greater likelihood of faculty regularly reading journals related to the search topic, and the greater likelihood that they had published a paper on the topic) is a factor leading to more stringent assessments in the areas of relevance, concern for recall, and perception of the searcher in the interview. Knowledgeability in the sense considered in the study does not appear to be a factor leading to greater information-giving activity in the search interview.

Interaction profiles developed in this study showed that information-gathering activity constituted the larger proportion of all searcher activity. This observation agrees well with the observation by Lynch (1978) that 'participating librarians (in reference interviews in public libraries) spent a significant proportion of their time giving information to users (patrons) rather than getting information from them'.

It appears that some relationship exists between user information-giving activity and relevance scores. Question-asking by the searcher has been suggested as a contributory factor in this relationship. Users in terminal session interviews exhibited more information-giving activity than those in non-terminal sessions. Searchers in terminal interview sessions exhibited more question-asking activity than did searchers in non-terminal sessions.

Wayne Crouch (1981) reports a study carried out at Syracuse University on the verbal behaviour of librarians and of users, and shortly describes a few papers giving an account of coding schemes used in communications, psychology and sociology.

Hawes (1972) described a coding scheme for verbal interaction, and found that conversations could be reliably coded and that consistencies in patterns of communication could be documented. In his scheme, verbal behaviours were coded every 10 seconds during an interview between a doctor and a patient.

Crouch and Lucia (1980) described in a codebook a scheme which was used in a study of verbal behaviour during interviews in seven libraries, involving 19 librarians and the coding of 82 interviews. They covered a wide variety of medical library requests. Most of the requests (69) did not involve the use of a terminal to carry out a search during the interview (the search was done later). Satisfaction of the users was assessed by nine individual measures. A factor-analytical study of requester responses to the nine measures identified four factors or indexes of satisaction:

focus on search results/information/problem
(measure 6, expect online search to be successful)

focus on librarian understanding
(measure 4, searcher understood my request, and
measure 8, searcher understood my purpose)

focus on the interview as an event
(measure 5, not a successful interview or,
measure 7, ill-at-ease, or
measure 9, fell short of my expectations)

focus on interview comfort
(measure 1, enjoyed working with searcher, or
measure 3, very dissatisfied with interview)

The main analysis consisted of running stepwise multiple regressions, with the criteria for each of the satisfaction indexes and measures for 52 verbal behaviours as potential independent variables in each equation. The analysis identified a number of verbal behaviours by librarians that were significantly related to requester satisfaction. Open questions were positively related to satisfaction, closed questions negatively. The first were associated with the user being able to express himself in his own terms, the second with being 'boxed in'.

Brooks and Belkin (1983) are in process of designing a front-end search processor that will act as an intermediary mechanism between the user and an online service. One component of the system aims to interact with the user to develop a pre-online search strategy. The paper presents the analysis of a dialogue that takes place between an end-user and a human intermediary. Tape-recorded interviews are transcribed according to a set of rules, a combination and modification of the rules of Crouch and Lucia (1980), Jefferson (1972) and Labov and Fanshel (1977), resulting in a coding into functions and tasks.

5.6 Some suggested approaches

The recognition of the importance of empathy between the user and librarian has led some investigators to see a strong relationship between the reference interview and counselling and therapy interviews, e.g. Peck (1975) and Pierce (1971).

Gavryck (1982) has suggested that an exploration of the literature on task groups, group interaction, social penetration theory, and uncertainty reduction theory could all help to illuminate further the reference interview relationship, and that such insight would enable librarians to create more cooperative atmospheres that would facilitate the flow of information that is so crucial to a successful search.

While the behaviours and roles of the participants have received considerable attention from some, others have concentrated on the techniques of structuring the reference interview. In the social sciences, the interview is a research instrument, and those using it in this capacity have tried to increase respondent participation, minimize situational determinants, reduce and control error. They have identified characteristics of the question-answer process that will yield reliable, unbiased, valid responses.

Another approach (e.g. Horn, 1974) is to turn to the sociological concepts of role and status. Quite typically in a reference interview, neither the librarian nor the user knows just what to expect from the other, there is a lack of control on the part of the librarian, and a need to establish relative status. The user is defensive about the librarian's ability to provide assistance. Such conditions present barriers to effective role relationships and reference transactions.

As well as verbal behaviour, investigators have been led to consider nonverbal communication factors (Auster, 1983). Body language, such as posture, facial expressions, hand gestures, eye movements and head nods, have been shown to influence the reference interview. For example, facial expression was said to be of importance in indicating approachability. Boucher (1976) summarized two extreme behaviours that librarians might adopt as the 'preoccupation' mode and the 'availability' mode. We have already referred to Gothberg's concept of 'immediacy'. Again, Kazlauskas (1976) confirmed that positive nonverbal behaviour exhibited by librarians generated similar positive responses from users, whereas negative behaviour inhibited user requests and interaction.

Munoz (1977) discussed the significance of nonverbal communication in the reference interview, and concluded by stating that the reference librarian 'has an obligation to become acquainted with the current research in nonverbal communication. ... Nonverbal communication is not just a matter of common sense; its study is a scientific enterprise which shows us how to use various communication modes as conscious techniques. It offers us a means to establish more effective contact between enquirer and librarian'.

Jahoda's (1977) list of good and poor ways to negotiate a request suggests that in good negotiation the librarian will make eye contact with the user, give him or her full attention, make the user feel at ease, show empathy, and be aware of nonverbal clues.

Auster and Lawton (1984) have reported the result of an exploratory study which has refined our understanding of the interaction taking place during the search interview. Findings suggest a model of the process with three component strands: the behaviour of the user, the questioning techniques of the search analyst, and the topic of the search.

The search analyst's methods included the use of empathy and nonverbal expressions, open and closed questions, and a loose structuring of the interview into five stages. On the user's part, it appears that his or her stock of knowledge, ability to express the content and type of information needed, and the value placed upon this information, were the important variables.

6 Human-computer interaction

6.1 Introduction

The literature on the interaction between computers and their human users is vast, encompassing topics as varied as the design of computer programming languages, the optimum viewing angle for display screens, the layout of keyboards, the relationship of display devices and input devices to user characteristics, the effect of system response time on user acceptance, the relationship of the task being performed to the nature of the interaction mode, the models that humans and computers hold of one another and their effect on interaction design principles, and so on and on. The disciplines which contribute to this literature are just as wide-ranging, from computer science to ergonomics to engineering to psychology to AI, and so on and on. Obviously, we cannot hope to review all this literature here, so once again we are forced to limit the scope of our review. In this case, we choose to concentrate on those areas which relate most directly to our model of information interaction; that is, on theories, methods and models which might help us better to understand the relationship between the human user and the computer system and to design interfaces between the two which help the user better to accomplish the information-searching tasks. Thus, we will not be reporting on investigations of parameters of particular devices, nor on research on programming languages as such, but rather on research on the conceptual foundations of the human-computer interface.

Even within this limitation, the literature is vast. We will ease our task further by taking advantage of the several excellent reviews in the various fields concerned, by being highly selective, and by attempting to limit detailed discussions to those studies or types of studies which seem especially relevant to information interaction. We will also not consider, except as specific examples of a particular theoretical approach, studies of particular task environments, such as text editing or help systems, with the exception, of course, of the IR task.

We begin by citing the review and text sources on which we have most heavily drawn. These will also generally be cited in our review proper, but should be taken as having shaped this chapter in general ways as well. This chapter should not be considered as a substitute for these reviews, but rather as a supplement. In chronological order, these basic sources are: J L Bennett (1972); Brenner *et al* (1981); Moran (1981);

Maguire (1982); Ramsey and Grimes (1983); and Gaines (1984).

The issue of the human-computer interface or interaction has been seen as significant in IR for almost as long as studies in such interfaces have been conducted. Gaines (1984) marks 1969 as the beginning point of serious work in human-computer interaction, and Bennett (1972) reports in his *ARIST* review of 1971 and earlier literature that '...vigorous search for literature that focused on the user interface in other applications [than bibliographic search] was often fruitless' (p 161). Despite this early intense interest in the problem, it seems as fair to say now, as it did then, that the problem is unresolved, and that there appear to be no really satisfactory interfaces to bibliographic search systems. Indeed, most such interfaces look very little different now from those used then. In this chapter, we would like briefly to investigate some possible reasons for this apparent lack of progress, and to describe some new directions in theory and research in human-computer interaction in several disciplines, which may offer hope for finally developing more effective human-computer interaction in IR.

6.2 The state of the human-computer interface in information systems

Bennett (1972) suggested that the design of an interactive system must, initially, take account of the properties of the following basic system components: (1) the task to be performed; (2) the user; (3) the terminal; and (4) the computer-stored information content. He also made the point that the task issue is certainly dominant over the others, and that perhaps the order of the components here reflects an hierarchical order for design specification. Although one might take issue with his specific terminology, it is clear that this statement of factors affecting design is generally reasonable, and certainly in accord with the current view of this situation. That is, there is now fairly general agreement among those working in all aspects of human-computer interaction that the nature of the task on which the user and computer are working is of paramount importance in interface design, then comes perhaps a specification of the respective roles of the two parties in the task to be accomplished, followed by characteristics of the user, of the hardware, of the information to be displayed, and finally of the database. Why then, if the general framework has changed so little in these 13 years, has there been so little genuine progress in constructing better interfaces in information systems?

One answer may lie in the fact that, although frameworks may be specified by someone quite well, this does not mean that research actually takes place within those frameworks. Thus, Bennett (1972) could cite only one paper that took a general look at task specification, and of the more substantial number of reports on systems in particular application areas, few seemed actually to have analysed the task performed in any detailed conceptual sense. For characteristics of the user, the situation then was much the same. More effort, for instance, appears to have been devoted to training users to use the interfaces, than to principled design from the user's characteristics, as suggested by Bennett and others. At the close of his review, Bennett suggests a reason for this state of affairs, that '...the theoretical basis for incorporating user problem-solving characteristics into analytical models is so rudimentary...', and closes by suggesting that '...the challenge for research is to ... [develop] an agreement on ways for characterising user tasks, for allocating interface resources to meet task requirements, and for evaluating user effectiveness in task performance'. That is, the rather poor state of affairs in 1972 (which was, nevertheless, substantially better than the previous work which was totally computer-dominated) may have been due to the lack of theories and methods, rather than failure to appreciate the fundamental issues. This being the case, one would expect to have seen some progress in the next 10 years in developing and applying such theories and methods to the design of human-computer interfaces in IR.

Unfortunately, as we and others have pointed out, this appears not to have been the case. In 1980, it was possible for a review of interface designs for information systems to state: 'Research has not yet provided a satisfactory solution to the problems of interfacing between the end user and large-scale databases' (Brenner et al, 1981, p 71). It appears to be commonly agreed that direct end-user use of information systems is highly desirable, yet that most such systems which are publicly available are extremely difficult to use in this way. What explains this stagnation, given the enormous amount of literature on the need for 'user-friendly' interfaces? One possible reason is the history of the large-scale information providers, whose interface systems were designed for use by information specialists, and which seem to be heavily constrained by costs and by the characteristics of the databases they search. But these are factors which could be overcome. Maguire's (1982) review showed that one appropriate design consideration is that using a human intermediary between user and database might be more appropriate than asking the user to interact directly with the computer. If we consider the case of IR interaction, this has certainly been the general response to the interface problem. Of course, the intermediaries still need to be trained, but at least they can specialize in the interface, and so adapt to its admitted faults.

This response appeared to be adequate up to the mid to late 1970s, and appears to have had the result of reducing the research effort suggested by Bennett (1972) in information science. It may also be the case that some of the issues raised by Bennett were too complex for the theories and methods available. That is, theories of goals and tasks, and of how they relate to user characteristics, just were inadequate or unavailable for the analysis of the highly complex information interaction situation. The evidence from other chapters of this review seems to support this interpretation.

The situation now and since the late 1970s has, however, begun to change. The shortage of trained intermediaries, increasing commercial pressure to incorporate the end-user into the information system, and the theoretical and practical attractiveness of direct end-user access, have combined to make the human-computer interface issue important once again in information science. Furthermore, research in fields outside information science, and some within, has begun to reach a state that might allow appropriate analysis of the information interaction situation. There are a number of recent projects in information science which concentrate on the human-computer interaction issue from various points of view, and an even more substantial research component outside information science. We first review some work from outside that seems most important, especially in terms of the design considerations mentioned, and then discuss a few representative projects in information science.

6.3   Human factors

Human factors, or ergonomics, is the field concerned with the relationships between humans and the tools they use, and especially with the design of tools for appropriate human use. It has become the cover discipline for studies of human-computer interaction by considering that computers are machines or tools, and thus can be studied according to human factors principles. Since the mid 1970s, with the advent of personal computing, there has been a substantial boom in research in human factors as related to human-computer interactive dialogue. This has led not only to a plethora of single-system designs and experiments, but also to some rather more generalizable work, following, at least to some extent, the design paradigm of Bennett (1972).

Most work in this field is aimed at investigating specific problematic aspects of the human-computer interaction. Ramsey and Grimes (1983) survey, for instance, the research on interactive dialogue design, and isolate a number of themes that have been recognized as especially important in good design. Maguire's (1982) survey of recommendations for the design of dialogues also isolated a number of themes which have arisen from studies of specific problems. The categories which the two surveys discover are different, but primarily because of differences in level of detail of analysis. Here we use Ramsey and Grimes (1983), because their scheme is more general, in most respects. The themes which they discovered were: flexibility; initiative; system response time; interactive graphics; and natural-language dialogue and voice input/output. In most of these themes there is now, in the human factors literature, some agreement and some evidence relating the system characteristics to user characteristics, and in some cases to tasks and goals.

Flexibility is perhaps too large a category, as Ramsey and Grimes admit, since there are so many ways it has been interpreted. They specify five: applicability to a broad range of tasks; allowing multiple approaches to a given task; allowing multiple ways of invoking the desired next computer operation; adapting well to different user classes; and allowing personalization of system behaviour based on user preferences (Ramsey and Grimes, 1983). The suggestion from the human factors literature is that all these types of flexibility are desirable in a human-computer interface, but that perhaps (according especially to Eason, 1980), task flexibility is most important. This accords with the idea that task specification, and therefore adaptation to task, is the most significant design variable. Eason (1980) proposes a classification of tasks based on the characteristics of frequency (how often the human performs the task) and structure (the extent to which the external parameters of the task are variable, being closed — non-variant, or open — highly variable). With this very basic classification, he suggests that different types of dialogue are required for the different categories. The frequent-closed situation may not, for instance, require much flexibility at all, but would work best with a formal, closed command language. The infrequent-open situation, as in libraries for instance, will require a degree of flexibility in the interface which a formal command language cannot provide. Thus, in the latter case, natural-language interfaces or human intermediaries are often suggested or used.

The category of initiative refers to which of the two parties 'initiates' each interaction. Thus, a system which is menu-based is computer-initiated, while one with a (non-displayed) command language is user-initiated. Mixed-initiative dialogue is that in which the roles can change. Initiative seems to be most directly related to the characteristic of user's experience, or frequency of use, with computer-initiated dialogue being suitable for inexperienced or infrequent users, and user-initiated for frequent or experienced users. But infrequent users, through use, become more frequent users, and so some work is being done on interfaces which adapt to changes in the user. What appears to be lacking in this area, however, is any appreciation of the effect of the task on the type of initiative to be used.

The classic ergonomic problem in human-computer dialogue is system response time. Although there are still many controversies in this field, it seems to be the case that instant response is not always the ideal, and that, indeed, the best response time seems to be related strongly to the nature of the task being performed by the user. For instance, problem-solving tasks, or tasks in which the user needs to attend to information presented, may be best served by delayed response times. Ramsey and Grimes make the point, however, that command language interactions on present systems are much more flexible in terms of system response time than any other mode. Since it is clear that evaluation of the effect of system response time is connected with how the system responds, then new technology which will allow different display and interaction modes may revise the results of system response time studies.

Interactive graphics is one of these potential new modes of human-computer interaction. Ramsey and Grimes point out that changes in computer technology now make such interaction realistic, and survey a number of studies which demonstrate the technology. Although they must conclude that there is little principled human factors work in this area yet, they maintain that the push of this particular technology will be important. Of interest to us, perhaps, is that a number of studies in this area use interactive graphics as a means of 'browsing' through information structures and 'selecting' from them.

Natural language and voice interaction have also been mentioned in the human factors literature, but there has been very little research done on this issue at all. This is, of course, primarily because the techniques of natural language and speech understanding are just not available. Nevertheless, there have been some principled suggestions as to when such interfaces are appropriate, and there are some design rules suggested for when to implement voice input and output. In general, they suggest that it is appropriate only in highly closed situations, although it is usually desirable in open situations.

So, overall, work in human factors on human-computer dialogues appears to have reached a stage now where some specific task and user characteristics can be related to particular interactive structures and system designs. There have been some suggestions as to how tasks can be analysed for this purpose, and what sorts of user characteristics are important. These generalizations appear to be based primarily on the results of experimental studies, rather than on any strong theory. This is not necessarily a disadvantage, and there appear to be some results of use to design for human-computer interaction for IR, especially in the issues of flexibility and initiative. Ramsey and Grimes (1983) conclude their review, however, by looking forward to the possibility of a new, more theoretically sound approach to the general problem, based on psychological principles. We consider some aspects of this approach in the next two sections.

6.4   User psychology

Moran (1981) has suggested that human factors research in human-computer interaction is actually a subset of a more general discipline, user psychology. This he takes to be an applied psychology of the users of computer systems; that is, the objective psychological study of user behaviour, with the goal of reliably assuring satisfactory user-computer interaction. Understanding the user's behaviour means investigating the determinants of that behaviour, which he identifies as: the user's goal; the task structure (that is, the restrictions on what the user can do); the user's knowledge; and the user's processing limits. Moran's view is that by investigating and understanding these aspects of the user (and the user's environment), it will be possible to make rational decisions about how to predict and control user behaviour, and how to adapt the interface to the user. It is worthwhile noting that Moran's viewpoint takes almost no account of the computer, except in the task structure which includes the constraints of the interface. But, once again, this view is in accord with Bennett's (1972), that the specification of the user's goal or task is of primary importance in investigating human-computer interaction.

Moran also makes the point that there is a difference between the designer's view of the human-computer interface, and that of the user. That is, the user's view is based on the user's entire experience within the system, and not just the interactive component. According to Moran, 'the whole conceptual organization of the computer system from the user's point of view' constitutes the user's conceptual model of the interface. He also suggests that it is possible, indeed necessary, for the interface designer to instil an appropriate conceptual model in the user, but that, because of the nature of this model, this can only be done early in the design process of the entire computer system. The user will become aware, through her or his entire interface with the system, of many internal characteristics of the system — the interactive component must be able to control this to some extent, but cannot do it alone. Thus, for instance, for Moran training and documentation are an important part of the human-computer interface. Notice that the user conceptual model in this sense is a description of the system as the user is intended (by the designer) to see it.

Moran's work is firmly within the information-processing paradigm of experimental cognitive psychology, and is perhaps best represented in Card, Moran and Newell (1983). In this work, models of how people perform particular tasks, or types of tasks, based on observation and experimentation, are built up at various levels of detail. The intention is to construct cognitive models of the tasks, which are seen as psychologically valid. If these models are made precise enough, and if the task is well enough specified, then given appropriate values for variables, it is possible to predict behaviour. So, for instance, using their Keystroke Level Model it is possible to predict error-free performance time for a given task, given specific values for characteristics of the user and the system response time. It is a very simple model, yet has been reasonably successful in its predictions. The great value of this approach is, of course, that one can not only design from principle, but also investigate the effects of changes to a given system without actually having to change it. In effect, this is cognitive simulation.

Moran's work is an example of the user psychology school, which focuses on empirical psychological testing or experimentation for model building, prediction and system design. Other examples of this school, not necessarily from the information-processing paradigm, include Shneiderman (1980b). The results of this work demonstrate that there are specific user and system characteristics that can be objectively investigated, such as functionality of the system, learning time of the user, task completion time of the user, errors by the user, adaptability of the user to the system, and so on, which can lead to specific design features for the human-computer interface. These characteristics will relate to factors such as the user's conceptual model of the system, the user's goals and the user's knowledge, especially about task and system. The tendency in this work, despite its very strong user orientation, is, however, toward controlling and predicting user behaviour, as for instance by training, and it tends not to take very detailed consideration of the actual interactive features of the human-computer interface.

6.5 Cognitive systems

Recently there have been a number of contributions to the study of human-computer interaction which we find it convenient to describe as fundamentally cognitive (e.g. Barnard and Hammond, 1982; Norman, 1982; Hollnagel and Woods, 1983). Although there are substantial differences among the various proposals in this work, there is a basic underlying agreement that the entire human-computer system ought to be viewed as a cognitive system, in order for effective interfaces (and even whole systems) to be designed.

In Barnard and Hammond (1982), the cognitive context of a human-computer dialogue includes factors such as the cognitive demands imposed by the system, information extracted from the wider task environment, the specific question or problem motivating the interaction, and the cognitive strategies mobilized in the course of learning or use. Thus, for them the cognitive context is interpreted strictly from the user's point of view. That is, all the factors are factors associated with the human being, or with the human's interaction with the computer. What distinguishes their work from the human factors work discussed previously is the shift in emphasis from just structure and content of the dialogue to interpretation of the dialogue in terms of the user's cognitive states and models. Thus, in order to understand specific interactions, and to design for good interactive systems, factors such as cognitive style and cognitive demands must be incorporated into the analysis. In empirical work, this group has demonstrated that such factors must be considered to explain particular experimental results. This work differs from that described by Moran (1981) primarily in that it takes the view that the user's cognitive models are not things to be pushed around or manipulated, but must be explicitly adapted to by the interface design. Rather than merely considering the nature of the specific task and the user's knowledge, this approach also expands consideration into the environment, and into the general goals and experience of the user.

Norman (1982) and especially Hollnagel and Woods (1983) take this adaptive cognitive approach even further. The latter suggest, indeed, that the whole human-computer system must be considered an adaptive, cognitive system, where both parties interact with and adapt to one another. This work is related to that of Hollnagel (1979), discussed in Chapter 4 on dialogue analysis, but extends it substantially in terms of general framework and specific recommendations. And, of course, it considers human-computer rather than human-human interaction. The basic tenet of this work is that not only does a user have a conceptual model of the system, in the sense defined above, and a mental model, meaning the user's own current, internal perception of the computer, but so does the computer have a model of the user. In addition, each has a model of the system as a whole, and of himself in that system. The viewpoint taken in this work is that to a large extent, successful interaction in complex tasks is dependent upon successful matching of the computer's model of the user and the user's own cognitive characteristics, and upon adaptation to agreement upon one another's models. Thus, this work represents a step beyond that of the user psychology school in that it suggests ways in which the roles of the two parties in the interaction can be assigned, and ways in which the cognitive characteristics of the user can be directly incorporated into the system design, as part of the computer's model of the user. They survey some work in cognitive task analysis to emphasize the validity of this point.

Thus, the cognitive systems work again suggests that the task being performed by the two parties is paramount in successful interface design, but makes more specific why this is the case, and how this can be accounted for. It also makes a principled argument for considering the computer as an active party in the dialogue. And, importantly, it suggests cognitive factors associated with users which will be significant for the design of effective human-computer interaction.

6.6   AI

Aspects of AI are surveyed in depth by us later in this review. Here we mention only two examples of a trend in AI approaches to human-computer interaction that has not been evident in other work in this field. Gaines (1984), from outside AI, identifies the AI position by the example of overcoming barriers to database access by casual users. The AI approach, he suggests, '... might be to build a better database system with understanding of the user, his requirements, and natural language communication, i.e. to put all the load on the computer and make it clever enough to deal with the casual user'. The human-computer interaction (human factors) approach, in contrast, would attempt '... to remove as much of the load as possible from both [human and computer] and share what is left between them'. (Gaines, 1984.)

Apart from research in natural-language understanding, most work in AI on human-computer interaction has been relatively unconcerned with the technical level of ease of use of computers by humans (one reason they have been able to do this is that the natural language interface seems always to be assumed). It has concentrated, rather, on the issue of the computer *understanding* the user, especially the user's goals, plans, knowledge, experience, and so on.

Rich (1979), for instance, designed an interactive system in which the user's goal (pre-specified) was to find a novel that he or she would like to read. Then the task of the system overall was for the user to get such a book, and the computer's specific role was to find out enough about the user to suggest one. Rich's hypothesis was that, in order for two humans to accomplish this task, the advisor would have to build up a *model* of the user, which would help to predict what a user of that *type* would like to read. The details of the system are relatively unimportant in our context. What is significant is the point that, for successful human-computer cooperation on a task, a part of the interaction must be devoted to the computer's understanding the user. It is also important that this point is made by analogy with, and study of, the equivalent human-human interaction.

Reichman-Adar (1984) takes a slightly different line in proposing an abstract computational structure for the human-computer interface which is derived from a functional analysis of human-human dialogue. She suggests that any interface capable of extended dialogue with a user must:

1. characterize the functionality of discourse utterances;

2. characterize the different implicit components of different types of conversational moves;

3. constrain inappropriate conversational development;

4. track the effects of preceding conversational moves on the discourse context;

5. predict and execute the most likely forms of subsequent development.

In this work, we have moved far beyond the idea of ergonomically effective human-computer interfaces, to one of a real human-computer dialogue, in which the computer not only understands the user, but participates with the user. But the reason that this complex dialogue is necessary is just so that the computer can build up models of the user which will help in cooperative resolution of the task which they share. This is a far cry from, for instance, the bald statement that the interface needs to be flexible, but it does demonstrate what real flexibility might mean, in an ideal human-computer interface. It is also interesting to note the strong connection of this work with that surveyed in the chapter on dialogue analysis.

6.7 IR

The study of human-computer interaction in the IR context has recently reappeared as a vital topic. There is a wide range of approaches to the general issue which, interestingly, appears to parallel some of the distinctions we have noted in our review of work from other disciplines. Accordingly, we will structure our somewhat cursory review of this work in a more or less logical progression, from attempts to deal with practical interface issues to research on the conceptual bases of information interaction.

There are a great number of practical problems in the interface between user and computer in IR, ranging from such issues as long, complex telephone or logon codes, to complex command languages, to costs and errors associated with constructing search statements online. There has been a good deal of work, and a number of systems have been constructed, for responding to such problems. The responses are generally of two sorts. One is to monitor user behaviour in interaction with the system, in order to discover what goes wrong and where, and then try to do something about it; the other is to insert an intermediary interface. Rouse and Rouse (1984) is a good example of the first approach. In this work, which is very much in the human factors paradigm, experiments are set up in which users have specific tasks to perform in a bibliographic retrieval environment. Their behaviour, particularly errors made and strategies selected in response to the interface, is monitored, and conclusions drawn as to the quality of the interface and the factors which lead to poor performance. The result of this type of work is then to modify the system in response to these particular problems with the interface design.

Williams (1980) is a good example of the approach of construction of intermediary systems. These systems are essentially front ends to large system hosts, which are intended to remove error-prone activities from the interaction with the end computer, and to reduce costs associated with such errors, and with slow response times and the necesssity for thinking about computer responses. Typically, such systems, although practically useful, do not actually make any changes in the logical structure of the interface. This approach is certainly needed, in order to make the current systems more usable, but it tends still to accept the framework of the human intermediary between end-user and computer. Also, it has very little to offer in terms of experiment or theory about significant factors in the interaction, relying primarily on intuition. There have also been some systems constructed specifically for ease of use in interaction. Bivins-Noerr and Noerr (1982) present an example of a user-friendly system based on menu selection with a touch screen terminal. This work responds to such issues as task structure, frequency of use and user skills, in terms of initiative, structure and input mechanism, but again there seems to be no theoretical basis underlying it, behind the usually highly refined and expert intuitions of the system designers.

More conceptually oriented systems are being designed and constructed, although only in a research environment. Meadow *et al* (1982), for instance, designed and tested an interactive system which instructed users in how to engage in the interaction as part of the interface itself,and then monitored their use in order to offer help when things went wrong. Although there were some novel features of this system, which required analysis of the tasks within the overall task structure, this work still fundamentally accepted the basic interface as a given, and tried to help users to overcome its most obvious disadvantages. The most interesting feature of this work, automatic search strategy error correction, was only very rarely involved, and was not capable of being evaluated.

Marcus (e.g. 1982a,b) has constructed and tested a similar system, but one with perhaps a more systematic task analysis and a stronger connection with human factors issues. This system also is an intermediary system; that is, it is intended to replace the human intermediary by performing that person's functions in the computer-intermediary-end-user interaction. These functions are identified primarily as having to do with the complex nature of the computer system information structure, with the problems of complex and heterogeneous interface languages, and with the inexperience of the end-users. Thus, this system interacts with the user in a mostly computer-initiative mode, includes tutorial aids for the interface, and automatically, and without further reference to the user, chooses an appropriate database and the appropriate search statement derived from the human-computer interaction. This work demonstrates a somewhat more sophisticated idea of what the task structure constitutes, but one should notice that it does not consider to any great extent the goals of the user (that is, it does not derive from any fundamental user task analysis). The system is, rather, primarily specified by an analysis of the functions of the intermediary, without reference to, for instance, the cognitive characteristics of the user.

Pollitt (1983) has constructed an intermediary system which is based primarily on traditional human factors principles, but which uses an extensive knowledge base, in keeping with the nature of the task. His is a menu-driven, touch screen system, with the menus reflecting the organization of knowledge in the database. The physical structure of the interface is chosen because the users are infrequent, because the knowledge relations are complex, and because the terms used in the the subject are long, leading to unacceptably high error rates if entered directly. The basis of this work, however, is that by making the knowledge structure of the database apparent to the user, a part of the knowledge that the human intermediary might have used has been replaced. In this sense, it goes somewhat beyond Marcus's analysis of the task, taking account of other kinds of knowledge in the system.

Brooks (e.g. 1984) has gone further in the analysis of the task performed by the intermediary than the systems mentioned above, relating at least some intermediary functions to the user's problem and goal. This work is still in its formative stages, but it suggests that an automatic intermediary, as well as being ergonomically comfortable, and capable of dealing with the vagaries of the databases and host interfaces, must be able to simulate the tasks which take place in the human-human interaction in the computer-human intermediary-end-user interface. These will include, at least, understanding the user's problem and interactively translating this into a form which can be the basis for searching. This work, thus, is the first we have reviewed in the automatic intermediary paradigm which attempts to take account of the user's task and goals in relation to the structure of the interactive interface, and especially to the functions of the intermediary.

Oddy (1977) proposed a rather different approach to the interface problem, by constructing a special-purpose IR system, THOMAS, which was designed specifically on the basis of the user's problem and characteristics. His insight was that users often cannot or do not want to specify what they want retrieved by an IR system, and, furthermore, that they might learn more about what would be useful to them through learning about what was available. He therefore constructed a system which was designed for browsing through the database. The interface was mixed-initiative, the user initially specifying an interest, the computer providing a response and prompting responses from the user. There was almost no command language at all, and, perhaps most interesting, the computer organized its responses according to an image it held of the user's (changing) interest, in relation to its database structure. Thus, THOMAS, from the interface point of view, was designed around a concept of the user's specific problem, and of some explicit user characteristics, and also managed to incorporate some aspects of the computer's model of the user. Given the state of research in human-computer interfaces, this was conceptually a highly advanced system.

This work was later incorporated with Belkin's (e.g.1980) ASK hypothesis, in a system design whose function was explicitly to take account of one particular user characteristic, related to the user's task: that the user cannot specify what she or he needs to have retrieved. The response to this characteristic was to try to develop a system which would not force the user to do this, but would rather use descriptions about the user's problem in order to conduct an initial search. It would use this description to construct a model of the user, which would be modified through a mixed-initiative dialogue (Belkin, Oddy and Brooks, 1982). This work extended the THOMAS idea by taking explicit account of the cognitive features of the user's situation and knowledge, and by attempting to involve the computer more directly in the dialogue.

Belkin, Seeger and Wersig (1983) discuss perhaps the most conceptually complex notion of the human-computer interface that we have seen. They start initially from a concept of why the user has entered the information system; that is, from a specification of the user's goal and cognitive tasks. They then specify the functions which the interface must perform in order to understand enough about the user's problem and situation to make a reasonable response to it. And they especially view the computer as an interactive, adaptive partner with the user in their mutual task of helping to manage the user's problem. We have discussed this work in the chapter on dialogue analysis. Here, we would just like to point out its similarities to the cognitive systems and AI approaches reviewed in the previous sections. It seems quite clear that using this type of cognitive, conceptual account of the information interaction situation as a basis for design of the human-computer interactive interface responds to the same criteria and issues as does the cognitively oriented human factors work, and perhaps even more to those of the AI approaches. Whether these will actually turn out to be useful remains to be seen (although Belkin, Hennings and Seeger, 1984, have reported on a simulation of such a system), but it certainly seems the case that they have the advantage of a theoretical model of the whole situation. And they appear to respond most directly of all the approaches we have seen to Bennett's (1972) system components to be considered in interface design, amplifying them as well in interesting ways.

6.8 Summary

This quick review of work in human-computer interface design seems to us to demonstrate a wide range of approaches in general human factors work, from intuitive system design for relatively naive technologically based concepts of user friendliness, through highly sophisticated experimental designs for investigating the human-computer interface, through increasing concern with and specifications of user characteristics, to highly complex cognitive analyses of the human-computer system, using the analyses for design specifications. At almost each level, there has been very high-quality work done, with some generalizable experimental techniques, analytic methods and design principles.

In IR, there seems to be evidence of the same sort of range of activities, with roughly parallel emphases. It seems to us that there is some reason to think that this range represents a progression, in both cases, since there is some temporal ordering on the various approaches, indicating a possible logical order. Given the parallelism, it seems that there now can and should be once more a strong interaction between general and information science human-computer interface work, and that there is some hope for strong research effort in this aspect of the IR interaction.

To conclude, we state once again the factors that research has identified as being fundamental in specifying design criteria for successful human-computer interaction. These are:

the overall goals and specific task of the user (in cooperation with the rest of the system, to include the external environment);

the respective roles of the two parties, and their models of one another;

the characteristics (especially cognitive) of the user, to include knowledge;

the limitations imposed on the task by its context;

the characteristics of the interface device;

the characteristics of the information to be displayed;

the structure of the database.

The consideration of many of these factors appears to have informed work on human-computer interaction in IR; we still await a fully integrated approach to the problem.

7 Search strategy

7.1 Introduction

Search strategy can be defined as a plan for the whole search on a question or topic, in contrast to search techniques which are methods, heuristics, tactics or plans that can be used by people in searching manual or automated information systems.

In this review, we understand under search strategy that part of a search process (manual or computerized) which follows the question statement by the end-user, together with question analysis and question formulation carried out by the end-user and/or intermediary (user-intermediary negotiation). Search strategy covers the planning of the search to answer the formulated question, continues through the process of passing through some kind of interactive mechanism, and ends when the user obtains the result of the search. It does not include the process of evaluating the search or satisfaction of user needs, both problems being handled in other sections.

Searching techniques on specific databases or online systems are not included in this section, the aim of the writers being to cover material which could be considered as an area of research, thus of a more general character.

The chapter is divided into the following sections: 7.2, the interactive mechanism (which includes the searching procedure in the computer itself); 7.3, search techniques (everything which further develops the search); 7.4, possible contribution from cognitive psychology; 7.5, AI and IR.

7.2 Search procedures

All search strategies are based on a comparison between the query and the stored documents. During a search, each term of the query statement is compared with the index terms of the inverted file, and if a match is made, the addresses of the documents are retrieved and the information (bibliographic or other) given to the user.

The retrieval function which determines the match between the query formulation and the indexed document terms can be represented in many ways. Terms can be assigned to the queries and to documents with weights and without weights, a threshold can be chosen to specify the cut-off point of a search or to retrieve the relevant documents above the threshold (and at the same time to reject non-relevant documents below the threshold point). This different treatment of a search implies different search strategies, and this problem will be discussed in this section of the review.

7.2.1   The Boolean search

In a Boolean search the query formulation is constructed using the logical combination of query terms whose relationship is expressed using the operators: AND, OR, and NOT, e.g.

$$Q = K1 \text{ OR } K2$$

means that query Q will retrieve all documents which have either keyword K1 or keyword K2 or both as their indexing terms.

While $\qquad Q = K1 \text{ AND } K2$

will retrieve only those documents which have both keywords, K1 and K2, as their indexing terms

the expression $\qquad Q = K1 \text{ NOT } K2$

will retrieve all documents indexed by the term K1 but not indexed by K2.

More complex combinations of query terms may be used, e.g.:

$$Q = (K1 \text{ AND } K2) \text{ OR } (K3 \text{ AND } K4) \text{ OR } (K5 \text{ NOT } K6).$$

In this case the Boolean search will retrieve all documents indexed by K1 and K2, as well as all documents indexed by K3 and K4, and those documents indexed by K5 which are not indexed by K6.

These are examples of Boolean searches, the most popular search strategies, available now on online systems from all large processors of information (e.g. Dialog, Datastar, Infoline). In most Boolean searches there is no ranking in order of preference, thus each retrieved item is assumed to be as important as any other.

Boolean strategies allow searches to be narrowed or broadened by giving the searcher access to structured dictionaries and thesauri.

Boolean searches are usually implemented on systems having inverted files. These systems offer the following facilities:

106

an alphabetical vocabulary of keywords;

a list for each keyword in the vocabulary, in which are stored addresses of documents having that particular keyword.

The searcher first formulates the search using query terms, as explained previously, and submits them to the system, which in turn finds the addresses of the documents, e.g.:

our search strategy is $\qquad$ Q = K1 AND K2 AND K3 AND K4

and the addresses of documents are as follows:

$\qquad$ keyword K1 and its list—D1, D2, D3, D4, D5, D6
$\qquad$ keyword K2 and its list—D2, D5
$\qquad$ keyword K3 and its list—D2, D3
$\qquad$ keyword K4 and its list—D2, D6

To satisfy the search statement K1 AND K2 AND K3 AND K4 we must find documents indexed by these terms, and this in the above cited case is just one document, D2.

There are many advantages and disadvantages normally attributed to a Boolean search. Salton (1975, p 121) gives the following disadvantages:

(a) The normal Boolean search formulation makes it difficult to vary the search depth in order to retrieve a greater or lesser amount of material, depending on user requirements. To obtain a desired level of performance, it is necessary to find just the right kind of query formulation — neither too broad nor too narrow — and ideally the searcher must be familiar with the properties of the vocabulary and the effects obtained by adding terms to and/or subtracting them from the query statement.

(b) It is awkward in a Boolean search environment to achieve the effect of the vector matching functions which provide a continuous spectrum of closeness between documents and search requests. This lack of 'partial matching' capability produces the 'all or nothing' quality of the Boolean search output. Although the construction of a set of nested subsearches can ideally produce the desired performance, the required multiple query formulations are difficult to generate.

(c) The set of output documents cannot be presented to the user in ranked order, for example in decreasing order of query-document similarity. Instead, a partial ranking must be simulated by using term weights when available and by listing the output in decreasing order of the matching term weights.

Bookstein (1980) gives the following three interpretations of Boolean retrieval:

(a) Logical. By means of well-defined rules applicable to any legitimate Boolean request, it is possible to state whether the request formally applies to any document, where each document is represented by a set of index terms. If the index record of a document is consistent with the request, we can say that the request makes a 'true' statement about a document, and all documents for which the request is true are retrieved.

(b) Set theoretic. Ultimately, in the approach described above, a set of documents, those for which the request is a true one, is retrieved. But the request can be analysed into a number of components, each itself a legitimate Boolean request, and one can associate with each component of the request the set of documents which would have been retrieved if that component had been offered in isolation. It is then possible to use well-defined set operations to combine these component sets to produced the final set of retrieved documents....Thus, a Boolean request can be thought of as instructions to the system to carry out a sequence of operations on sets of documents to yield the set of documents that is ultimately retrieved.

(c) Operator. A related approach is to interpret a request as an operator acting on a set to produce an altered set. This definition permits us to break up the operator into simpler operations until we have only operators made up of simple terms, and these can be evaluated immediately. Thus, the definition is general and can be applied to any request acting as an operator on any set.

Thus, a request made up of basic index terms and logical connectives is seen by Bookstein as a set of instructions telling the system how to act on its document store so as to reduce its size and produce a set meeting its user's needs.

Bookstein however admits that, although using Boolean expressions permits one to represent accurately the logical relationships among concepts involved in an information need, it does so with some loss in flexibility. For this reason some attention has been given to an approach in which one issues Boolean requests while independently assigning weights to each term in the request to indicate how important that term is. Norealt, Koll, and McGill (1977) reported some success in the use of such a method. However, the use of weights, while increasing the system's flexibility, 'deprives it of its aesthetic appeal'. According to Bookstein (1978, 1980) it is better to generalize the definition of Boolean requests by merging some of the strengths of Boolean and weighted systems, while 'eluding the perils that such a process usually entails'. Bookstein suggests introducing the notion of a fuzzy set into a Boolean search. He states rightly that it is sometimes difficult to say whether a document ought to be indexed by a specific term. The indexer hesitates to represent the document by a term which according to his understanding is neither a firm yes nor a firm no. Bookstein refers to Zadeh (1965) who developed the concept of a fuzzy set to satisfy the need for a set that permits partial membership. Bookstein relates the classical Boolean systems to the notion of fuzzy sets. The fuzzy set concept forms then the basis of the concept of the fuzzy request in which weighting is an intrinsic component of the logic of the system.

To define a fuzzy set, each potential member of the set is assigned a degree of membership between zero and one, with zero denoting non-membership and one full membership. The values between zero and one denote partial membership. Bookstein (1982) gives the following characteristics of fuzzy-set retrieval:

1. The fuzzy-set approach is intrinsically deterministic. The weights that are assigned to documents represent degrees of relevance, and these are conceived of as being made with no degree of uncertainty.

2. The fuzzy-set approach concentrates on the logic of retrieval, just as does the Boolean approach.

The fuzzy-set approach differs from the Boolean approach in the method of indexing. Indexing terms are not simply assigned or not assigned. 'Each assigned term is given a weight indicating the system's assessment of the extent to which that term describes the document.' The retrieval of documents is similar to Boolean operations, except that the set operations take now a form determined by fuzzy-set theory.

Waller and Kraft (1979) developed a generalization of a mathematical model for a weighted Boolean retrieval system. The authors suggested several criteria for the evaluation mechanisms used to determine the relevance of a given record to a given query. The self-consistency criterion anticipates that different logically equivalent query formulations yield equal retrieval status values. A new fuzzy connector known as 'ANDOR' for the Boolean operator 'AND' and 'OR' can be analysed and compared with other formulations. It is expected that more research in this direction will follow to evaluate these mechanisms.

7.2.2. Cluster-based retrieval of documents

The idea of document clustering has been advocated by many people, but usually without any attempt at theoretical justification (Robertson, 1977a). Van Rijsbergen and Sparck Jones (1973) propose a Cluster Hypothesis which postulates that the documents relevant to one request are on the whole more like each other than they are like the non-relevant documents. They suggest that this Cluster Hypothesis might improve the retrieval process.

A classification method can construct a system of clusters. This relationship is called 'association' or 'similarity'. The measure of similarity is designed to quantify the likeness between objects (Van Rijsbergen, 1979). Many of the more sophisticated search strategies are implemented by means of a matching function. This is a function similar to an association measure. The difference between the two functions (as defined by Van Rijsbergen) lies in the following: the matching function measures the association between a query and a document or cluster profile, whereas an association measure is applied to objects of the same kind. Mathematically the two functions have the same properties; they differ in their interpretation.

A matching function associated with the simple matching search strategy is given below (Van Rijsbergen).

$$M = \frac{2|D \cap Q|}{|D| + |Q|}$$

Where M is the matching function, D the set of keywords representing the document, and Q the set representing the query.

Serial searches provide a convenient demonstration of the use of matching functions. Suppose that there are N documents Di in the system. In this case the serial search proceeds by calculating N values $M(Q,Di)$ for $i=1$ to N. In other words, the matching function is evaluated for each document for the same query Q. On the basis of the values $M(Q,Di)$ the set of documents to be retrieved is determined. There are two ways of doing this:

1. The matching function is given a suitable threshold, retrieving the

documents above the threshold and discarding the documents below the threshold.

2. The documents are ranked in increasing order of matching function value. A rank position R is chosen as cut-off and all documents below the rank are retrieved. It is expected that the relevant documents are contained in the retrieved set.

In the serial search there is a need to match queries with each document in the file, while in a search of a clustered file we need to be able to match queries with clusters. For this purpose clusters are represented by some kind of profile — a cluster representative.

'A cluster representative should be such that an incoming query will be diagnosed into the cluster containing the documents relevant to the query. In other words one expects the cluster representative to discriminate the relevant from the non-relevant documents when matched against any query' (Van Rijsbergen). There is no theory guiding the selection of the right kind of cluster representative. One can only proceed experimentally. There are various ways of characterizing clusters.

One way is to select a 'typical' member from the cluster. A simple way of doing it is to find a document which is linked to a maximum number of other documents in the cluster. This is the *maximally linked document*. If there is more than one candidate, one either makes an arbitrary choice or one maintains a list of cluster representatives for that cluster.

Another way is to find a method of representation which in some way 'averages' the descriptions of the members of the clusters. Both of these methods of representation are effective when used in conjunction with appropriate search strategies.

Another theoretical way of looking at the construction of cluster representatives is through the notion of a *maximal predictor* for a cluster (Gower, 1974). Given that the documents Di in a cluster are binary vectors, then a binary cluster representative for this cluster is a predictor in the sense that each component Ci predicts the most likely value of that attribute in the member documents. It is maximal if its correct predictions are as numerous as possible.

Although the main reason for constructing these cluster representatives is to lead a search strategy to relevant documents, it should be clear that they can also be used to guide a search to documents meeting some condition on the matching function (Yu and Luk, 1977; also Luk, Siu and Yu, 1979).

'Cluster-based retrieval has as its foundation the Cluster Hypothesis, which states that closely associated documents tend to be relevant to the same requests.' Clustering picks out closely associated documents and groups them together into one cluster. Supposing that there is a hierarchical classification of documents, then a simple search strategy may proceed as follows.

The search starts at the root of the tree at some node and proceeds down the tree by evaluating a matching function at the descending nodes. A decision rule directs the search, comparing the values of a matching function at each stage. A search is terminated following a stopping rule. Then retrieval follows.

A few remarks from Van Rijsbergen may be quoted about this search strategy:

1. We assume that effective retrieval can be achieved by finding just one cluster.

2. We assume that each cluster can be adequately represented by a cluster representative for the purpose of locating the cluster containing the relevant documents.

3. If the maximum of the matching function is not unique, some special action, such as look-ahead, will need to be taken.

4. The search always terminates and will retrieve at least one document.

There are searches which may be described as top-down searches because they enter at a certain node and proceed down the tree. A bottom-up search is one which enters the tree at one of its terminal nodes, and proceeds in an upward direction towards the root of the tree.

If we abandon multi-level clustering and accept single-level clustering, we end up with the approach to document clustering which Salton and his co-workers have worked on extensively. Rocchio's algorithm typifies the appropriate cluster method. The search strategy is in part a serial search. It proceeds by first finding the best (or nearest) cluster(s) and looking within these. The second stage is achieved by doing a serial search of the documents in the selected cluster(s). The output is frequently a ranking of documents retrieved in this way.

7.2.3. *Interactive search formulation*

It happens very seldom that a user confronted with an automatic retrieval system is able to express his information need in one single step. He usually becomes involved in a trial-and-error process in which he reformulates his query on the basis of an answer to the initial query. If the user discovers that his search result is too voluminous he may wish to make it more specific by choosing more narrow terms from an appropriate thesaurus. On the basis of a small sample of retrieved references and their index terms he can get some idea of the kind of documents which are likely to be retrieved; he can also evaluate how effective his search terms have been in expressing his information need. He may modify his query. He operates using the method of feedback (Oddy, 1977a,b).

The word feedback is usually used to describe the mechanism by which a system can improve its performance on a task by taking account of past performance. In other words a simple input-output system feeds back the information from the output so that this may be used to improve the performance on the next input. The process of feedback has been popularized by Norbert Wiener's book *Cybernetics.*

In IR, a typical relevance feedback system operates by first processing the initial query statement and retrieving a number of documents. The user examines the documents, identifies one or more relevant items and on this basis formulates a new improved query by adding to the original query vector the relevant document vectors and subtracting the non-relevant vectors. The query alteration process may be applied iteratively several times. Experiments have revealed that it is not practical to carry out feedback operations beyond the third iteration. Two major variants exist in the relevance feedback process. One is the so-called positive feedback, which uses only the retrieved relevant documents to alter an original query. The second, called negative feedback, uses both relevant and non-relevant items to alter the query (Ide, 1971).

One problem affecting both positive and negative feedback strategies arises when the set of relevant items is not adequately clustered in the document space. The result is a low recall performance. If the non-relevant documents are insufficiently separated from the relevant, a loss in precision may also occur (Ide and Salton, 1971).

When the user's view of the subject area reflected in the query formu-

113

lation is incompatible with the document indexing, then the only method which could bring a remedy to a search formulation is the query split method. This process breaks up a given user query into several subqueries so that each subquery approaches a separate set of relevant items (Borodin, Kerr and Lewis, 1968).

It is the aim of every retrieval strategy to retrieve the relevant documents A and withhold the non-relevant documents not-A. Relevance is defined with respect to the user's *semantic interpretation* of his query. From the point of view of the retrieval system the user's formulation of a query may not be ideal. An ideal formulation would be one which retrieved only relevant documents.

In the case of a serial search the system will retrieve all D for which $M(Q,D)>T$ and not retrieve any D for which $M(Q,D)<=T$, where T is a specified threshold. Nilsson (1965) has discussed at length how by modifying weights QI, the correlation function may be 'trained' to discriminate correctly between the two categories. Supposing that A and not-A are known in advance, then the correct query formulation $Q0$ would be one for which

$$M(Q0,\ D)>T \text{ whenever } D \text{ equals } A$$

and

$$M(Q0,D)<=T \text{ whenever } D \text{ equals not-}A$$

There is a theorem (Nilsson, 1965, p 81) which states that providing $Q0$ exists there is an iterative procedure which will ensure that Q will converge to $Q0$ in a finite number of steps. The iterative procedure is called the fixed error correction procedure. It is sometimes necessary to proceed through the set of documents several times before the correct set of weights is achieved, namely those which will separate A and not-A linearly (providing a solution exists).

The situation in an operational IR system is not so simple. One does not know the sets A and not-A in advance. However, given a query formulation Q and the documents retrieved by it, we can ask the user to tell the system which of the documents retrieved were relevant and which were not. The system can then automatically modify Q so that at least it will be able to diagnose correctly those documents that the user has seen. The assumption is that this will improve retrieval on the next run.

It is often difficult to fix the threshold T in advance so that documents are ranked in decreasing matching value on output. It is also more difficult to define what is meant by an ideal query formulation.

Robertson and Sparck Jones (1976) described a weighting technique which provides a basis for an interactive strategy. The user submits a query to the system. Initial weights are assigned to each of the terms in the query and the document collection is ranked according to the degree of match between document and query. The initial weights are derived from the frequencies of the terms in the whole collection (Sparck Jones and Bates, 1977). The first few documents, at the head of the ranked list, are shown to the user, who then indicates the relevance (or non-relevance) of each of the documents. Using this feedback information the weights are adjusted and the collection re-ranked. The process is repeated until some criterion for stopping has been satisfied. Four different formulae have been suggested by Sparck Jones and Robertson for calculating the relevance weights. Not enough attention was given during the experiments to some questions relating to interaction; for example how should the initial weights be assigned to query terms when no relevance information is available? This problem was elucidated in subsequent work by Harper and Van Rijsbergen (1978) and Sparck Jones (1979).

W Goffman (1969) suggested a method of retrieval based on the dependence between documents. He postulates that there exists a probability that document A is relevant given that document B is relevant. Goffman estimates the transition probabilities on the basis of the number of terms the documents have in common.

Vernimb (1977) described a procedure for automatic adjustment of queries. The starting point for the automatic procedure consists of a few documents known to the user as being relevant to his query. These documents or representations of the documents are in the store of the IR system. The search strategy is then performed as follows:

Phase I   Mode

step 1 —   establishment of partial queries
            on the basis of relevant documents   (automatic)
step 2 —   establishment of total query   (automatic)
step 3 —   relevance assessment for the   (user's
            document retrieved   judgment)

Phase II

step 4 —   selection of the most effective
            partial queries   (automatic)

| step 5 — | establishment and loosening* of a new query and retrieval | (automatic) |
| step 6 — | relevance assessment for the document retrieved | (user's judgment) |

*loosening means broadening

The automatic query adjustment made use of a combination of Boolean query formulation and weights.

Other methods of retrieval and search strategies have been considered by Oddy (1975, 1977a,b). He described a technique in which the user interacts with the computer. Preece (1973) described a post-retrieval clustering of documents.

Jamieson and Oddy (1979) received a grant from the British Library Research and Development Department to build an intelligent terminal at the University of Aston and to test interactive retrieval strategies in real life. In the first instance, automatic term weighting was chosen to be tested on MEDLINE. During the experiment the user was to enter a list of keywords without Boolean operators and without weights. The system would calculate initial weights, retrieve and display references, ranked according to similarity with the query. Next, the user was to decide on the relevance of the retrieved references, in response to which the system would compute new weights and modify the query accordingly. The interaction would continue until a satisfactory search had been completed.

The experiment was planned to be carried out on a microprocessor-based terminal which would automatically assign weights to the query terms and produce the ranked output. The sum of the term weights common to the query and the document would be used to determine the rank of the document, and the top-ranking documents would then be displayed. Having calculated weights for all the terms in a query, the microprocessor would then determine a sequence of Boolean conjunctions of terms to send to the host system (MEDLINE) which should yield references in order of decreasing matching value. A special algorithm was developed by Jamieson (1979) for this purpose. The experiment has so far not been implemented.

Preece (1980) describes an online system of associative information retrieval. The system uses a network representation of the information in a bibliographic database, and a processing paradigm modelling a continuous flow of user interest through the network to implement associative retrieval and query modification. The Online Associative

Query System (OAQS) assists the searcher in formulating and modifying his query. An automatic query modification facility offers an improved access to databases by identifying a vocabulary related to the words of the query. It is a query expansion incorporated in an iterative process of search and modify cycles. Negative activation is also available in the system, in which an item is used as a negative example. The Boolean searching capability is implemented as a weighted search, using term weights that are powers of two.

Stibic (1980) employs unlimited ranking in operational online systems. In the DIRECT system, the Philips in-house online retrieval system, the association value ('weight') of a document depends on the number of matching terms, and on the relation between the frequencies of the respective terms in the query, in the document, and in the whole file. The value is increased if the respective terms occur in a specific part of the document, e.g. in the title.

All documents containing at least one of the query terms are potential 'candidates' for display; all are evaluated and the most relevant ones are submitted for display in a descending order of their association values. If Boolean operators AND or NOT (ORs between the query terms are considered as default values) are used, then documents not meeting the Boolean constraints are rejected, the others are ranked. The ranking of documents permits display of those documents with high probability of being relevant at the top of the set of retrieved documents.

7.2.4 Probabilistic retrieval

The probabilistic retrieval approach rejects the Boolean approach altogether. Documents are as before represented by records. Index terms are also used in the majority of projects but any property of a document is a candidate for inclusion. Quantitative features, taking arbitrary numerical values, can also be useful. An example is the number of times a term or concept appears in the document (Bookstein, 1983). Each feature represents a clue to the relevance of a document to a query. The number of clues is large. Each clue in itself gives rather weak evidence regarding the relevance of the document to a query, but collectively they make a strong case for retrieving or not retrieving a document. Boolean search is characterized by features unambiguously associated with documents and the effort of a searcher is directed to expressing the logical relation of features in relevant documents. In the probabilistic search, the presence of features is probabilistically related to the request and the searcher seeks for methods of combining and 'balancing' evidence that the document is relevant to his query. The idea of uncertainty in indexing was first proposed by Maron and Kuhns (1960).

The clues in each document can either be assigned by a human indexer or they will be assigned automatically, as will certainly happen in the near future. A user, in turn, will provide the system with a request in the form of a list of features that would characterize the documents he would expect to receive. This list would not have Boolean operators as logical connectors. The system, given the clues, will be able to compute the probability of document relevance. The objective of the system is to provide each user with a list of documents ordered on the assumption that they are relevant. The ideas that probabilities could be used to design an IR mechanism, and that such a retrieval system can, in some cases provide optimal retrieval, and the initial development of the pertinent mathematics, appeared independently in papers written by Robertson (1977,b), Robertson and Sparck Jones (1976) and Bookstein and Swanson (1977).

As compared to a fuzzy-set retrieval, the weights assigned to the document and the query features in a probabilistic system have a different meaning. In fuzzy-set logic, no probabilities are involved and the weights represent the actual degree of relevance of each document to the request. In a probabilistic approach, there is no distinction between different levels of relevance — the weight represents the probability that the document is relevant. The weighting mechanism indicates how much the presence of each feature contributes to this probability, and how to take feedback information into account in changing these weights.

The disadvantage of the probabilistic approach as presented by Bookstein are as follows:

1. All logical connections between terms are lost.

2. Increased storage capacity is required.

3. The detailed assignment of weights are model-dependent. There does not exist operational experience to indicate the value of these models.

7.2.5 *Mapping relations between terms*

One method of modifying a query is to replace one term by a broader, narrower or otherwise related term. The new terms are not necessarily provided by the feedback methods discussed above. The searcher needs to be able to consult some map of term relationships.

For this purpose different term dictionaries and thesauri are used, especially thesauri which provide a classification of terms used in a given subject area, which proved to be very helpful. Thesauri may broaden a query or a document term by adding more general subject descriptors and in this way enhance the recall in a retrieval situation. In the same way the searcher may use a narrower term from a thesaurus making the search more specific.

Doyle (1961) in his search for a mental 'contact between the reader and the information store' suggested the construction of semantic road maps for literature searchers. He wanted to make books and documents 'visible' to the searcher and the computer a tool for analysis of books and papers by arranging and labelling things so that humans could search them. The things to be searched were not the documents themselves, but only proxies 'which adequately mirror the nature of documents.' The characterization and organization of information is to be derived from analysis of frequencies and distribution of words in libraries.

Doyle suggested the use of an association map whose organization would be decided by humans, and whose details would be determined by computer analysis. He differentiated between two kinds of association maps, psychological and empirical. A psychological association map would result if some eager human decided to organize in detail all knowledge. Such a psychological association map would result if all literature searchers were asked to draw a small map of the associations which lead to their search request statements and then all these small maps were to be integrated to form a big one. This map should have some similarity to an empirical map, determined by computer analysis of text. Each person would find an empirical map different from his expectations (i.e. his psychological map); and to the extent that it was different it would convey information. If knowledge is the state of the association network in a human mind, then information is that which alters this state.

The association map should lead to a document and in this sense convey information on what is available in the document collection (or document representation collection).

Doyle further compared the association map to a cardiovascular system (arteries, arterioles, capillaries of the system). Arteries can be thought of as associational relationships involving thousands of documents such as that between 'computer' and 'programming'.

Arterioles, pathways of much smaller scale, lead to a specific aspect of a subject, such as 'programming' and 'chess' which may involve dozens to hundreds of documents. Capillaries, the smallest pathways, can involve from a few dozen documents down to, at the least, one document (not zero, since we are dealing with an empirical map). Most of the expected associations will naturally be concentrated in the arteries and arterioles.

Because changes in the artery region are not rapid, there will be minimum need for flexibility and maximum opportunity for human design. Such design should have as its goal good overall routing of searches to arterioles. Presumably, searchers can find an arteriole by looking in an index of terms, but there are undoubtedly many times when productive starting points for a search are not in the mind of the searcher. At these times a map of the gross structure will guide the searcher's imagination.

The arteriole-sized elements (and smaller) are the ones strongly affected by year-to-year changes in the literature, and have to be organized in a flexible way, and it is at this level that we expect the computer to do most of the work. The arterioles lead one to capillaries and the best principles (heuristics) for this remain to be worked out. In some areas, document search frequences will provide a basis for organization; in other areas meaningful organization will not be possible, and simple serial searching and recognition by humans of automatically generated proxies for documents will have to be relied upon. Some of the arteriole-sized elements will be 'unexpected', but they will not be unexpected for long in the minds of searchers.

The capillaries are the smallest elements and, according to Doyle, should have the most interesting function. It is hoped that these links will answer the searcher's question: 'What does this document talk about that no other document talks about?' Very often, individual documents will only reinforce already well-populated linkages; some work must be done by the searchers. The main task at this level is to give the searcher enough information about each undiscriminated document to permit him to narrow his focus by recognition.

In coordination systems, one cannot cope with lack of precision by bringing additional ordinates into play; bringing in the fourth and often just the third ordinate is likely to lead to inaccuracies, that is to rejection of relevant documents. The cause of this state is that both librarians and authors generate words and terms from their own 'psychological association maps'.

In his conclusions, Doyle stated that the method described could not only help to clarify the picture of a specific search, but could serve as the basis of highly systematic and rapid browsing. The searcher would be given the advantageous illusion of proceeding along ordinates of meaning and browsing, rather than along the usual irrelevant ordinates of page length and shelf location.

7.3 Search techniques

In the actual practice of information search, the searcher is often not the actual enquirer but an intermediary of some kind, and many studies of searching are concerned with the performance of the intermediary.

The work of the reference librarian has been recognized since the turn of the century, but little literature was published on the subject till 1944 (Hutchins). Neill (1975) applied the psychologist Guilford's 'Structure of Intellect' model to the reference process, and Benson and Maloney (1975), in their analysis of the search process, focus on building a 'bibliographic bridge' between system and query. WA Katz (1978) reviewed eight models of the reference process. The paper of Josel (1971), 'Ten reference commandments', is one of the first describing in more detail the work of the reference librarian.

Jahoda (1974) tried to answer a question of interest both to manual and computerized searching: Can a machine be instructed to perform question analysis and search strategy development for reference questions? A small sample of 28 questions was examined to find out whether rules for performing the selected reference process steps could be developed by machine. Each of the 28 questions was first analysed manually then by machine, using nine steps. Jahoda concluded that it would be very difficult, if not impossible, to automate the processes involved in question analysis and search strategy. Today, it is possible to develop search aids and create intelligent front-end peripherals that will facilitate the searcher's effort, but we are still far from using a machine to replace the cognitive processes involved in searching.

Smith (1976a,b) compared online bibliographic searching to a complex problem-solving activity. She suggested dividing a difficult problem (the initial search request) into a group of simpler subproblems (subsearches) that can be solved more easily. The solution to the initial search request is achieved by combining the results of subsearches. This is usually done in real life, although the process is not as straightforward as presented by Smith. An experienced search analyst proceeds in this direction intuitively without realizing the steps he or she is taking. This is also the way presented to future online searchers during courses organized in various institutions.

Markey and Atherton (1979) presented five models of the more predominant approaches to search strategy (we would call it tactics):

1. Building blocks. This is the straightforward problem reduction model as suggested by Smith (above).

2. Citation pearl growing. The searcher starts with a search on the most specific terms derived from the query. The aim is to retrieve at least one relevant citation, check the index terms of this citation (or citations if there are more than one), and then use the index terms to retrieve further 'similar' citations. It is an iterative process.

3. Successive fractions. Having retrieved a set of citations too large, the searcher reduces the set using narrower index terms.

4. Most specific facet first. The searcher starts a search with the most specific concept, and stops searching if the first result of the search is acceptable.

5. Lowest postings first. A similar approach to 4. It involves beginning the search with the concept that has fewest postings and not searching further if the size of the initial set retrieved is satisfactory.

Markey and Atherton admit that the list of the five mentioned search tactics is not exhaustive and that it is possible to develop a combination of all five techniques. In real life, one uses a search technique appropriate to the search carried out. The choice of a technique is a spontaneous process and not consciously adopted as a result of careful analysis. One analyses the content of a query and its subject and not the technique.

The IIDA project members (Meadow, 1977) developed a structural model of the search process based on the classification of commands into six types according to function:

1. commands that begin or end a search;
2. commands for retrieving information about search terms;
3. commands for combining terms;
4. commands for displaying references online;
5. commands for printing references offline;
6. commands for processing saved searches.

Morrow (1976) used a generalized flowchart of the search process as a teaching aid. The flowchart was used to display support commands for browsing and vocabulary and reviewing search strategy (search tactics).

Adams (1979) presented useful and practical instructions for designing search strategies (search tactics) for online searching in libraries. As computer searching is used to 'retrieve concepts through the use of imperfect surrogates, words, and a word may mean different things in different contexts', these words (terms) must be chosen carefully. He gave the following advice:

1. Minimize the number of intersections and choose just 'key concepts'.

2. Adapt the search strategy to the database; the number of access points in a database varies. Some contain just the title words, while others have titles, descriptors, concept codes, abstracts, etc.

3. Anticipate methods for narrowing or broadening the search.

4. Fill in the details: codes, commands, etc.

Psychological aspects of searching reviewed by Bates (1981) deal with the process of thinking. In her paper (1979a), she presented a model of search strategy that is intended primarily as a facilitation model and secondarily as a teaching model. The model consisted of four types of tactics:

1. monitoring tactics, to keep the search on track and efficient;

2. file structure tactics, techniques for threading one's way through the file structure of the information facility to the desired file, source, or information within the source;

3. search formulation tactics, to aid in the process of designing or redesigning the search formulation;

4. term tactics, to aid in the selection and revision of specific terms within the search formulation.

There is a table of 29 tactics which in this paper were restricted to those dealing with search proper.

A second paper by Bates (1979b) dealt with idea tactics, i.e. tactics to help generate new ideas or solutions in information searching. These tactics were applicable to all types of searching, both bibliographic and reference searches, and in both manual and online systems. Bates stated that the focus of the tactics is psychological: they should improve the searcher's thinking and creative processes in searching. Idea tactics were presented as part of a facilitation model of searching. The tactics presented in the paper were grouped into 'idea generation' and 'pattern-breaking' tactics. The tactics were intended for beginner searchers.

Blair (1980) based his research on the work of two psychologists: A Tversky and D Kahneman. He stated that searchers may show systematic biases during the process of search modification. They may stick to the terms chosen initially, i.e. they may be reluctant to drop their initial terms in search formulation and even when revising a search they will probably drop the terms accepted during the later stage of searching.

Pejtersen (1980) identified five patterns of searching, the most significant being 'empirical search strategy'. On the basis of manual search observation in public libraries, she noticed that librarians stereotype users and suggest material of similar nature to persons classified in the same category.

Ingwersen and Kaae (1980) presented a model of 'the public library communication system from a cognitive viewpoint'. The authors discuss their detailed description and analysis of 'thinking aloud' protocols taken from 20 librarians and non-librarians. Using this technique, certain elements related to the formulation of user needs, interaction and information search activities were recorded on tape. The user-librarian conversations were directly recorded (analysis of this search stage has been reviewed in the section on human-human interaction). Analysis of the librarian's search process was based on written queries directed to the participating librarians. Ingwersen (1982) itemized nine steps in the retrieval process: (1) information need of user; (2) the formalized information need of the user; (3) user-librarian negotiation; (4) developing the search profile; (5) choice of tools; (6) looking up: systematic or alphabetic; (7) judgment based on index (terms); (8) judgment based on descriptions, abstracts, titles; (9) evaluation of the documents themselves.

This section of our review covers only points (4) to (6). These steps depend on thought processes linked to mental processing of entries in tools or documents. Different kinds of knowledge influence these steps, namely knowledge regarding the actual topic and/or regarding library and information work.

Ingwersen regards search as a problem-solving task. Thus, besides behavioural phenomena involved during search negotiation, other problems concerning the processing of information in the IR process are mainly of a linguistic and psychological nature.

Experimental search testing involved 13 librarians and five non-librarians. The subjects were asked to verbalize their thoughts during the search procedure and, to avoid misinterpretation, thinking aloud was supplemented by observation of the subjects' behaviour and actions and by self-confrontation. This means that the subjects and the observer made repetitive runs of the recorded tape immediately after recording.

Before analysing the protocols in depth, it was necessary to identify search routines and to analyse subject relations, search and solving possibilities for each search. The analysis was based on a heuristic model developed in connection with the project.

The analysis revealed three different and specific search modes on which the information search depends. The treatment of a retrieval problem depends on the motives underlying the librarian's way of attacking the search and on the expectations concerning the tools and documents. Two decisive motives were discovered:

1. open search motive, to gain information useful to the librarian in the future IR process;

2. fixed search motive, to locate the document or tool which includes the answer.

Motive related to expectations concerning both (a) whether a document may provide an answer at all, and (b) in what form the answer may exist.

The open search mode is characterized by a heuristic IR process in which the librarian from the start is concerned to extend his conceptual knowledge structures. This extension may again serve as a basis for further search by formulating lack of knowledge about part of the topic. The librarian is open to new information from the environment. The search routines — which form a part of the knowledge of documents and tools — are applied in order to obtain information throughout the search process. When sufficient information items are perceived and processed, the application of search routines changes to the means of solving the original information problem.

The fixed search is carried out as an algorithmic IR process. The librarian searches at first for a direct solution to the query, aiming to find the document that includes the answer immediately. To solve the information task search routines are applied in relation to the different search possibilities, but always within the framework of the fixed motive. This motive continues throughout the search process and the formulation of the query is accepted and maintained as originally stated.

The semi-fixed search starts by following the pattern of the fixed search. The librarian, however, may reach a certain degree of openness caused by the search process itself which momentarily leads to a kind of open search during the IR process. In such moments reformulations of parts of the query may appear owing to either expected but missing answers or problems encountered during the search.

In summary of the paper, Ingwersen stated that online IR work and training will change the search routines and thereby the librarian's search procedures in general. For online assistants employment of some kind of open search mode seemed likely to be most efficient, because it combined heuristic features at the beginning of the search process with more formal solutions later, using the search algorithms built into the IR system in a flexible way.

Quite a number of studies during recent years have been dedicated to enabling the end-user to be a searcher, i.e. to giving him or her direct access to the database without an intermediary. These issues are reviewed in the section on human-computer interaction.

7.4 Cognitive maps

The reference of Doyle to the psychological association maps of individuals directs us to examine studies made in cognitive psychology related to personal knowledge structures.

De Mey (1977) presented an evolutionary view of such areas of knowledge related to information science as: perception, represent-ation of knowledge and philosophy of science. He stressed that the adoption of the cognitive view is a recent stage in the frame of four stages within information-processing development: (i) a monadic stage during which information units are handled separately and independently of each other, as if they were single self-contained entities; (ii) a structural stage which views information as a more complex entity consisting of several information units arranged in some specific way; (iii) a contextual stage, where in addition to the structural analysis of the information-bearing units, contextual information is required to disambiguate the meaning of the message; and (iv) a cognitive or epistemic stage, in which information is seen as supplementary to a conceptual system, that represents the information-processing system's knowledge of its world.

Loftus (1976) and Lindsay and Norman (1977) represent the input of data into the mind as follows:

ENVIRONMENT
▼
SENSORY STORE
▼
SHORT-TERM STORE WITH REHEARSAL BUFFER
▼
LONG-TERM STORE FOR SEMANTIC AND EPISODIC MEMORY

Although the following account refers to this series of 'stores', these are not necessarily physically separate areas of the brain, but may be seen as stages or levels in the processing of incoming data.

There is evidence first that data are, as it were, held in a sensory store, comprising all the sense data momentarily impinging onto the body from the environment — a large quantity indeed, but they decay quickly, and each datum is lost within a second or so unless it is transferred onward through the system.

In any given situation, the mind's attention is focussed on a small proportion of the data in sensory store, and this is transferred to a short-term store of very limited capacity. Here it will decay in about 15 seconds unless there comes into play the 'rehearsal buffer' (as when one remembers a telephone number by repeatedly rehearsing it to oneself). The final stage of the system is the long-term store, apparently of virtually unlimited capacity. A distinction has been made between its content of 'episodic' memories — records of individual life experiences — and the 'semantic memory', structured knowledge going beyond remembered episodes, though the two sets of memories are clearly interrelated. In our review we are particularly concerned with the long-term memory.

As a physical mechanism, the brain is very complex — about 10^{10} nerve cells in the human cerebral cortex, multiply interconnected. Perhaps we may say, following Young (1978), that each cell corresponds to '(1) a small part of one particular feature of change going on in the outside world, (2) some small part of a memory record of a past external change, or (3) some small part of the instructions for an action that can be done by the body, say to initiate the movement of a few fibres of one muscle,' though this description deliberately simplifies the matter. Some mapping of the cortex to show the locality of different sensory and motor areas has been possible.

But no such mapping is yet possible for memory records — and indeed there is no physiological evidence that a specific memory is stored in a specific part of the brain — many brain areas seem to contribute to it (Lindsay and Norman, 1977).

Clues to memory structure can only be provided by human behaviour — and in particular by verbal output. The knowledge expressed in behaviour, speech and writing must be correlated in some way with the mental structure of the actor, speaker or writer.

Analysis of speech or text, and of the structure of public knowledge, therefore gives an indication of memory structure. Experimentally, psychologists have sought clues from the responses of subjects to questions: for example, words commonly associated with a stimulus word, or the speed of response to questions of the type 'Is it true that an A is B?' Examples below are taken from such texts as Kintsch (1978), Rumelhart (1977), Loftus (1976) and Baddeley (1976). An excellent review of cognitive psychology from an information-processing viewpoint, is the book by Lachman and Lachman (1979).

If the same word is presented to a large group of experimental subjects, there is usually considerable consensus among them on the list of words spontaneously associated with the stimulus. For example, the following words are all likely to occur frequently among responses to the word BUTTERFLY. In a particular study, the numbers of occasions on which each word was associated with the others are also shown.

	Moth	Insect	Wing	Bird	Fly	Cocoon
Moth	—	2	2	—	10	—
Insect	4	—	—	—	18	—
Wing	—	—	—	50	24	—
Bird	—	—	6	—	30	—
Fly	—	10	—	8	—	—
Cocoon	16	6	—	—	—	—

Such an association table suggests that a common pattern of

association links in the mind is as follows:

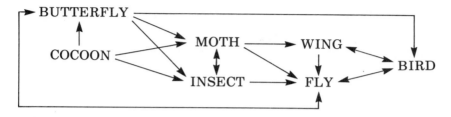

The numbers in the table above give some indication of the 'strength' of association, the closeness with which two words are associated, their *semantic distance*. Strength of association has also been used as a measure of 'typicality'. If a number of people are asked to give a set of examples of BIRD, different birds will be mentioned with different frequency. In one experiment, frequencies such as the following were obtained:

Robin	377		Ostrich	17
Sparrow	237		Swan	14
Eagle	161	*but*	Crane	13
Crow	149		Geese	12
Canary	134		Pelican	11
Blackbird	89		Stork	10

The high-frequency items are more widely considered as 'typical' birds than the low-frequency, and are more readily recalled in response to the request 'Name a bird.'

Another approach to indication of semantic distance is to ask subjects to rate the 'similarity' of words. For example, from a list of 30 mammals, subjects were asked to rate each possible pair on a similarity scale between 1 (identical) and 10 (maximally different). In the course of the study it became clear that two criteria of similarity were seen as of most importance: how like or unlike a human the animal was judged to be, and how fierce. From the results a spatial representation of semantic distance was established.

Semantic distance has also been explored by measuring the time taken by a subject to verify statements of the kind: 'An A is B — true or false?' Some representative results are given below, where L means 'verification takes less time than ....'

(1) Canary is a — bird L animal L fish

(2) The following is a bird — canary L ostrich L butterfly

(3) Collie is a — dog L animal L mammal

(4) Canary — is yellow L flies L eats L has gills

(5) Flower is a — chair L oak

A simple interpretation of such results is to distinguish between entities (such as canary, bird, dog, chair) and properties (such as yellow, flies, eats). The entities are linked hierarchically in a generic chain (animal-bird-canary-particular canaries), and at each link in the chain are attached properties common to entities at a higher level. An example of a hierarchical network from Collins and Quillian (1969) is shown below.

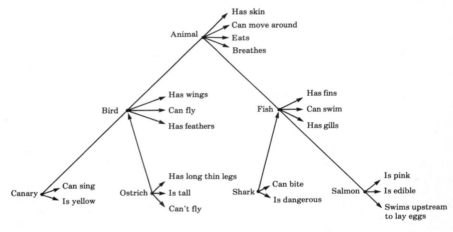

Figure 7.1 Illustration of a hypothetical memory structure for a three-level hierarchy (Collins and Quillian, 1969). Reproduced by permission.

It is assumed that to verify that A is B, the mind accesses both A and B, and traces the chain of links between them: the longer the chain, the greater the response time. Thus 'canary is bird' takes less time than 'canary is animal', 'canary is yellow' less time than 'canary eats', and the latter less time than 'canary has gills'.

Some experimental results support the Collins and Quillian model, but others do not. The example (3) given above shows that 'collie is mammal', which should hierarchically come between dog and animal, takes longer to verify than either, and this has been ascribed to the relative lack of familiarity of the term MAMMAL — i.e. it is less likely to be semantically close to COLLIE in a word association experiment. CANARY and OSTRICH are equidistant from BIRD in the pictured model, but example (2) shows that it takes longer to verify that ostrich is a bird — canary is more familiar, typical and closely associated. In example (5), FLOWER and OAK are in the same general area of knowledge, and the memory structure between them is explored to verify that a flower is not an oak, but the unrelated words FLOWER and CHAIR are more quickly assessed. It is evident that memory structure is more complex than the Collins and Quillian model, and in particular (a) semantic distance is influenced by strength of association as well as by hierarchical links, (b) we need not assume that a property is linked only to the highest level of entity to which it applies — for example, 'has wings' might be linked directly to a number of bird-names — and (c) the model makes no provision for direct linkages between properties.

An alternative model for memory does not stress hierarchical linkages but concentrates on associations. For example, we might have the following sets of features associated with various concepts. The nearer the top of a list, the stronger the association.

BIRD	CANARY	OSTRICH	BUTTERFLY
Feathers	Sings	Neck	Wings
Wings	Yellow	Long legs	Flies
Flies	Cage	Beak	Flowers
Eggs	Feathers	Runs	Nectar
Nests	Beak	Feathers	Moth
Beak	Small	Eggs	Coloured
Sings	Wings		Insect
			Cocoon

In response to the question whether A is B, the feature sets of A and B are compared. It is clear that CANARY — with four features in common with BIRD — is likely to be more readily verified as a bird than is OSTRICH. When BUTTERFLY is compared with BIRD, there is an overlap of two features so there can be some initial doubt — hence perhaps the long reponse time in example (2) above. A feature model of this kind can be refined by distinguishing between 'defining' features (essential aspects of meaning) and other features playing a decisive role in cases of doubt. For example, if feathers were the defining feature of BIRD, it would act to include OSTRICH but exclude from the category of birds BUTTERFLY.

It should be stressed here that the models discussed above are considered to represent the conceptual knowledge structure. It seems likely that there are in addition (a) a lexical structure of *words*, separate from though necessarily linked to the structure of concepts, and (b) a linked *image* store, since a sight, a sound, a smell calls up both a corresponding concept and its name. In the experimental work reported earlier, input stimuli in the form of words must first be matched in the lexical system before being transferred to the conceptual structure. Other experimental work has explored the structure of the lexicon itself by asking people to name pictures of objects, and measuring the speed of response.

It has been found that the speed varies according to the frequency of occurrence of the name in general English usage — for example, the picture of a book or chair was more rapidly named than one of a bagpipe or gyroscope. There is another factor at work: everyone responds in the same way to a picture of a book ('it's a book'), but the names supplied for the picture of a gyroscope include spinner, top, whirler, circumrotator and machine. As uncertainty about a name increases, so does the time taken to give a name, and this has been shown to be independent of the effect of usage frequency of the name. It appears that more frequently occurring names, and the names of more readily identified images, are more easily accessed in the lexicon.

After taking into account further lingustic considerations, cognitive psychologists have developed some considerably more complex — and more speculative — models of personal knowledge structures. The Lachmans note a number of cognitive characteristics that a 'global' model must represent. People can quickly retrieve any one of a larger number of facts. For example, an educated person has about 100,000 words in his productive vocabulary, yet while speaking he or she can locate and express about two concepts a second. A model must suggest how efficient search and retrieval are achieved. Second, the model must allow for rapid inference. If knowing X and Y makes possible inference Z, then something about the way X and Y are stored and linked to each other must contain the implicit information that Z is probably true. A model should also allow ready conversion of simple ideas into complex ones and provide for such abilities as classification and detection of similarities. Finally, it should permit accretion: the growth of knowledge by assimilation of external information and by generating new information.

Let us look at one particular global model of knowledge structure, and that of the LNR research group as described by Lindsay and Norman. They start with the hierarchical pattern previously illustrated:

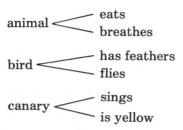

animal — eats, breathes

bird — has feathers, flies

canary — sings, is yellow

They go on to name the relations shown by the linking lines (class and property) and then to represent class by 'isa' and property by 'applies-to'. An example is:

animal --- breathes
                                    applies-to

isa

dog ---barks
                                    applies-to

isa

Bingo --- is sick
                                    applies-to

To take account of the fact that the lexical image and conceptual structures seem to be separate though linked, the LNR model then represents concepts by numbered nodes, linked to lexical elements by the 'name' relation and also linked to images:

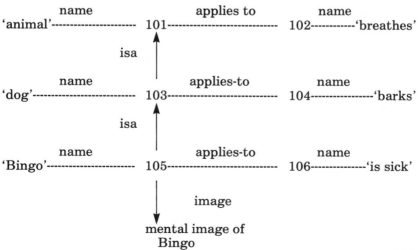

Further, to take account of the 'typicality' effect, the group suggests that each familiar concept might be associated with a 'prototype', with a set of 'standard' features.

The model implies that the more closely the characteristics of a particular bird match those of the prototype, the more readily would it be named or classed as a bird.

Lindsay and Norman accept the distinction between episodic and semantic memory — concepts in semantic memory are often accessed readily, without apparent search or effort, whereas it is often difficult to recall episodic information. Yet they see the two as intimately related. The following figure is an example of the structure of personal knowledge as they represent it (each concept and name has been coalesced into a name mode to simplify the picture).

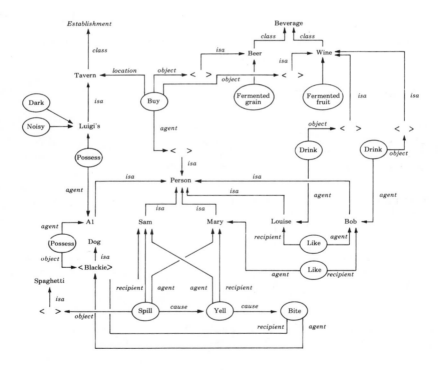

Figure 7.2   Episodic and semantic memory (Lindsay and Norman, 1977). Reproduced by permission.

134

This figure represents some semantic information — beer and wine are beverages, made respectively from fermented grain and fermented fruits, a person can buy them from a tavern, such as Luigi's — but much more such information could be linked on. Embedded within this is the memory of an episode at Luigi's where Bob and Louise were drinking wine, Mary spilled spaghetti on Sam, he yelled at her, and Blackie (the dog of Al, the owner of the tavern) bit Sam.

To represent events, the LNR model uses the following series of relations.

The Parts of the Event

Action	The event itself. In a sentence, the action is usually described by a **verb**:
	The diver was **bitten** by the shark.
Agent	The actor who has caused the action to take place:
	The diver was bitten by the **shark**.
Conditional	A logical condition that exists between two events:
	A shark is dangerous **only if** it is hungry.
	Linda flunked the test **because** she always sleeps in lectures.
Instrument	The thing or device that caused or implemented the event:
	The **wind** demolished the house.
Location	The place where the event takes place. Often two different locations are involved, one at the start of the event and one at the conclusion. These are identified as **from** and **to** locations:
	They hitchhiked **from La Jolla to Del Mar.**
	From the University, they hitchhiked **to the beach.**
Object	The thing that is affected by the action:
	The wind demolished the **house.**
Recipient	The person who is the receiver of the effect of the action:
	The crazy professor threw the blackboard at **Ross.**
Time	When an event takes place:
	The surf was up **yesterday.**
Truth	Used primarily for false statements:
	No special suits had to be worn.

Overall, then, Lindsay and Norman represent personal knowledge structures as a multiplicity of concept nodes, linked by various relations that are themselves concepts — 'isa', applies-to, name, prototype, location, object, agent and so on. As they put it:

> The memory system is an organized collection of pathways that specify possible routes through the data base. Retrieving information from such a memory is going to be like running a maze. Starting off at a given node, there are many possible options available about the possible pathways to follow. Taking one of these paths leads to a series of crossroads, each going off to a different concept. Each new crossroad is like a brand new maze, with a new set of choice points and a new set of pathways to follow. In principle, it is possible to start at any point in the data base and by taking the right sequence of turns through successive mazes, end up at any other point. Thus, in the memory system all information is interconnected.

The knowledge structure of each individual is unique, built up in accordance with his or her own life experience. The search strategy adopted in retrieval from an external database will be influenced by interaction between the semantic structure of public knowledge and the searcher's personal knowledge structure.

7.5 AI and IR

Linda Smith (1980a,b) has presented an interesting review on AI in IR.

The areas which she compares for similarities between various concepts in AI and IR are: pattern recognition, representation, problem-solving and planning, heuristics and learning. We will concentrate here on aspects relevant to the search process.

1. *Pattern recognition* in AI is concerned with the problem of extracting useful information from data, which are most frequently of a sensory character. The feature extraction involves conversion of the sensory input into discrete features (attributes, properties) which are more easily interpreted by the system. Pattern classification involves assignment of an object to one of a predetermined number of classes based on the results of the feature extraction phase. In scene analysis, one wants a description of a picture rather than a classification.

In IR, pattern recognition relates to both the content analysis operation and the matching operation during the search phase, when query formulations and document surrogates are matched one against another. Content analysis may be viewed as a feature extraction problem; determination of the subset of the file to be retrieved may be viewed as a pattern classification problem; and the shifting emphasis in pattern recognition from an interest in classification to an interest in scene description analysis is reflected in IR in more flexible document descriptions no longer limited to index terms, assigned or extracted at the time of data input.

Pattern classification can be viewed as a categorizing activity. There is a finite set of pattern prototypes and the problem to be solved is to avoid errors in the assignment of samples to classes.

Sidorov (1969) has analysed qualitatively and quantitatively the relationship between the retrieval problem and classification problem in the following way:

Retrieval problem, (e.g. retrospective bibliographic search)

1. Natural language for describing characteristics of objects not used owing to fundamental and practical difficulties in algorithmic implementation of a matching criterion.

2. Use of an IR language:
   (a) permits simple algorithmic implementation of a matching criterion; but
   (b) it is hard to implement methods for translating from the document to the IR language.

3. Use of methods reducing number of inspections of the search file necessary for practical reasons.

4. Number of elements in search file $= 10^4$ to 10^6

5. Number of possible search features $= 10^3$ to 10^4

6. Average number of search features per document $= 10^2$

7. Most important technical parameter is volume of the search file.

Pattern classification problem (e.g. letters of the alphabet)

1. 'Exact' photographs of patterns for their subsequent identification are not used owing to the practical difficulty of algorithmic implementation of a matching criterion;

2. Use of quantized patterns:
   (a) permits complex algorithmic implementation of a matching criterion;
   (b) no complex methods required to quantize patterns.

3. Use of methods reducing number of elements in the search file inspected not required.

4. Number of prototypes $= 10^2$

5. Number of possible identifying features $= 5 \times 10^2$ to 10^3

6. Average number of identifying features per pattern $= 5 \times 10^2$ to 10^3

7. Most important technical parameter is identification time of one pattern.

In the case of IR, feature extraction yields a search pattern for each document in the file, and a search pattern for the request.

Retrieval of a particular item from the file is determined by the measure of closeness calculated between the search pattern of that item and the search pattern of the request.

In pattern recognition a measure of closeness is calculated between the quantized input pattern and each prototype with assignment of the input to the class to which it is most similar. The success of each task depends on definition of a satisfactory matching criterion by which similarity can be measured.

Smith (1976a,b) summarizes her comparison by stating that the pattern to be identified is the analogue of a request in the retrieval problem and the prototype plays the same role as the search pattern (features) of a document. The prototype file is the analogue of the retrieval file. The main parameters determining the specific nature of each of these problems are the number of features of documents or prototypes and the number of items in the file.

Whereas in the retrieval problem there is usually a large number of documents each described by a small number of features, in the pattern classification problem the volume of the file is much smaller with a large number of features describing each prototype. In both retrieval and the AI pattern recognition, success depends on the matching criterion or similarity measure used.

If one turns to more complex patterns, in which it is desired to reflect varied relationships among parts of the whole, the finite number of classes available in the classificatory approach is insufficient. This has led to a growing interest in scene analysis in pattern recognition. Pattern classification is adequate when there is a finite set of objects to be recognized, as in the case of alphanumeric characters. Scene analysis is necessary when one wants to perform actions on the sets of objects analysed, as in the case of a robot performing some task. A similar distinction exists between reference retrieval and question-answering systems. Feature extraction followed by classification may be adequate in reference retrieval, but different techniques must be developed for question-answering. We will leave aside Linda Smith's discussion of representation in AI and IR, and go on to consider her next theme.

2. *Problem-solving and planning.* The concept as used in AI is that a problem exists whenever a problem solver desires some outcome or state of affairs that he does not immediately know how to attain. A genuine problem-solving process involves repeated use of available information to initiate exploration, which discloses, in turn, more information until a way to attain the solution is finally discovered (Newell and Simon, 1972). In AI, the basic idea is that solving a problem involves selecting a good action from the space of possible actions. Evaluation of the best action necessitates tracing through consequences of alternatives, a process referred to as search.

In IR the problem to be solved is how to decide for each item, relative to a given query, whether or not it will be relevant. The problem-solving process is one of forming and executing a search strategy. It is interesting to consider techniques used in AI to formulate searches for solutions to problems, since it may be desirable to incorporate such techniques in retrieval systems to aid requesters in the task of search strategy development.

The search for a problem solution in IR is well represented by the problem reduction approach. The query is the initial problem. It can be reduced to subproblems by segmenting it into elements which make up the request formulation. Separate elements are linked by AND and OR. VanderBrug and Minker (1976) define the problem reduction representation of a problem as a specification of the structure of the description, description of the original problem, a characterization of the problem whose solutions are immediately known (primitive problems) and a set of operators which map problems into sets of problems. It is a partitioning of difficult problems into two or more simpler problems each of which may be further partitioned. The problem reduction space can be illustrated by an AND/OR graph.

Planning and search strategy development. Planning is a heuristic and, as other heuristics, does not offer a guarantee that it will always work, since it may generate no plan, a single plan or several plans. However, subplans that make up a plan are collectively simpler than the original one. Planning gives the machine system a technique with which to analyse problem structure in the large, using a simplified model of the problem situation. The process of translating from the planning space to the full detail of the problem space is conveniently expressed by the notion of structured programming (Dykstra, 1975).

The planning heuristic describes a process quite similar to that of search strategy formulation, the analysis and formulation of optimum methods by which specified requests for information may be answered in a retrieval system. Till now, the process of strategy development is carried out by the human in most existing retrieval systems; it would be interesting to suggest methods by which the machine could assume at least some of the burden of planning.

As for questions versus commands, or ill-defined versus well-defined problems, in the retrieval system, the search strategy formulation takes the form of a command to the machine, specifying what elements are to be searched and their logical relationships. A command assumes either (or both) of two things on the part of the enquirer: (a) he knows exactly what he wants and can describe its form (book, paper, etc.) and its label (author, title, specific subject combination etc.); (b) he knows the organization of the system, the rules for formulating queries so that they may be obeyed as commands (Taylor, 1968). The use of commands in communication with the system ignores the whole process of question negotiation which precedes statement of the command. Question negotiation begins with an initial statement of the problem which may be highly unstructured and loose. In the systems of today, the requester, sometimes with the help of a trained intermediary, must transform this initial statement into a command which the system can follow.

Existing systems exploit the advantages of imperative sentences (procedural description in imperatives is already laid out and is carried out faster; one does not assume previous knowledge on the part of the machine).

New techniques must be developed to facilitate machine handling of declarative sentences which is a necessary capacity if the machine is to participate in the question negotiation process.

140

The distinction between command and question is closely related to that between well- and ill-defined (or structured) problems. In general, problems which requesters bring to retrieval systems can best be regarded as ill-defined problems which become well-structured only in the process of being prepared in a form which the system can handle.

Open constraints are one or more parameters, the value of which is left unspecified as the problem is given (Reitman, 1964). Open constraints are the source of ill-definedness in problem statements. Some sources of open constraints which must be handled in question negotiation are as follows: (a) ambiguity; (b) analogical attributes — in retrieval an example would be to find all documents 'like' one already known to the user; (c) available vocabulary — is it possible for the requester to express his query without resorting to utterances which are not included in the subset of natural language interpretable by the system?

If one considers systems capable of handling a wider class of IR problems than reference retrieval, the notion of 'hearer program' is of interest. A hearer program accepts input in natural language and performs some task on the basis of the input. In a typical form of hearer program the inputs represent queries that the program interprets and answers. Within a certain subject area, the program exhibits 'understanding' of inputs in the operational sense that it frequently makes appropriate responses to them.

3. *Heuristics.* The next area discussed by Linda Smith is heuristics. The concept in AI is that heuristics are things that aid discovery of solutions to the problems. The development of problem-solving programs in AI has led to recognition of several heuristics, some of them being problem-specific and some having wider applicability. Associated closely with the notion of heuristics is that of an evaluation function used to select among alternatives in the search for a solution.

The significance for IR is that human searchers use various heuristic techniques to guide searches in IR, but they have not yet been implemented for machine searching.

Index language devices have been employed to introduce more flexibility in subject searching. Certain devices allow one to broaden the scope of a search or to increase precision. To improve the quality of searching, certain recall and precision devices may be used and although actual selection of a device to be used may still be left to the human searcher, the machine could consult its table of connections to determine what devices are available to reduce the difference identified

141

by the searcher. The means-ends analysis was one of the general-purpose heuristics used by GPS (General Problem Solver) in a wide range of tasks. Linda Smith discusses the use of this analysis and suggests that it may prove useful in IR.

4. *Learning.* Finally, she turns to the concept of learning. The concept in AI is that feature extraction routines, representations, problem-solving and planning techniques, and heuristics are initially selected and programmed by a human designer when an AI system is developed for some applications. Learning systems can also be used to improve any of the aspects mentioned above, and to evaluate system performance.

The significance to IR is that the availability of online computer systems makes it reasonable to speak about dynamic systems which can change and improve performance over time.

There are several techniques implemented in AI systems.

1. Modes of learning:

(a) incremental adaptation — adjustment of weights based on favourable or unfavourable outcomes. The program learns by successive modifications of parameters, e.g. in evaluation functions;

(b) trial and error — an *ad hoc* technique which involves a series of questions at each decision, e.g. Have I been in this situation before? If so, what did I do? What were the consequences of my action? If satisfactory, choose the same action again. Otherwise choose something else. The technique is limited in its scope since there is no generalization from experience;

(c) procedural learning — learn procedure which allows one to deduce facts;

(d) aggregation and generalization. Aggregation is accomplished by chunking pieces of information into larger units and generalization is a form of learning where results of one unsuccessful problem solution are saved in a form applicable to solve subsequent problems;

(e) learning with a teacher (with supervision, with performance feedback). The simplest example of this method occurs in the development of pattern classification algorithms;

(f) learning by building descriptions — from various examples, the program determines the minimal description of a concept in terms of objects and their interrelations;

(g) learning without a teacher (without supervision, without performance feedback, cluster-seeking techniques, mode-seeking techniques, clumping techniques.

2. Learning retrieval systems:

The measure of adequacy of a system is the ability of the system to satisfy users' needs as they arise (Lipetz, 1966). A learning system can be directional, a system which seeks goals or at least recognizes a goal when it is reached and transitional, a system which introduces changes with time.

8 Question-answering and expert systems

8.1 Introduction

Question-answering as well as expert systems employ many techniques developed by AI, techniques of search, knowledge representation, and natural-language processing.

Linda Smith (1980b) defined research in AI as efforts aimed at studying and mechanizing information-processing tasks that normally require human intelligence. Avron Barr (1982) sees in AI that part of computer science which is concerned with creating and studying computer programs that exhibit behavioural characteristics identified as intelligence in human behaviour: knowing, reasoning, learning, problem-solving, language-understanding, etc. Nilsson's (1980) definition of AI is as follows:

> AI has embraced the larger scientific goal of constructing an information-processing theory of intelligence. If such a science of intelligence could be developed, it could guide the design of intelligent machines as well as explicate intelligent behaviour as it occurs in humans and other animals.

AI started to evolve in the 1930s and the two subjects which helped to develop this new science were mathematical logic and computation. Formal, mathematical logic should not be equated with human thinking.

> From the logician's viewpoint, logical inference has objective, formal standards of validity which exist in Plato's heaven of ideas and not in human heads .... From the psychologist's point of view, thinking must not be confused with logic because human thinking frequently is not rigorous or correct, does not follow the path of step-by-step deduction — in short, is not usually logical (Newell and Simon, 1972).

The contribution of formal logic to information-processing psychology was to demonstrate by example that the manipulation of symbols (at least some symbols) could be described in terms of specific, concrete processes quite as clearly as the manipulation of pine boards in a carpenter's shop. Formalisation of logic showed that symbols can be copied, compared, rearranged and concatenated with just as much definiteness of process as boards can be sawed, planed, measured and glued (Newell and Simon, 1972).

Parallel to the development of formal logic was the progress within economics of formal theories of rational decision making. Hand in hand with economics emerged statistical decision theory, and statistics had, in turn, close historical links with philosophy, especially through the theory of probability and the problem of induction. Just before the Second World War, the logicians became more explicit in manipulating symbols. Alan Turing described the processor, now known as a Turing machine, while Carnap, Church, Curry and Post were introducing formalizations of the syntax in logic, models for 'formal grammar'.

The application of mathematics to biology, psychology and even to social sciences followed an earlier similar phenomenon in the physical sciences. Lotka's *Elements of physical biology* foreshadowed some of the main concepts of cybernetics. The term 'cybernetics' devised by Norbert Wiener (1948) includes such elements as (1) information theory, (2) the theory of feedback systems (servomechanism theory, control theory) and (3) the electronic computer. In Eastern Europe the term cybernetics is used more broadly to include addition to the above mentioned topics also (4) game theory,(5) mathematical economics and statistical decision theory, and (6) management science and operational research.

Newell and Simon (1972) in their *Historical addendum* present Wiener's version of the history of the development of cybernetics (1948), adding their own interpretation:

1. From the beginning, cybernetics had a strong concern with physiology and biological feedback mechanisms, being thus linked strongly to the homeostasis concepts of Claude Bernard, Lotka, Cannon, and Henderson.

2. The ties with formal logic were especially evident in the early cybernetic publications, preceding the war and during the early years of the war: Shannon's thesis (1940) employed Boolean algebra for the analysis of switching circuits; the Pitts-McCulloch paper (1943) provided a Boolean analysis of nerve networks. The cyberneticians influenced many fields by linking ideas about the functioning of the nervous system with information theory and control theory.

3. Most of the prominent men who contributed to these developments had early in their careers been deeply immersed in modern symbolic logic. Wiener had been a student of Russell's in Cambridge; much of

von Neumann's work in the 1920s and 1930s was in logic. Computers played only a small role in these first years of cybernetics. The main emphasis was on feedback and on the information theory of Wiener and Shannon.

What brought together all these ideas was the development of computers, conceived by Babbage and guided by Turing, von Neumann, and others. The brain-computer metaphor suggested itself almost immediately. The analogy applied was between the neurological organization of the brain and the wiring of the computer (von Neumann, 1958). Turing was one of the first to see that there was another level, the more abstract level of information processing, at which the analogy was more appropriate.

Feedback concepts had an impact on psychology. The information theory was clear and precisely defined. Hick (1952) undertook testing of a relation between response time and amount of information contained in the response. Others attempted to measure the information capacity of the human sensory and motor 'channels'. But the limits of applicability of information theory to psychology gradually became clear, certainly by the time of Garner's monograph on uncertainty and structure (1962).

The formalism of information theory, statistical decision theory, and game theory had stimulated new interest in the classical research area of concept formation seen clearly in the paper by Hovland, a 'communication analysis' of concept learning (1952) and in the book by Bruner, Goodnow and Austin (1962). This book, *A study of thinking*, states that inputs and outputs of a communication system could not be dealt with exclusively in terms of the nature of these inputs and outputs alone nor even in terms of such internal characteristics as channel capacity and noise.

One should mention that the revival of cognitive sciences was not entirely due to the influence of information theory. Another strong influence was the deep changes in psychology itself, the development of personality theory from the time of Freud. Psychoanalysis and personality theory have become increasingly interested in what has come to be called 'ego psychology'. Together with the interest in 'ego', a search has been initiated for links between general laws of perception and cognition on one side, and general laws of personality on the other.

The Second World War produced also an increase of research into human skills and performance. Much of this work was concerned with the human side of complex man-machine systems: pilots, radar personnel, etc. The researchers observed the analogies between human information processing and the behaviour of servomechanisms and computers. Broadbent (1957) describes a mechanical model which illustrates a formal theory of attention and immediate memory in information theory terms.

In the years which followed the Second World War, computers were viewed mainly as mathematical machines but it was not long before people started to write programs that enabled them to play chess and other games, and to provide translations of text from one language to another. This was the beginning of AI.

Pamela McCorduck in her historical study of AI — *Machines who think* (1979) — underlined the link between the intelligence of the human and the complicated devices developed by the human. There is and there always has been a tendency to construct, or rather a dream of constructing, an automaton in the image of the mental life of its creator.

People started to explore the capabilities of computers with greater insight. For example, could computers solve problems? From the first chess program, initiated by Newell in 1948, it was felt that the problem-solving process is an important step towards the programming of more complex processes for a variety of intellectual tasks. Could computers, for example, prove theorems, or retrieve information? They could but under one condition, namely that step-by-step instructions would be given to them. And these instructions could and can be given providing that people understand and can explicate the tasks they themselves perform. The drive to understand what intelligence is initiated research in AI.

Soon after computers became available, research in computational linguistics had been initiated. The machine's ability to handle symbols was applied to written text. Machine translation was suggested by Weaver in 1949. The method then applied was based on looking up each word in a bilingual dictionary and post-editing the output in the right word order. Later on, Weaver introduced an idea that all languages have many features in common and a conference in 1952 recommended work towards a universal language, called Machinese. Weaver proposed Machinese as an intermediate language for machine translation. Shortly, it became evident that using just syntactic rules produces only a low-quality translation. It became clear that high-quality translation systems must 'understand' the input text before transforming it into a second language. This, in turn, involved the accumulation of a great deal of knowledge about the world. For the first time the researchers realized the need for a 'world knowledge' base. (Barr and Feigenbaum, 1981, pp 233-238.)

The work of Chomsky (1957), in which transformational grammars were introduced, redirected linguistics from a concern with structure to a concern with processing. New computer languages, such as ALGOL and LISP, were introduced into computing with their features of lists and recursion. Concurrently, considerable progress was made in understanding natural language. New attempts in language translation led Schank and Wilks to develop programs which perform translation tasks. A fully automated machine translation has not yet been realized. The general belief exists that a machine translation program must first understand the subject before it can translate material written about the subject. Schank and Abelson (1977) express this in the following way:

> For both people and machines, each in their own way, there is a serious problem in common of making sense out of what they hear, see, or are told about the world. The conceptual apparatus necessary to perform even a partial feat of understanding is formidable and fascinating.

The previously mentioned achievement of chess playing by computer was a big step forward for AI. Techniques such as looking ahead several moves and dividing difficult problems into easier sub-problems evolved subsequently into other AI techniques, such as those of search and problem reduction. Considering once more the chess game, the human player is still superior in his ability to see the board configuration as a meaningful pattern. Another open question in problem-solving is the 'original conceptualization of a problem', called in AI *choice of problem representation*. Human beings often solve a problem without realizing how they do it. Humans can also solve a problem finding the easiest way of doing so. Computers must be told how to solve a problem. It is quite clear that human intuition and the so-called rule of thumb are not yet transferred into the machine and maybe this domain will always be the prerogative of human beings. As AI progresses, there have arisen ideas of linking machines, each of them with a special knowledge system, into one coherent entity. However, this creates serious problems of designing 'social' systems with units able to communicate with each other.

8.2 Question-answering

The attempts to develop rules that would enable logical expressions to be automatically derived from natural sentences, and natural sentences to be derived from these expressions, directed the computational linguists and computer scientists to a new goal — the design of question-answering systems. The intention of these systems was to simulate the linguistic behaviour of humans. All early question-answering programs were restricted to simple English and ignored the complex grammatical constructions of unrestricted English. These programs followed the first attempts at machine translation in the 1950s and were precursors of the much more sophisticated semantic-based natural-language systems of today.

Martin Kay and Karen Sparck-Jones (1971) describe question-answering programs in the following way: Question-answering programs are those:

> that are intended to simulate some or all aspects of human linguistic behaviour .... Suppose that a machine could be built that understood English perfectly, that remembered what it was told about as well as human beings do, that could respond to questions, and so forth. Suppose, in other words, that the machine was able to demonstrate reasonable command of human linguistic competence. There would be no necessary connection between the inner structure of the machine and the way humans operate, but the prima facie case for such a connection would be strong and compelling. Most models of this kind that have actually been proposed or are being worked upon make use of a formal grammar of one kind or another and of sentence-generation and parsing techniques. To this extent, they belong to the same field of endeavour as grammar testing .... The computer program that mimics human performance would at least have to remember what it was told and be prepared to answer questions about it .... The first problem of such a system is to make it understand, remember and respond .... People working on question-answering systems wish on the one hand to throw some light on questions of human psychology and, on the other hand, they would like to be able to provide a practical, useful computer system that could communicate with untrained users in their own language.

Raphael (1976) believes that an ideal question-answering system should be able to:

1. accept facts and questions, and make appropriate responses, all in the form of natural English;

2. store, remember and make efficient use of a large amount of data — at least thousands of elementary facts;

3. answer questions that require it to figure out the logical consequences of the facts stored explicitly in its memory;

4. operate conversationally.

Programs which attempted to answer simple English questions have existed only from 1960. It is difficult to group natural-language programs into a coherent scheme. One such attempt was made by Winograd (1972) who grouped them according to how they represent and use knowledge of their subject matter (Barr and Feigenbaum, 1981).

The earliest examples were natural-language programs which limited their knowledge base to very specific domains. The programs below belong to this group.

The CONVERSATION MACHINE is a program written by L Green, E Berkeley and C Gotlieb in 1959. It can converse about the weather. The conversation machine deals with three factors: meaning, environment and experience. The meaning of each word is stored as an attribute-value pair. The meaning of a remark (combination of words) is derived by looking up each word and coding it by its attribute-value pair from the dictionary. The program compares the meaning of a remark with its own store of knowledge and experience coded in a similar way, and selects a stereotyped reply frame.

The conversation machine avoids the whole problem of syntactic analysis and is limited to a few simple constructions. It is able to analyse a statement into a set of meaningful parameters which are then used to select an answer.

The ORACLE resulted from an MSc thesis by A V Phillips and was written in 1960 in LISP. It first produces a syntactic analysis of both the question and the text which can contain the answer to the question. This analysis transforms both the question and the text into a canonical form which shows the subject, the verb, the object, and the nouns of place and time. At the end of the analysis a match is performed to determine whether the elements of the text match those of the question. The ORACLE is an example of answering questions by structural matching of syntactic and semantic codes.

SAD-SAM (Syntactic Appraiser and Diagrammer—Semantic Analyzing Machine) was written by Robert Lindsay (1963) at Carnegie Institute of Technology in the IPL-V list-processing language. SAD-SAM accepts Basic English sentences (a subset of English limited to a vocabulary of 300-1600 words and the simplest grammatical constructions), builds up a list-structured database, and answers questions using stored facts. The SAD module parses the input, creates a derivation tree structure, and passes this structure to SAM. SAM extracts the semantically relevant information on kinship relationships (the domain of the program) to build out of them family trees, and answers questions. The algorithm employed permits storing definite links but not possible inferences. SAM cannot handle ambiguities.

The BASEBALL system was written by Bert Green at Lincoln Laboratories in 1963 in IPL-V programming language. It is a system which answers questions about the scores, teams, locations and dates of baseball games from lists which summarize a Major League's season's experience. The database is essentially an IR system. The requests from the users must have only one clause, no logical operators (AND, OR, NOT), no comparatives (higher, longer), no sequence of events. The parsing system uses 14 categories of parts of speech. The answer is found by searching the database, and storing relevant items on a 'found' list. BASEBALL does not interrogate the user for clarification of semantic ambiguities, it simply asks him to rephrase a question.

BASEBALL is of particular interest because of its detailed analysis of questions. Simmons (1966) summarizes the description of the system:

In the BASEBALL system three aspects of the question-answering problem stand out clearly. A first phase of syntactic analysis merges into the second phase, semantic analysis. However, for the first time a third logical processing phase becomes explicit. In this phase, even though the relations between words are already known, a wide range of operations are performed as the function of these meanings.

DEACON BREADBOARD (Direct English Access and Control) has been developed by F Thompson and J Craig (1966) at General Electric's TEMPO. It is a databased question answerer which is part of a man-machine communication system that according to the envisaged plans may eventually allow the operators to communicate with each other and with the computer in a subset of natural English. The program is written in a special list-processing language, KLS-II, developed at TEMPO. The programs do not break neatly into a parsing system, a semantic analyser, and a data processor, although these units are distinguishable. The system has a well-understood data structure and introduces a principle of equivalence between the word classes of syntactic analysis and the semantic categories of the database.

The TEMPO system is self-contained in that it both reads its own data and answers questions. DEACON makes explicit the principles of structure and question analysis which, although implicit in such systems as BASEBALL and SAD-SAM, were not yet fully conceptualized.

THE PICTURE LANGUAGE MACHINE (PLM) was devised by R Kirsch, D Cohen *et al* in 1964 for the National Bureau of Standards. The system has the power of translating from English or from graphic data into a subset of predicate calculus. The program accepts both pictures and text as input that is then translated into a common intermediate logical language.

PLM is composed of three sub-systems: a parser, a formalizer and a predicate evaluator. The parsing system is based on an immediate-constituent grammar. Parsing is done by a recognition routine which substitutes symbols for the dictionary words in the sentence or for an intermediate symbol string until the top of the parsing tree is reached. After the parsing of a sentence is completed and one or more tree structures representing the sentence are produced, the formalizer translates the parsed sentence into a formal language which is a first-order functional calculus with a small number of predicates. The formalizer is designed to work with each parsing which the grammar produces. For each rule of the grammar, there is a corresponding rule of formalization. For each parsing of a sentence the translation into a formal language results in a unique, unambiguous, well-formed formula. The predicate evaluator translates input from pictures to the formal language. It is designed to accept inputs that have been processed by SADIE, a scanning device which is used as an input to a computer.

SIR (Semantic Information Retrieval) was written in LISP by Bertram Raphael (1968) at MIT. It is a prototype of an 'understanding' machine. It accumulates facts, makes deductions about them and then answers questions. SIR accepts a subset of English and matches sentences against 24 matching patterns. The program has certain built-in knowledge and can interact with the user to gather more information.

The Raphael program is another example of a system which uses a limited set of logical predicates, such as subset, part-whole, left-right, to allow study of deducing answers into questions. The program ignores syntactic problems but tests the sentence for consistency before accepting it as data and makes explicit the interaction with the questioner. SIR recognizes when information is missing and demands it but is limited to those relational terms for which it has corresponding functional routines.

STUDENT is a pattern-matching natural-language program developed by D Bobrow for an MIT doctoral thesis in 1964. The program is written in LISP and is based on the MIT's Project MAC. It is an algebra problem-solver that accepts problems phrased in a subset of English and transforms these into equations which can be solved arithmetically. STUDENT is based on a theoretical relationship model whose objects are variables such as words, numbers, or phrases which name numbers. 'STUDENT's simple pattern-matching scheme, combined with a small set of well-chosen heuristics, does an impressive job of parsing typical high-school algebra word problems .... It solved the problems submitted as fast as humans could' (Barr and Feigenbaum, 1981).

ELIZA written by Joseph Weizenbaum at MIT in 1966 is an attempt to explore the possibility of programming computers to conduct natural-language conversation with humans. It is a 'pattern-matching' program. The program assumes the role of a Rogerian psychotherapist in dialogue with a patient. The programming language is SLIP developed by Weizenbaum in 1963. ELIZA is based on keyword searching. 'Each of the keywords is associated with a list of relevant transformation rules, and the context of the key determines the selection of one rule from the list in a particular case '(Boden, 1977). Weizenbaum provided ELIZA not only with a list of keywords but also with ranking of keywords relative to one another. Later versions of ELIZA have several subsets of sentence decomposition and reassembly rules; control is passed to one subset rather than another in the light of the particular context of discussion.

ELIZA has been studied in application to a number of computer-aided instruction problems (Taylor, 1968) and to a computer simulation of counselling behaviour (Ellis and Teideman, 1968) and in each case has shown promising capabilities. The system includes limited features for remembering previously mentioned topics, for tagging keywords in the dictionary, and for operating rules that refer to tags.

All these early natural-language programs were restricted to specific domains in simple English, and their input sentences were limited to simple declarative and interrogative forms and were scanned by the programs for pre-declared keywords or patterns that indicated known objects and relationships (Barr and Feigenbaum, 1981).

The text-based systems represent yet another approach to natural-language processing. They try to find answers to questions not from well-structured databases but from English text. They resemble IR systems in their use of indexing and term-matching techniques but they deal at the level of English questions instead of term sets and documents. In addition, there are also syntactic and semantic processing phases which evaluate the material discovered in the retrieval phase. These systems are not tied to any specific domain, since the textual database could cover any subject. Three examples of these text-based systems are described below: PROTOSYNTHEX-I, THE AUTOMATIC LANGUAGE ANALYZER and THE GENERAL INQUIRER.

PROTOSYNTHEX-I, developed by Simmons, Burger and Long in 1966 at SDC, attempts to answer questions from an encyclopaedia. The system accepts natural-language English questions and searches a large text to discover the most acceptable sentence, paragraph or article as an answer. Both the question and the retrieved text are parsed and compared. In the final state of the analysis the program checks the semantic correspondence of words in the answer with words in the question. There is an index to all words in the text and all words in the question. The human operator interacts frequently with the parser to avoid errors and ambiguities. The actual matching is accomplished by a fairly complex set of programs which build a matrix containing all the words from the question and from the possible answers. A semantic evaluation system is essentially a dictionary lookup whose entries can grow as a function of use.

The approach of PROTOSYNTHEX-I is to filter out successively more and more irrelevant information, leaving just statements which have a high probability of being answers to the question. The system is an attempt to deal with a large and syntactically complex sample of text. PROTOSYNTHEX-I is recognized as a symbiotic system in which a man works with a computer to help to resolve both syntactic and semantic ambiguities (Simmons, 1967).

THE AUTOMATIC LANGUAGE ANALYZER (ALA) was designed by Thorne in 1965 to handle the text found in a book on astronomy. It is a text-based system which translates the English language into a metalanguage FLEX.

THE GENERAL INQUIRER developed at Harvard University was

useful for analysing the content of text. As a question-answerer, the General Inquirer recovers all sentences containing a given set of concepts. The most interesting feature of the system is its dictionary and thesaurus operation. A special thesaurus is constructed for each text according to its subject. Each of the words in the main dictionary is defined by thesaurus tags or clusters. The dictionary includes 3,000 common English words plus terms of special interest to any particular subject. The semantic portion of the General Inquirer may be used separately for text analysis. The General Inquirer differs from most of the earlier systems in that any syntactic manipulations are done as a manual pre-editing phase for the text and the questions.

In the early 1970s, two systems were built, both aiming at a comprehensive treatment of syntactic as well as semantic aspects of language processing. These were LUNAR and SHRDLU.

The LUNAR system is an IR system created by W Woods (1972). The system has been developed to help geologists to evaluate data from chemical analyses of moon rock and soil composition brought from the Apollo-11 mission. It was one of the first programs which dealt with English grammar, using an augmented transition network parser (ATN can be considered as a versatile representation of grammars for natural languages). The procedure used in LUNAR is as follows: a question entered in English is translated into an expression in a formal query language. The translation is done using an ATN parser coupled with a rule-driven semantic interpretation which guides the analysis of the question. The 'query' that results from the analysis is then applied to the database to produce the answer to the request. The query language is a generalization of the predicate calculus (Barr and Feigenbaum, 1981).

The LUNAR language processor contains an ATN grammar for a large subset of English, semantic rules for interpretation of database requests, and a dictionary of approximately 3,500 words. It is able to deal with tense and modality, some anaphoric references and comparatives, restrictive relative clauses, certain adjective modifiers, and embedded complement constructions.

The formal query language contains three types of objects: designators which name classes of objects in the database, propositions which are formed from predicates with designators as arguments, and commands which initiate actions.

Terry Winograd's SHRDLU (1972) was based on a doctoral research project completed at MIT. The program carries on an interactive dialogue via teletype with a user. The dialogue refers to the activity of a simulated 'robot' arm in a 'tabletop world of toy objects.' SHRDLU is written in LISP and in MICRO-PLANNER. The knowledge representation in SHRDLU is not represented by syntax and meaning as rules in grammar, or as patterns to be matched against the input, but is dependent on the task domain chosen by Winograd. The question-answering techniques used by SHRDLU are limited by the task ('toy') domain of the system. The system consists of four parts: a parser, a recognition grammar in English, programs for semantic analysis, and a problem solver. The user can specify his own heuristics and strategies for a particular domain. The knowledge is embodied in the MICRO-PLANNER programs. The problem solver of SHRDLU consists of a group of 'theorems' about the robot's environment and actions.

SHRDLU combines a sophisticated syntax analysis with a fairly general deductive system. It provides a framework in which it is possible to study the interactions between different aspects of language. It emphasizes the relevance of non-linguistic knowledge to the understanding process (Winograd, 1980).

To write the parser for SHRDLU, Winograd first wrote a special programming language embedded in LISP, which he called PROGRAMMAR. PROGRAMMAR operates basically in a top-down, left-to-right fashion and uses neither parallel processing nor backtracking strategy in dealing with multiple alternatives.

In the technical dimension, SHRDLU incorporated a number of ideas: (1) use of reasoning formalism based on the 'procedural embedding of knowledge'; (2) an emphasis on how language triggers action; (3) a representation of lexical meaning (the meaning of individual words and idioms) based on procedures that operate in the building of represen-tation structures; and (4) an explicit representation of the cognitive context.

The model of language understanding included additional structures labelled 'model of the text' and 'model of the speaker/hearer'.

In addition to reasoning about the world (the world of toy blocks), the system reasons about the structure of the conversation, about the hypothesized internal structure and state of the other (user) participant.

LUNAR and SHRDLU thus integrated syntactic and semantic analyses with a world knowledge about a limited domain. Knowledge representation is structured as procedures within the system; the meanings of words, phrases and sentences are embodied in procedural structures. Barr and Feigenbaum (1981) describe these programs as 'a significant step forward in natural language processing research, because of their attempts to combine models of human linguistics and reasoning methods in a language understanding process.'

The MARGIE system developed by Roger Schank and others (1975) is based on the Conceptual Dependency representation of the meaning underlying natural language. The basic axioms of conceptual dependency theory are:

1. 'For any two sentences that are identical in meaning, regardless of language, there should be only one representation of that meaning in CD' (Schank and Abelson, 1977, p 11).

2. 'Conceptual Dependency representations are made up of a very small number of semantic primitives, which include primitive acts and primitive states' (Barr and Feigenbaum, 1981).

3. 'Any information in a sentence that is implicit must be made explicit in the representation of the meaning of that sentence' (Schank and Abelson, 1977, p 11).

The MARGIE system, programmed in LISP 1.6, consists of three parts: the first, written by Christopher Riesbeck, is a conceptual analyser, which takes English sentences and converts them into an internal conceptual dependency representation. The second part, written by Charles Rieger, is an inferencer designed to accept a proposition (stated in conceptual dependency form) and deduce a large number of facts from the proposition in the current context of the system's memory. The inference knowledge is represented in memory in a modified semantic net. The third part of the system is a text generation module written by Neil Goldman.

Conceptual Dependency is used in MARGIE as an interlingua, a language-independent representation scheme for encoding the meaning of sentences. The review article by Schank (1980) is a discussion of the development of his ideas about natural language.

SAM (Script Applier Mechanism) and PAM (Plan Applier Mechanism) were written by Roger Schank, Robert Abelson and their students at Yale University to demonstrate the use of scripts and plans in understanding simple stories.

A script is a stereotypic event sequence which describes common everyday behaviour in culturally stylized situations. The role of plans and goals was investigated in PAM (Schank and Abelson, 1977). Not all human behaviour can be understood in terms of stereotypic event sequences. Some situations require an interpretation of events in terms of underlying goals and general strategies to achieve these goals. A strategy relies on the nature of the specific task desired, the relationship with other persons, and a range of social conventions which act to constrain behaviour.

PAM understands stories in terms of general knowledge about typical human goals and general strategies for achieving these goals (Lehnert, 1980).

QUALM is a computational model of a question-answering system. It runs in conjunction with the two larger systems mentioned before, SAM and PAM, both being comprehensive story-understanding systems that input stories in English and generate internal memory representations for what they read. These story representations can then be accessed by processes designed to paraphrase, summarize and answer questions about stories read (Lehnert, 1978). QUALM is responsible for the question-answering capacities of SAM and PAM. Both systems are modularized so that parsers and generators can be attached for different input and output languages. Lehnert (1978) described SAM and PAM as having English input and producing paraphrase output in English, Spanish, Russian, Dutch and Chinese. QUALM itself is language-independent.

QUALM is a four-stage system consisting of: (1) question analysis; (2) inferential analysis; (3) content specification; and (4) retrieval heuristics.

1. Question analysis. QUALM begins its processing with an initial stage of question analysis. The question analyser is a discrimination net (a kind of binary decision tree) which categorizes a question into a uniquely defined question type. The question category assigned to a question will decide on all subsequent processing for that question. SAM required 13 question categories to answer questions about script-based stories. PAM required some expansion in the number of categories. The question analyser performs one other task in addition to assignment of a category to each question. In addition a question concept is extracted from the conceptual representation of the question. Thus, at the end of the first processing stage, the question has been transformed into two representational components: a question category and a question concept.

2. Inferential analysis. Inferences are made on the basis of knowledge about the world. If we expect a computer to make inferences, then it must have knowledge structures in its memory similar to those in human memory. Inferential analysis is responsible for finding the intended meaning of a question when the literal meaning does not provide the most appropriate interpretation. Inferential analysis is most useful in an interactive conversational context. In each sentence there is a script describing the overall context of the question. Once the scripts have been identified, the unknown conceptual components in each sentence can be associated with their appropriate script role. After identification of the proper script roles, the retrieval heuristics have to be instructed to look for answers within these role bindings.

3. Concept specification. Up to this point, the analysis of the question concentrated on classifying the question in a manner which will determine which retrieval heuristics should be invoked to produce the appropriate response. But, before the retrieval heuristics can be executed, one must determine how much information is needed in the answer. For any given question there may be many appropriate and even correct responses. One must specify the retrieval heuristics according to the system's 'intentionality'. QUALM had originally three 'intentionalities': talkative, cooperative, and minimally responsive.

Content specification in QUALM consists of a module which inputs the question concept and question category produced by the inferential analysis, checks the intentionality of the system, and produces a strategy of retrieval heuristics which then examines the memory for an answer. The strategies vary: they may be very simplistic and in this case a response to a question may just check for the presence of a concept in the question, or they may be very involved (a talkative response to a verification question may involve the generation of a new question) — (Lehnert, 1977).

In 1980, Lehnert wrote that she would like to introduce new elements into QUALM, e.g. a strong theory of personality interactions which would determine whether the system would provide an honest answer or a deceptive one, be hostile and give uncooperative response, or be benignly misleading. She also thinks that it would be worth while to consider assumptions about the questioner's knowledge state in content specification, since one would like to produce answers which could provide the user with new information.

4. Retrieval heuristics. The last process within QUALM is responsible for extracting a conceptual answer from the memory. Each question

category dictates a search strategy for memory retrieval. A search strategy is then refined by content specification according to the system's intentionality. The initial retrieval strategy for nearly all question types involves the specification of an 'answer key' in the story representation. An answer key is a concept which matches the question concept according to standard pattern-matching conventions (Cullingford, 1978). Once the answer key has been located, retrieval proceeds according to the question category. The outline of retrieval heuristics in QUALM's initial implementation is given in Lehnert (1978).

The natural-language systems described till now fall into two categories: those built to study natural-language processing issues and those built with a particular task domain. In 1977, Gary Hendrix designed the first off-the-shelf program for implementing a 'natural language front-end' that could be used in any subject domain. The system, called LIFER, can be used by system designers to interpret the English input and to produce a sequence of commands, e.g. a formal query for an IR system (Barr and Feigenbaum, 1981).

The LIFER system consists of two parts: (1) a set of interactive functions for specifying a language (any subset of English appropriate for interacting with the application system) and (2) a parser. The system designer who is going to use the interface must specify the language in terms of grammatical 'rewrite rules'. LIFER translates them into transition trees (a form of augmented transition network) which, in turn, are used by the parser during interpretation of the input into the application language. The technique is used to embed the semantic information into the syntax. This technique, which is usually referred to as semantic grammar, increases the performance of LIFER. LIFER has been used by many systems proving that it is possible to construct natural-language systems for a wide variety of domains without a large programming effort.

8.3   Expert systems

In the complex and specialized world of today, human expertise about diverse subjects, scientific, economic, social and political, plays an important role. We rely heavily on the human expert's ability to identify and synthesize factors to form judgments and decisions. We use years of our experience to gain expertise in some specific narrow area of science, engineering or medicine and then apply this specialization in problem-solving.

Expert systems are knowledge-based systems which attempt to solve

160

problems in the way human experts do. They are called knowledge-based because their performance depends on the use of facts and heuristics provided by experts. One of the most important characteristics of expert systems is the way they search for solutions. Expert systems are based on research relating to such fundamental questions as the nature of knowledge both in terms of formal representational systems and as social phenomena (public knowledge). They are also characterized by interactive dialogues between men and machines, dialogues that are an integral part of the system. Typically the user interacts with an expert system in a form of a consultation dialogue, in the same way as he would interact with the human expert: thoroughly explaining his problem, defining the uncertainty as to how to deal with the problem and discussing possible solutions. Expert systems can be viewed as intermediaries between human users and human experts; the human expert giving his expertise, and hence being in a knowledge-acquisition mode with the system, and the human user taking advice from the system, and hence interacting with the system in a consultation mode. Expert systems exist now in many areas of knowledge: e.g. medicine (diagnostics), geological and chemical data analyses and detection of faults in computer operation.

Relying on the knowledge of human experts to build expert systems is helpful for several reasons:

1. the decisions and recommendations of a program can be explained to its users and evaluators in terms which are familiar to the experts;

2. because we hope to duplicate the expertise of human specialists, we can measure the extent to which our goal is achieved by a direct comparison of the program's behaviour with that of an expert;

3. within the collaborative group of computer scientists and experts engaged in AI research, basing the logic of the programs on human models supports each of the three somewhat disparate goals that the researchers may hold (Szolovits, 1982 — on expert systems in medicine):

a) to develop expert computer programs for clinical use, making possible the inexpensive dissemination of the best medical expertise to geographical areas where that expertise is lacking, and making consultation help available to non-specialists who are not within easy reach of expert human consultants;

b) to formalize medical expertise, to enable physicians to understand better what they know and to give them a systematic structure for teaching their expertise to medical students;

c) to test AI theories in a 'real world' domain and to use that domain to suggest novel problems for further AI research.

Encoding human expertise in the computer is very difficult. The difficulty lies in our lack of understanding of how people know what they know and in technical problems of structuring and accessing large amounts of knowledge in the machine. This is one of the reasons for a more pessimistic evaluation of AI applications held by some researchers and often shared with practitioners, that expert consultant programs cannot meet the challenge of general competence and reliability until much more fundamental progress is made by AI in understanding the process of reasoning and common sense.

In 1979, Barr, Bennett, and Clancey stated:

A key idea in our current approach to building expert systems is that these programs should not only be able to apply the corpus of expert knowledge to specific problems, but they should also be able to interact with the users and experts just as humans do when they learn, explain, and teach what they know .... These social interactions — learning from experts, explaining one's reasoning, and teaching what one knows — are essential dimensions of human knowledge. They are as functional to the nature of intelligence as expert-level problem-solving, and they have changed our ideas about representation and about knowledge.

With the DENDRAL system in the mid-1960s, the problem-solving systems have developed beyond the constrained domains of chess and puzzles. They started to be used in symbolically expressed problems that were known to be difficult for the best human researchers (Lindsay, Buchanan, Feigenbaum and Lederberg, 1980).

In production rules of the form IF <condition> THEN <action> Shortliffe (1976) encoded information about reasoning processes of physicians. The IF part of the rules contains clauses that attempt to differentiate a certain situation, and the THEN part describes what to do if one finds oneself in that situation. This production-rule knowledge representation in MYCIN was able to perform its task in a specific area of infectious-disease diagnosis as well, or nearly as well, as human experts.

AI concentrates on building expert systems, each of which exhibits knowledge in only a very small subject area. Each expert system can only solve an associated set of problems in a particular subject domain. The use of knowledge in computer information systems involves three stages: (i) acquisition of knowledge; (ii) retrieval of facts from a stored database; and (iii) interacting with these facts and programs in search of a solution to a problem.

Knowledge acquisition involves not only adding something to the existing store of information, it means relating and assimilating the new fact to the knowledge already available. AI systems are usually built in the same way. What kind of knowledge needs to be represented in AI systems? Barr and Feigenbaum (1981) distinguish between the following types of knowledge:

(i) *Objects* (facts about objects in the world around us). The AI system must have a way to represent these.

(ii) *Events* (actions and events in the world). These events have to be encoded, but also a representation formalism may need to indicate their cause-and-effect relations as well as the time sequence of events.

(iii) *Performance* (knowledge of how to do things, the performance of skills). Most cognitive behaviours, like writing a letter, or riding a bike, involve performance knowledge.

(iv) *Meta-knowledge* (the extent and origin of our knowledge of a particular subject or reliability of certain information). Metaknowledge also includes how we evaluate our own performance, our weaknesses and strengths and feeling of progress during problem solving.

Retrieval means the recovery of relevant information from the memory. Two basic ideas related to retrieval as used in AI systems are known as *linking* and *lumping*. If one data structure is in some way related to another 'in an expected reasoning task', a link is made between the two data structures. This operation is called linking and is used to make this relation retrievable. If several data structures are going to be used together, they are lumped, or grouped together into one larger structure.

When the system is told to do something that it was not programmed to do, it must reason and plan how to do it on the basis of information it has. The system must be able to deduce and verify new facts beyond those it has been explicitly told.

There are various knowledge representation schemes and till now there is no theory of when to apply a particular scheme. It is not possible to prove why one scheme captures some aspects of human memory better than another. One thing is certain, namely that the suitability of a scheme depends on the particular application. The problems of knowledge representation research are reviewed by Boden (1977) and by Brachmann and Smith (1980).

One of the earliest representation formalisms used in AI programs was the state-space representation, developed for problem-solving. The basic idea of state-space representation is as follows: assuming one has reached a certain state in a problem, next states (alternatives) can be found with a small set of rules, called transition operators. The solution adopted in AI is to limit the number of alternatives searched at each stage of problem-solving to just the best possibilities.

Logic-based representations have been very popular in AI research, one reason being that, using this method of knowledge representation, one can move from old facts to new ones, by employing mechanistic theorem-proving techniques, especially in cases of relatively small databases. The results of deduction in logic systems are nearly always correct, and the database can be kept logically consistent, a state not yet reached in other representation schemes.

In a procedural representation of knowledge, knowledge about the world is contained in procedures, small programs that know how to do specific things. For example, in a parser for a natural-language understanding system, the knowledge that a noun phrase may contain articles, adjectives, and nouns is represented in the program by calls to routines that know how to process articles, nouns and adjectives.

Semantic nets (Quillian, 1968) were developed as explicitly psychological models of human associative memory. A net consists of nodes and links between the nodes, leading to interrelations. (A semantic network has been implemented in 'Teachable Language Comprehender' described by Bell and Quillian, 1971). However, there is some unreliability in employing semantic nets, because interpretation of net structures depends on the program under control of which the nets operate. Therefore, inferences drawn by manipulation of the net are not assuredly valid, in the sense that they are assured to be valid in a logic-based representation (Barr and Feigenbaum, 1981).

A modular knowledge representation scheme — Production System — developed by Newell and Simon in 1972 for their models of human cognition, is very popular in large AI systems. The database consists of rules, called production rules, in the form of condition-action pairs: 'If such a condition occurs, then do this...'. Production systems have been implemented in MYCIN, DENDRAL and PROSPECTOR.

Frames are data structures that 'include declarative and procedural information in predefined internal relations. For example, a generic frame for a dog might have knowledge slots for facts that are typically known about dogs, like the breed, owner, name, and an "attached procedure" for finding out who the owner is.' (Minsky, 1968.)

Many expert systems employ large and proficient decision-making models that relate observations to conclusions with little concern for the underlying subject domain that supports these relations (Hart, 1980). Such systems are unable to recognize and deal with problems for which their own knowledge is insufficient. They have no independent means of checking the plausibility of their conclusions and normally their explanatory capabilities cannot identify the fundamental principles behind their reasoning process. Apte (1982) states that it would be very useful to develop hierarchical knowledge bases that allow a representation of the fundamental knowledge of the domain in addition to the compiled knowledge that is dominantly used in most current expert systems. The compiled knowledge (typically represented in some form of production rules) could then be used to obtain answers for straightforward problems. The underlying fundamental knowledge would be involved in checking conclusions, providing guidelines for explications or analysing problems that cannot be handled by the compiled knowledge alone.

For example, in engineering problems there are systems at various levels of complexities. Hart (1980) introduces the notion of surface and deep systems in this context. Surface systems associate input states with actions; deep systems represent fundamental concepts such as causality, intent or basic physical principles. Surface and deep systems have different properties. As the task difficulty increases, the complexity of the surface system grows up to a barrier beyond which it is simply inadequate. In contrast deep systems have a higher start-up cost for tasks of modest difficulty but are capable of doing tasks of greater difficulty. Surface systems tend to use compiled/qualitative knowledge in their problem-solving, while deep systems tend to use analytical/quantitative knowledge (Apte, 1982). MYCIN is an example of a surface system; DENDRAL and CASNET represent models of deep systems.

8.3.1 Expert systems in medicine

There are three steps in medical decision taking: data gathering, diagnosis and prescription of treatment. Data consist of patient's history, laboratory and clinical data. To make a diagnosis, it is desirable for the physician to determine the aetiology (original cause of disease) and pathogenesis (the way the disease developed from its causes).

Knowledge representation in medical diagnostic systems

Two types of medical knowledge must be available in these programs: (i) general knowledge of diseases and (ii) specific knowledge about the patient. The usual representation formalisms of AI, such as semantic maps, frames, production rules, are not directly applicable in medicine because of the inexact nature of medical knowledge. In all medical consultation systems, these representations have been supplemented by incorporating some way of expressing strength of belief or strength of association.

The following descriptions of specific medical systems are based closely on the exposition of Barr and Feigenbaum (1981).

MYCIN

The MYCIN system (Shortliffe, 1976) is a rule-based diagnostic system, designed to assist physicians with the selection of antibiotics for patients with serious infections. MYCIN's strategy in rule selection is goal-oriented. The program reasons backwards from its recognized goal of determining therapy for a patient. It therefore starts by considering rules for therapy selection, but the premise portion of each of these rules in turn sets new questions or subgoals. These new goals then cause new rules to be invoked and a reasoning network is thereby established. MYCIN is programmed in LISP.

The knowledge representation used is a set of production rules augmented by certainty factors.

Clinical reasoning: production-rule-based inference mechanisms are used to determine parameters e.g. of the patient's infections and the causative organisms. The parameter is considered true if the combined value of the associated certainty factors exceeds a predefined threshold. Each rule is a 'chunk' of domain-specific information. The premise of each rule is a Boolean combination of one or more clauses, each of which is constructed from a predicate function with an associative triple (attribute, object, value), as its argument.

Explanations are provided by printing out an English version of the chain of rules used.

Certainty factors: the rules make inexact inferences on a confidence scale of −1.0 to 1.0, where −1.0 represents full confidence that a proposition is false and 1.0 represents complete confidence that it is true.

Reasoning: rules are invoked in a simple backward-chaining fashion that results in an exhaustive depth-first search of an AND/OR goal tree (because rules may have OR conditions in their premise).

Therapy selection: after MYCIN determines the significant infections and the organisms that cause them, it proceeds to recommend an antimicrobial regimen. The MYCIN therapy selector uses a description of the patient's infections, the causal organisms, a ranking of drugs by sensitivity, and a set of drug-preference categories to recommend a drug regimen. The algorithm will also modify dosages in the case of renal failure in the patient. The program can provide detailed explanations of how it made a regimen choice and can accept and criticize a regimen proposed by the physician (Barr and Feigenbaum, 1981).

The expert physician can communicate with MYCIN. MYCIN allows the expert to inspect faulty reasoning and then add and modify the rules or clinical parameters required to augment and repair the medical knowledge of MYCIN. This interactive facility permits the system to communicate directly with domain experts without intervention of a programmer.

MYCIN compares favourably with experts on infectious disease in the diagnosis of the disease and prescribing treatment to the patient.

CASNET

CASNET, the Causal ASsociational NETwork program (Weiss, Kulikowski, and Safir, 1977) is a consultation system developed at Rutgers University. The application of CASNET has been the domain of glaucoma. The disease in CASNET is not in a static state. It is a dynamic process that can be modelled as a network of causally linked pathophysiological states. The system diagnoses a patient by determining the pattern of pathophysiological causal pathways present in the patient and identifying this pattern with a disease category. The treatment is then prescribed and a prediction of the likely course of a disease is made in the two cases, if the disease is treated and if untreated (Barr and Feigenbaum, 1981).

Knowledge representation: causal network representation (a semantic network with one relation, CAUSES) in which each CAUSES link is qualified by a number representing the strength of causality. There are three planes of knowledge: the plane of pathophysiological states which represent the elementary hypotheses about the disease process; the plane of observations containing nodes representing evidence gathered from the patient; the third plane containing the classification tables for the disease. A classification table defines a disease as a set of confirmed and denied pathophysiological states and a set of treatment statements for that disease.

Clinical reasoning: a status measure is associated with each state in the causal network. Weights are propagated in both forward and backward directions depending on disease causality. A state is considered confirmed if its status exceeds a specified threshold.

Explanation: the detail of the explanation can be controlled by the program. CASNET is able to summarize the consultation by displaying the scores of the hypotheses and the status measures of states in the causal network.

Justification: CASNET can cite references to literature to support diagnoses and treatment recommendations.

Validation: CASNET has undergone extensive clinical trials and has been rated in experimental evaluation as performing at human-expert level.

CASNET adopts a strictly bottom-up approach to the problem of diagnosis, working from the tests, through causal pathways, to a diagnosis. The program is continually being tested and updated by a computer-based network of collaborators.

Researchers have attempted to use variations and/or extensions of the causal representation in other problem domains. QUAL (De Kleer, 1979) attempts to represent the causal and teleological relations associated with electrical networks. ABEL (Patil, Szolovits and Schwartz, 1981) uses multi-level causal representation to provide expert consultation for electrolyte and acid-base disturbances in patient illness.

168

INTERNIST

INTERNIST is a consultation program in the domain of internal medicine. It has been developed at the University of Pittsburg by H Pople, a computer scientist, and J Myers, a specialist in internal medicine. The program only formulates diagnoses without recommending treatments. Diagnosis in internal medicine is complicated because the patient may suffer from more than one disease.

Knowledge representation: a taxonomy of diseases is stored as a huge tree hierarchy of diseases with each node representing a disease. Associated with each disease node is a list of manifestations, with numerical weights reflecting the strength of association between the disease and the manifestation. Diseases and their manifestations are related in two major ways: (i) a manifestation can evoke a disease, and (ii) a disease can manifest certain signs and symptoms. These relations can be thought of as probabilities. The strength of these relations is given by a number on a scale of 0 to 5, where 0 means that no conclusion can be drawn about the disease and manifestation, and 5 means that the manifestation is always associated with the disease. The data about diseases and their associated manifestations are constructed and maintained separately from the diagnosis program.

Clinical reasoning: at the beginning of a consultation, a list of manifestations is entered. As each manifestation is entered, it evokes onr or more nodes of the disease tree. A model is created for each evoked disease node. Disease hypotheses are scored by a procedure that takes account of the strength of association among (i) the manifestations exhibited by the patient and the disease, (ii) the manifestations associated with the disease which are not present in the patient, and (iii) the confirmed diseases causally related to this disease. Disease hypotheses are ranked, and the top-ranked diseases are further investigated. When the difference between the scores of the top two disease hypotheses reaches a threshold, the top-ranking disease is confirmed.

Explanation: the INTERNIST system is able to summarize the consultation by displaying the scores of the hypotheses and the status measures of states in the causal network.

INTERNIST's hypothesis generation strategy attempts to limit the number of hypotheses by two methods: first, it activates a disease node only when it contains a finding of evoking strength greater than zero (the evoking strength is a weight associated with each disease; it is a subjective estimate, on a scale from 0 to 5; a 0 indicates that the finding is too non-specific to lend support to that disease; 5 indicates that the finding is pathognomonic for that disease); second, INTERNIST activates a superior node in the disease hierarchy if findings which would differentiate between the inferior nodes are not known. This allows the INTERNIST to generate one general disease hypothesis until more specific information is known.

The INTERNIST—I and INTERNIST—II (a revised program) combine a bottom-up and top-down approach to medical diagnosis. INTERNIST has a large knowledge base, containing 500 of the diseases of internal medicine (75%). It has displayed expert diagnosis capabilities even in complex cases.

PRESENT ILLNESS PROGRAM (PIP)

PIP has been developed at MIT (Pauker *et al*, 1976). It is a typical consultation of a patient with his general practitioner. It simulates the reasoning of physicians. The system takes present illnesses of patients with renal disease and the diagnosis is based on patient's history, physical examination and routine laboratory tests. The present version of PIP is written in MACLISP. It is a frame-based diagnostic program. It uses a pseudo-Bayesian hypothesis-driven approach to diagnosis.

Knowledge representation: network of frames centred around diseases, clinical states, and physiological states and containing data on typical findings, relationships to other patient situations and rules for judging how well a set of findings exhibited by a patient matches the situation given in a frame. The slots used by PIP in the disease frames include: type, scoring-function, must-not-have, in-sufficient, triggers, findings, differential diagnosis and some causal and associational link slots (e.g. major-cause-of). Matching is the key strategy in the diagnosis.

Clinical reasoning: the clinical reasoning of PIP is based on the manipulation of hypotheses and findings. There are three kinds of hypotheses: confirmed, active and semiactive. Hypotheses with ratings higher than a preset threshold are considered as confirmed hypotheses. Active hypotheses are those with at least one trigger finding. Semiactive hypotheses are the immediate neighbours of the active hypotheses in the frame system. They are not strong enough to be investigated but are 'at the back of the consulting physician's mind.' PIP combines two methods of reasoning: categorical and probabilistic, categorical decisions being based on logical criteria rather than on numerical values. The probabilistic reasoning involves scoring the disease. The applicability of a disease frame to a particular patient can be confirmed on either logical or probabilistic criteria.

The two systems described above, the INTERNIST and PIP, are often described as hypothesis-driven systems. Although there is no precise accepted definition of hypothesis-driven systems, they are understood as those which, given a set of findings, select a small set of hypothesized diagnoses which are used to guide a search for the correct diagnosis by controlling the search for further evidence. This is often a useful approach when searching a large state space with many possible transitions between states. The associations between findings and diseases are then used to identify the likelihood of a disease being present. The systems use these likelihoods to select a strategy from which to proceed. This strategy is used to select an unknown finding to ask the user. The process continues in an iterative way until the system has found a satisfactory match between findings and diseases. A matching algorithm is used to determine the likelihood.

IRIS

The aim of IRIS was to design a tool for building and experimenting with an expert diagnostic system. IRIS was developed at Rutgers University and written in INTERLISP (Trigoboff and Kulikowski, 1977). It was intended that the system should permit easy experimentation with alternative representations of medical knowledge, clinical strategies, and modes of interaction and be used by computer specialists in cooperation with domain experts.

Knowledge representation: combination of two knowledge representation formalisms — semantic nets and production rules. The semantic net consists of nodes representing patient information and uses a large and extendable set of link types to build associations with the medical database. A set of production rules associated with each link of the network controls the transmission of information between the nodes and the semantic network. The nodes in the general medical knowledge net represent clinical concepts. The links represent relations between the nodes, e.g. causes, treatment. The patient-specific knowledge collected during a consultation is represented as a set of knowledge structures called Information SPECifications (ISPECs). ISPECs are associated with the nodes of semantic net and are essentially frames.

Clinical reasoning: at the beginning of a consultation, IRIS runs through a set of questions and the user answers them. Symptom nodes are linked to the disease nodes, and disease nodes to treatment nodes. IRIS uses a forward-chaining reasoning process. The production rules are encoded as decision tables. A consultation system for glaucoma has been developed with IRIS.

IRIS was designed to represent medical knowledge from any domain and to implement a variety of clinical strategies. This is possible because the representation of medical knowledge in IRIS is very general.

DIGITALIS THERAPY ADVISOR

Gorry, Silverman and Pauker (1978) describe a system that advises physicians on the administration of the drug digitalis. Digitalis is used to slow and stabilize the cardiac rhythm of patients who are experiencing arrhythmias and to strengthen the heartbeat of patients who are in heart failure.

Digitalis Therapy Advisor is not concerned with diagnosing the need for the drug in a patient. The program decides on the treatment regimen and its subsequent management for patients known to require digitalis. The amount of digitalis varies from patient to patient, depending on the state of the disease of the patient and the patient's history of digitalis administration. The normal strategy in administration of digitalis is to give the patient relatively large doses over a period of one to four days and then to give smaller daily doses to replace the digitalis which is excreted. Digitalis is widely administered by physicians with little training in cardiology. For many years, research has been carried out on the best method to estimate the dose of digitalis. Various aids, such as mathematical models, have been tested but unfortunately, such models give only the amount of digitalis in the body and not the amount of the drug needed by the patient.

The MIT group has been developing a program directed at the continuing management of the drug intake by each patient. The Digitalis Therapy Advisor interacts with the physician to select models appropriate to the patient. The program asks about the state of the disease and proposes a dosage and asks the physician to interact with the program again after some time to find out about the patient's progress. The follow-up sessions continue till the appropriate dosage for the particular patient is adjusted. The goal of the feedback process is to maintain the highest level of therapeutic effect with the minimum dosage of digitalis.

The programs have been evaluated several times and the results were judged by a panel of five experts. The panel stated that the results achieved by the system were the same or better than those obtained by human experts.

EXPERT

The EXPERT system is a general-purpose facility for helping investigators design and test consultation models. It is a domain-independent system, developed at Rutgers University in 1979. Models based on the EXPERT system have been developed in medicine, chemistry, oil-well log analysis and in car repair. EXPERT, like EMYCIN and PROSPECTOR (discussed later), is best suited for classification problems which have a predetermined list of possible conclusions from which the program may choose. It is written in FORTRAN and there are versions of EXPERT available on DEC and IBM computers.

Knowledge representation: there are three sections in the consultation model: hypotheses, findings and decision rules. Findings are facts about the patient collected during a consultation — the patient's illness history, symptoms, and results of laboratory tests. These are reported in the form of true, false and unavailable and are represented as attributes that can be present, absent, or undetermined in the patient, or as numerical variables. Hypotheses are the conclusions that may be inferred by the system: diagnostic and prognostic decision categories and therapy recommendations. The major hypotheses are structured into a taxonomic classification scheme.

Reasoning: when an assertion about a finding is made to the system, the rules in which this result appears are evaluated to produce weights that rank the hypotheses.

The two systems developed at Rutgers University, CASNET and EXPERT, attempt to provide a general framework for describing the knowledge of expert consultants. The experience with CASNET showed that although it was possible to arrive at a correct set of diagnostic and prognostic conclusions on the basis of strictly causal reasoning, there was a need for a more flexible and general scheme of reasoning. The EXPERT system attempts to introduce such facilities of representation and reasoning. The EXPERT system uses a simple strategy of prompting the user to acquire patient information in a sequence which can be either constrained by the model-builder or else is guided by the system's criterion of pursuing the 'best' leads at least cost.

173

EMYCIN

EMYCIN (Van Melle *et al*, 1981) is used to construct and run a consultation program that offers advice on problems within its domain of expertise. The consultation program elicits information about a particular problem by asking questions of a user. It then applies its knowledge to the specific facts of the case and informs the user of its conclusions. The user can ask the program questions about its reasoning in order to understand better the advice given.

There are two 'users' in EMYCIN: the system designer or expert interacts with EMYCIN to produce a knowledge base for the domain. The knowledge base is made up of two basic components: factual knowledge about the case under consideration and rule-based knowledge about how to carry out the consultation. EMYCIN interprets this knowledge base to provide advice to the client or consultation user. Thus the combination of EMYCIN and a specific knowledge base of domain expertise is a new consultation program.

Knowledge organization: facts. The factual knowledge about a case is stored in the same way as in a traditional database, as context-parameter-value triples. A context is a conceptual entity in the domain of the consultant: a patient, an aircraft etc. A set of parameters is associated with each context, such as age, sex, location. Each parameter of each context can take on values.

The expert uses the EMYCIN knowledge acquisition aids to define these record structures (context, parameters, and values). An important difference between traditional record structures and EMYCIN's factual knowledge structure is that parameters can take on multiple values. A certainty factor (CF) is attached to each fact triple, a number between -1 and 1 indicating the strength of belief in, or importance of, that fact. A CF of 1 represents total certainty, while a CF of -1 represents certainty in the negation of the fact.

Knowledge organization: rules. The system reasons about a domain using knowledge encoded as production rules: IF premise THEN action (CF). Each rule has a premise which is a conjunction of predicates over the fact triples in the knowledge base. Rules also have a CF, reflecting the degree to which the premise facts imply the action facts. If the premise is true, the conclusions in the action part of the rule are drawn, updating one or more fact triples in the knowledge base.

At any given time during a consultation, EMYCIN is working toward the goal of establishing the value of some parameter of a context.

EMYCIN evaluates the premise; if true, it makes the conclusion indicated in the action.

The advantage of having rules as primary representation of knowledge, in which each rule is a single 'chunk' of information, lies in its modular character. Individual rules can be updated, added, deleted or modified without drastically affecting the overall performance of the system.

Explanation capabilities: EMYCIN's explanation program allows the user to interrogate the system's knowledge, either to find out about the inferences made during a particular consultation or to examine the static knowledge base in general, independent of any specific consultation.

Another form of explanation is available through the Question Answering (QA) Module, which is automatically invoked after the consultation has ended. The QA Module accepts simple English-language questions dealing with any conclusion drawn during the consultation and about the domain in general. Explanations are based on rules. The questions are parsed by pattern matching and keyword lookup, using a dictionary that defines the vocabulary of the domain.

Knowledge acquisition: the system designer's principal task is entering and debugging the production rules and the fact triples in the knowledge base. EMYCIN provides a terse stylized, but easily understood, language for writing rules and several high-level knowledge base editors for each of the additional knowledge structures in the system. As EMYCIN exhibits some human engineering features, the system builder is relieved of tedious concerns of acquiring and debugging a knowledge base.

The most important part of the knowledge base is the context tree. It is the backbone of the consultant, organizing both the conceptual structure of the knowledge base and the basic flow of the consultation interaction. The largest component of the knowledge base for an EMYCIN consultant is the rule base, a collection of production rules that instruct the computer about how to make inferences and arrive at conclusions for the values of parameters in the context tree. The rules capture the expert's problem-solving methods and judgmental rules of inference. They determine the ordering of the goals and subgoals to be explored during consultation.

Several consultation systems have been written using EMYCIN. The PUFF program (Kunz *et al*, 1978) performs interpretation of measurements from a pulmonary function laboratory. In this system, over 100 cases were used to create some 60 rules diagnosing the presence of pulmonary disease. The PUFF program was expanded and converted into a BASIC program to run on a PDP-11 at Pacific Center at San Francisco.

The HEADMED program (Heiser *et al*, 1978) is an application of EMYCIN to clinical psychopharmacology. The system diagnoses a range of psychiatric disorders and recommends drug treatment.

CLOT (J S Bennett and Goldman, 1980) is an experimental system dealing with the diagnosis of disorders of the blood coagulation system. GRAVIDA assists the physician during a patient's pregnancy, LITHO is a consultant that interprets geology surrounding an oil well, and DART is a system that gives advice on computer telecommunication system failures (J S Bennett, 1980).

The limitations of EMYCIN derive largely from the fact that EMYCIN has chosen one basic, readily understood representation for the knowledge in a domain: production rules applied by a backward-chaining control structure, with facts about the case represented as associative triples. While the rule representation is quite general, this choice of control structure is unsuitable for problems of constraint satisfaction, or those requiring iterative techniques.

8.3.2 Applications in chemistry

The AI techniques have been applied to two areas of non-numeric chemical reasoning problems: determining the molecular structure of an unknown organic compound, i.e. the analysis or structure-determination problem; and planning a sequence of reactions in order to synthesize organic chemical structure, i.e. the synthesis problem (Barr and Feigenbaum, 1981).

DENDRAL

In 1964, Joshua Lederberg developed the DENDRAL algorithm that allowed an exhaustive approach to structure elucidation. Structure elucidation programs are designed to help organic chemists to determine the molecular structure of unknown compounds. The DENDRAL project started in Stanford University in 1965. The aim of the project was to prove that algorithmic programs can be augmented by some of the heuristic knowledge of experts to produce the same results with just a fraction of the effort.

The HEURISTIC DENDRAL program augmented the structure enumeration algorithm with data from mass spectrographic analysis of the unknown molecule and a set of rules used by expert chemists to infer constraints on molecular structure from the data obtained. Mass spectrometry is a particularly useful technique when the quantity of the sample to be identified is very small. It was difficult to receive rules about mass spectrometry from expert chemists and therefore, in 1970, the META-DENDRAL system was initiated.

The META-DENDRAL, which is described later, inferred automatically the rules of mass spectrometry from examples of molecular structures that had been analysed by humans. The HEURISTIC DENDRAL was based on the DENDRAL algorithm and could generate only acyclic structures: ketones, alcohols, ethers, thiols, thioethers and amines. In 1976, the CONGEN program replaced Lederberg's original acyclic structure generator with the generator which did not have the acyclic limitations. The HEURISTIC DENDRAL has two sets of rules that encode the mass spectrometry knowledge: (i) rules applied during planning that interpret mass-spectral data and infer molecular fragments and (ii) rules applied during testing that simulate the action of the mass spectrometer on the structure or structures imposed by CONGEN and that predict peaks that should be observed in the spectrum of the molecule.

The DENDRAL PLANNER uses a large amount of knowledge of mass spectrometry to infer constraints. It allows for cooperative man-machine problem-solving in the interpretation of mass spectra. It uses the chemist's relevant knowledge of mass spectrometry and applies it systematically to the spectrum of an unknown. The HEURISTIC DENDRAL program is given the mass spectrum and the atomic constituents of a molecule. From these data, it can infer the molecular weight of the molecule.

An important part of the DENDRAL system involves the generation of candidate structures, given the chemical formula of the compound. The system for generating candidate structures can be viewed as a production system. The global database is a 'partially structured' compound. The production system operates on this database to increase its degree of structure. The structure generator essentially 'grows' molecules, starting with a small fragment of the molecule and adding pieces of the composition to it.

In DENDRAL, there are two programs which employ a large body of knowledge about the process of molecular fragmentation in a mass spectrometer to make predictions from each plausible candidate molecule. Predicted data are compared to the unknown compound, and some candidates are thrown out as not fulfilling the matching conditions, while others are ranked.

CONGEN (CONstrained GENerator) was designed to replace the old DENDRAL generator. The purpose of CONGEN was: (i) to allow the user to specify interactively certain types of structural information determined from any of several sources, and (ii) to generate an exhaustive and non-redundant list of structures consistent with this information. Unlike the HEURISTIC DENDRAL, CONGEN does not infer constraints from mass spectra but allows the chemist to specify them. There are two algorithms in CONGEN, designed to determine all topologically unique ways of assembling a given set of atoms, each with an associated valence, into molecular structures.

CONGEN has an interactive 'front-end'. The system is on the SUMEX computing facility at Stanford University and is available nationwide in the United States over the TYMNET network.

DENDRAL was one of the first programs to demonstrate the power of encoding domain-specific, heuristic expertise and was one of the first projects to recognize knowledge acquisition as a major problem in AI.

The HEURISTIC DENDRAL and CONGEN have shown that it is possible for a computer program to be as good as some experts in a very specialized area of science.

META-DENDRAL

Because of the difficulty of extracting domain-specific rules from experts for use by DENDRAL, a more efficient means of transferring knowledge into programs was sought. Two methods have been explored: interactive knowledge transfer programs and automatic theory formation programs. The latter method has been employed in META-DENDRAL. The DENDRAL programs are structured to read their task-specific knowledge from tables of production rules and execute the rules in new situations under elaborate control structures. The META-DENDRAL programs have been constructed to aid in building the knowledge base, i.e. the tables of rules.

META-DENDRAL utilizes a semantic model of the domain. This program provides guidance for a rule formation program in a space of rules that is too large to search exhaustively. It also provides a check for the meaningfulness of associations produced by the program in a domain in which the trivial associations outnumber the important ones.

The program is based on a generator of production rules that uses predetermined syntax operating under the constraints of a semantic world model.

One measure of the proficiency of META-DENDRAL is the ability of a DENDRAL program to predict correct spectra of new molecules. The META-DENDRAL program has successfully rediscovered known, published rules of mass spectrometry for two classes of molecules. It has also discovered new rules for three closely related families of structures for which rules had not previously been reported.

CONGEN has attracted chemists who consult it for help with structure elucidation problems. The DENDRAL and META-DENDRAL programs are not used outside Stanford University and represent rather a demonstration of scientific capability. The achievement is considered significant in that the task domain was not tailored to fit existing AI techniques (Buchanan and Feigenbaum, 1978).

CRYSALIS

The CRYSALIS system has been developed to apply the AI methodology to the task domain of protein crystallography. In the course of deriving a protein structure, a crystallographer generates an electron density map, a three-dimensional description of the electron density distribution of a molecule. The crystallographer interprets the map using auxiliary data and general principles of protein chemistry in order to obtain a description of molecular structure. The goal of the CRYSALIS system is to interpret the electron density map. To achieve this goal, there is required: (i) a representation of an electron density function suitable for machine interpretation; (ii) a substantial chemical and stereochemical knowledge base; (iii) a wide assortment of model-building algorithms and heuristics; (iv) a collection of rules and associated procedures for using this knowledge to make inferences from the experimental data; and (v) a problem-solving strategy for applying these knowledge sources effectively, so that the appropriate procedures are executed at the times that they are most productive.

A problem-solving paradigm which is used in CRYSALIS is the 'blackboard' architecture of HEARSAY-II, in which an 'iterative guess-building' process takes place; a number of different knowledge sources, such as facts, algorithms, and heuristics, cooperate when

179

working on various descriptions of the hypothesis. To use the knowledge sources effectively, a global database, the 'blackboard', is constructed. The hypotheses are represented in a hierarchical data structure.

Knowledge representation: the system draws on many concepts that have been developed in the design of other large knowledge-based systems, e.g. production rules and blackboards. Knowledge consists of facts, algorithms, and heuristics. The facts required for protein-structure inference are physical, chemical, stereochemical and crystallographic constraints. Algorithms and heuristics comprise both the formal and the informal knowledge that generates or verifies hypothesis elements. The representation of this knowledge in CRYSALIS follows two general principles: (i) identifiable areas of knowledge are decomposed into elementary units; (ii) the elementary units are represented as situation-action rules.

Event-driven rules: the CRYSALIS system uses an event-driven control structure. In this scheme, the current state of the hypothesis space determines what to do next.

The formal and informal procedures that comprise the knowledge sources are expressed as rules. These rules are collected into sets, each set being judged appropriate to use when particular kinds of events occur. The events generally reflect the level at which the inference is being made. The correspondence between event classes and rule sets is established by another set of rules, the task rules.

Once a task either is completed or fails, the system looks to a higher level of control to determine what to do next. Strategy-level decisions are also expressed as rules and make use of the current state of the blackboard and event list. The control structure is rule-based and employs three distinct levels of rules (or knowledge): the specialists (the knowledge sources), the task rules (representing knowledge about the capabilities of the specialists), and the strategy rules which know when to use all available knowledge to solve the problem.

CRYSALIS is capable of performing only a small portion of the total task of interpreting electron density maps. CRYSALIS contains a relatively small knowledge base that permits the interpretation of portions of high-quality, high-resolution electron density maps. New knowledge sources are continuously being added to the system, so that it is expected to be a significant helping tool in the determination of new protein structures.

SIMULATION AND EVALUATION OF CHEMICAL SYNTHESIS — SECS

Organic synthesis is the activity of producing new chemical compounds, such as those for use in drugs, fuels, plastics, dyes and superconductors. The design of an organic synthesis requires knowledge of many reactions and a lot of factual data. Over 250,000 chemical papers appear annually in the chemical literature and according to *Chemical Abstracts,* the chemical literature is increasing at 8.5% per year. Over 4,000,000 different chemical compounds have been reported in the literature. It would be very useful and time-saving to have a computer with a program which could help the chemists to digest the available information, evaluate and extrapolate the existing data and solve synthetic problems.

SECS is written in FORTRAN with a few assembly language functions for handling sets, lists and dynamic arrays. SECS has its own software virtual memory system for data structures which grow with the search tree.

The knowledge base includes information about structural theory, chemical reactions, chemical reactivity, and principles of chemical synthesis. SECS has a large knowledge base of reverse chemical reactions (starting with the target molecule, and determining which reactions might produce it) called transforms (production rules). SECS knowledge base contains 400 separate transforms. New transforms can be added by the users without changing the program. The SECS transforms are externally stored, which allows the knowledge base to be tailored to a 'specific' problem domain.

To communicate with the SECS program, the chemist uses a graphics terminal with a CRT, a minicomputer, a keyboard, and a light pen. The chemist draws with the light pen the graphical structure of the target molecule to be synthesized.

Two other synthesis-research programs are LHASA and SYNCHEM. The earliest of the three programs is LHASA (Logic and Heuristics Applied to Synthetic Analysis) written by Corey and Wipke at Harvard University. SYNCHEM (SYNthetic CHEMistry) was written by Gelernter and his research group at the State University of New York.

PROSPECTOR

PROSPECTOR has been developed at SRI International to assist geologists working in 'hard rock' mineral exploration. PROSPECTOR attempts to represent the knowledge and the reasoning processes of experts working in this field.

In PROSPECTOR, the geological knowledge base is clearly separated from the mechanisms that employ this knowledge. The main function of PROSPECTOR is to match data from a particular geological situation against models that are formal descriptions of the most important types of deposits. The available data are assumed to be uncertain and incomplete, so that the conclusion is expressed as a probability or a degree of match.

A dialogue session between the user and the system begins with the user giving the system the information about the most significant features of his prospect: rock types, minerals, and alteration products. At the end of this description, PROSPECTOR asks the user for additional information. At any time during the dialogue, the user can stop giving new information, change previous statements, or request an evaluation. After the model is matched, the system prompts the user to different interpretations of the data and suggests additional observations to be made, if these are needed for reaching more definite conclusions.

Knowledge representation: the geological knowledge is represented in the form of an inference network, in which the nodes refer to various assertions. In any particular run, any assertion may be known to be true, known to be false, or suspected to be true with some probability. Most of the arcs in the inference network define inference rules that specify how the probability of one assertion affects the probability of another assertion. These inferences rules correspond to the production rules of other systems, e.g. MYCIN.

To allow certain kinds of logical reasoning by the system, each assertion is represented as a space in a partitioned semantic network. A typical space asserts the hypothetical existence of physical entities having specific properties (e.g. being composed of a certain mineral) and participating in specific relations (such as an alteration relation).

Probabilistic reasoning: the various inference rules form an inference network. Thus, if the user provides some evidence, this information may change the probabilities of several hypotheses, which in turn can change the probabilities of hypotheses that depend on them. In the system, there are built in some probability formulas, which determine exactly how these probability changes propagate through the inference net.

MACSYMA

MACSYMA was designed to help mathematicians, scientists and engineers in solving mathematical problems. MACSYMA runs exclusively on a Digital Equipment Corporation KL-10 at MIT and may be accessed by ARPA Network. It has a wide range of algebraic manipulation capabilities, all working on symbolic inputs and yielding symbolic results. It has also a large numerical subroutine library (IMSL) and plotting package. MACSYMA can perform 600 mathematical operations and consists of 230,000 words of compiled LISP code and an equal amount of code written in the MACSYMA programming language.

The aim of creating MACSYMA was to invent and analyse new mathematical algorithms and to extend previously known numerical algorithms to symbolic manipulation. Two other capabilities of MACSYMA are a new representation for algebraic expressions using data abstractions and a knowledge-based, plan-based 'mathematician's apprentice'. One of the ways that the apprentice can be of use is in keeping track of the user's plan for solving his problem. If the apprentice knows the steps involved and the significance of various results, it could inform the user of potential errors, make suggestions and, in some cases, carry out steps by itself. MACSYMA is an example of a knowledge-based programming approach.

TEIRESIAS

TEIRESIAS is a system that assists in entering and updating the large knowledge bases used in expert systems (e.g. MYCIN). The system was developed by Randall Davis at Stanford University. Through TEIRESIAS, the human expert can 'educate' the program just as he would tutor a student who makes mistakes. TEIRESIAS is a tool which asks experts for their opinion about accumulated but still not complete knowledge. 'What do you know that the program does not know?' In this way TEIRESIAS helps in transfer of expertise. The transfer starts when the expert identifies an error in the performance of the program and invokes TEIRESIAS to track down the error.

To identify faulty reasoning steps in the performance program, the expert can use the WHY and HOW commands to ask TEIRESIAS to back up through previous steps, explaining why they were taken. When the expert has identified an error in the knowledge base, TEIRESIAS questions the expert in order to correct the error. The process relies on meta-level knowledge, which is simply the representation in the program of knowledge about the program itself. This knowledge is represented in the same formalism as the domain knowledge, yielding a program containing object-level representations that describe the external world and meta-level representations that describe the internal world of the program, its self-knowledge. Meta-level knowledge is also used to encode problem-solving strategies, in particular, to order the invocation of rules so that those that are most likely to be useful (given the current knowledge of the system) are tried first. TEIRESIAS assists in finding the source of error in the database by explaining the program's conclusions — retracing the reasoning steps until the faulty (or missing) rule is identified. Thus, TEIRESIAS helps in knowledge acquisition, modifying faulty rules or adding new rules to the database.

8.4 AI in database management

AI has been applied to database management systems in three ways: (i) introducing an interface for the user to interact with the system; (ii) making it possible to increase the efficiency of the DBMS system — to find the best expression in the data manipulation language for what the user wants to know, considering how the data are distributed among files in the database; and (iii) exploiting the similarities between AI and database management, both of which involve representation of information, to extend the capabilities of a DBMS, allowing it to answer different kinds of questions about the data and about itself (Barr and Feigenbaum, 1981).

(i) The user interface. The importance of easy and user-friendly interaction between man and machine was realized some time ago. The user should interact with the system without paying any attention to the actual organization of the database. The following aspects have been considered:

(a) natural language for accessing the database. Several attempts have been made to introduce natural language as a query language, including LADDER in 1977, PLANES in 1978, ROBOT in 1977 and TQA in 1979. Each of these interfaces functioned in a different way, but all used a grammar of a particular language and a parser. All have explored the ability of an elliptic input, correction of spelling errors, handling of pronouns, and the look-up of unknown terms in the query;

(b) automatic derivation of a natural-language front-end. The TED system, 1981, functions similarly to LADDER, but instead of employing extensive programming to build a natural-language interface, it uses the database schema and a dialogue with the user to achieve similar objectives;

(c) incremental query formulation. Instead of specifying the query in detail, the user may be helped by the system in constructing the profile. Such interactive query formulation was aimed at by RENDEZVOUS (1978) which passed the initial query through the parser. The parser converted it into a logical form and initiated a clarification dialogue with the user, mainly to resolve any ambiguity. Output from this phase was processed by a menu driver, which offered a list of choices at each point in the dialogue, attempting to fill in any gaps in the query specification by interrogating the user. The processed query was then passed to a generator which printed out an English translation of the final form of the query for the approval of the user;

(d) a more sophisticated interface. KLAUS, under development at SRI International (1980) is intended to help the user. It acts as an intermediary between the user's needs and the resources of the computer system. A pilot implementation, NanoKLAUS, can build a model of the query domain by engaging the user in an interactive dialogue in natural language. The natural-language component of NANOKLAUS is based on LIFER, discussed in Section 8.2. The dialogue results in the building up of a tree-like data structure that represents the knowledge of the query domain that has been assimilated by the system from user input. Once developed, the data structure can be consulted in interactive mode to answer questions about the domain. A later system, MIKROKLAUS, will replace LIFER with a more sophisticated grammar.

(ii) Query optimization. AI techniques are sometimes used to improve the system behaviour in ways not noticeable to the user. In the QUIST system (J I King, 1981), a semantic constraint is used to improve the execution of queries. The semantic constraint may cause limitations on the value of a particular attribute, on the number of entities that can be related to other entities, etc. Furakawa (1977) developed a deductive database query system DBAP that used a theorem prover to plan its access to the database. The theorem prover was designed to make the access efficient by observing a number of heuristics. The heuristics used in DBAP are syntactic, referring only to the structure of the database. Methods employed here are referred to as syntactic and semantic query optimizations.

(iii) Enhancing DBMS capabilities. Database management is concerned with representation, retrieval and use of information. The same elements are used in AI. Two improvements have been made in database management owing to the involvement of the AI techniques: improved data models which describe the structure of the database in the database schema, and the use of formal logic to reveal restrictions on the ability of database systems to represent certain kinds of information or to perform certain operations.

Data models: DBMS incorporate a database schema that describes organization of the database. The schema includes a description of the objects in the database, the operations permitted on them (for retrieval and update purposes), and the constraints that the database must satisfy. The schema is described in a descriptive language called a data model. The idea of a language for encoding knowledge about the database is identical to knowledge representation language in AI.

Sowa (1976) and Roussopoulos (1977) developed data models based on the semantic representation formalism. Special algorithms were specified for answering queries by matching the graph encoding the query against the graph representing the data model. This technique provided the system with the capabilities of question-answering, including the use of inferencing, the ability to use a procedure instead of the database, and the ability to answer queries phrased in a high-level form.

TAXIS (1980) is a language for the design of information systems such as databases. It covers both the description of the structure of the database and the formal specification of the procedures for operating on the data. TAXIS uses the semantic net representation formalism and also implements the principles of data abstraction.

Logic as a conceptual framework: a recent trend has been to use first-order logic to express certain aspects of a database. Reiter (1978) underlines in his study that a database is merely a collection of well-formed formulae. He states that a current database is unable to represent many kinds of quantified information, e.g. facts about the existence of an unspecified entry. Databases also do not contain extensive capabilities for inference. Certain forms of deduction are performed by means of constraints and views, but general inferencing

186

capabilities do not exist in current DBMS. Shaw (1980), Reiter (1978), Minker (1978), and Kellogg, Klahr and Travis (1978) have proposed a number of enhancements to incorporate deduction into databases for query processing; J I King (1981) and Furakawa (1977) suggested incorporating deductions for query optimization. Gallaire and Minker (1978) collected and edited a series of articles discussing more advanced techniques of AI applications in database management systems.

9 Evaluation and user satisfaction

9.1 Introduction

The evaluation component of the IR interaction has a rather special status, since it must, in some sense, refer to all the other components. That is, in principle, the success or failure of any one of the components will be reflected in the overall performance of the interaction as a whole. Thus, the extent to which the user's reasons for initiating the interaction are understood, the type of question put to the system, the quality of the interaction between the user and the intermediary, and between the humans and the computer (or other mechanism), the types of representation and of search strategies, will all affect the nature of the response to the user, and the user's evaluation of that response. Each of the components is also capable of being evaluated separately, either in terms of the eventual overall response, or in terms of criteria associated strictly with itself, or one or more of the other components.

The literature of evaluation in library and information science reflects the multi-faceted character of evaluation of the IR interaction, there being studies, or at least evidence of some thought, on the evaluation of almost all the components which we have discussed in this review. Indeed, almost any serious research in this field will have an evaluative component.

In this chapter, we will focus primarily on one basic characteristic of evaluation, which has been the subject of much debate, and which appears to us still to be unresolved. This is the issue of the criterion of evaluation. Having discussed this in some detail, we will briefly consider the related issues of who should be the evaluator, and what aspects of the interaction should be evaluated. Although these three aspects are strongly related to one another, in the sense that a positive choice in one facet may imply particular solutions in the others, we will attempt to indicate the range of solutions that have been proposed for each separately. As usual in our review we will consider exemplar contributions, rather than attempting to be exhaustive, and we will concentrate on papers which deal explicitly and solely with the issue of evaluation. We refer the reader for general reviews on the topic to the many relevant chapters in the *Annual review of information science and technology*.

9.2   Criteria of evaluation

There have been basically four approaches to the issue of the criterion by which the IR interaction should be evaluated: retrieval effectiveness*; utility; satisfaction; and use. Although there are connections between these ideas, notably the concept of relevance, they have been seen as competitors in the issue of evaluation. In particular, they have been interpreted as leading to different measures of the success of information interaction.

9.2.1   Retrieval effectiveness

This is the oldest evaluative criterion for IR, and the best established. Its basic premise is that the function of an IR system is to retrieve documents *relevant* to the user's information problem, and that any IR system should therefore be evaluated according to the extent to which it is *effective* at retrieving all and only the documents in its database which are relevant. Before we go on to discuss retrieval effectiveness, we look at the concept of relevance, which underlies it, and some of the other criteria as well.

The idea of relevance in information science has been much discussed, and even investigated, almost from the beginnings of the field. In its most general IR sense, it describes the appropriateness of a text to a specific information problem. Saracevic (1975) has written a fine review of research and speculation on this concept in information science, and we refer the reader to it for details. Here we wish only to mention a few problems with the concept, which bear upon the issue of evaluation, and proposals which have been made to deal with them.

A major difficulty in evaluation of IR systems has been to obtain reliable and reproducible relevance judgments. The problem has been that the ultimate judge of relevance in the real world is the person with the information need, and this person's formal question to the IR mechanism (which is all that mechanism has to work with) may not encompass all the factors which bear upon her or his eventual relevance judgement. So relevance as a general concept has tended to be divided into two or three separate concepts (see, for example, Kemp, 1974, or P Wilson, 1973). These include *logical relevance* (Cooper, 1971), which requires that the propositions of the request or query be included in or logically deducible from the text; *destination's relevance* or just *relevance* (Saracevic, 1975), which depends solely upon the relationship

---

*We should note that our use of 'retrieval effectiveness' and 'utility' separates two approaches to evaluation that are often subsumed in the literature under the single term: 'retrieval effectiveness'.

between the topics of the formal question and the texts retrieved, usually as evaluated by an external judge (see also Farradane, 1974); and *situational relevance* or *pertinence,* which is the judgment by the user of the appropriateness of text to need based not upon the question put to the system but rather on the user's entire desire and problem state at the time of receiving the text for judgment (see, e.g. Kemp, 1974; P Wilson, 1973).

Each of the concepts of relevance proposed is obviously quite different from the others, and each has special advantages and problems in the evaluation situation. Our major point here is that the choice of relevance concept will radically affect evaluation of IR interaction by any measure of retrieval effectiveness, since these measures all operate with given relevance decisions.

Retrieval effectiveness, as a criterion for IR evaluation, was developed in the context of offline batch searching of databases. In this context, there was a given query to the system, and the problem was seen as discovering how well the system responded to the query. This was, as many have noted (e.g. Cleverdon, 1974), very much a management view of evaluation, since the only variables capable of being manipulated were those associated with the system. The success (or comparative success) of a system depended upon some measure of retrieval effectiveness, as defined above. All tests of IR systems well into the 1970s used this basic paradigm for evaluation, with the basic problem being perceived as what *measure(s)* should be used to judge retrieval effectiveness. There is a large literature on the problem of how to test for retrieval effectiveness (see, for instance, Sparck Jones, 1981, for a collection of papers devoted to this issue), and an equally large one on the problem of what measures should be used. Robertson (1969) surveyed the classical measures of retrieval effectiveness, and argued for some particular combinations; Van Rijsbergen (1981) presents an elegant argument on the nature of the relationship between evaluative measures and the models of IR on which they are based.

A basic problem with retrieval effectiveness has always been the issue of how to discover the relevance of all the documents in a document collection to any query put to the system. This is because *recall* has been considered a fundamental measure or component of any measure of retrieval effectiveness, since soon after the very first retrieval tests. Recall is the proportion of relevant documents retrieved to all the relevant documents in the collection, and it can be seen that its significance is at least to some extent dependent upon the batch-mode context of early IR systems. That is, it is a static measure which can be applied only to a fixed collection with definable characteristics, and which is strongly, although not completely, dependent upon the idea of a fixed query, put to the system at one time. Furthermore, it is strongly dependent upon the assumption that the appropriate system response to any query is *all* the relevant documents in the collection.

Thus, we can see that recall, as a fundamental measure of retrieval effectiveness in information interaction, has two major built-in deficiencies. First, it requires at least estimates of relevance for all the documents in the collection, an extremely difficult problem which in effect limits its usefulness to experimental collections. Although there have been attempts to apply recall in operational environments, such as that by Lancaster (1969), where different sources and methods were used to do a presumably exhaustive search, which gave an estimate of all the documents relevant to a query, most have seemed at best unreliable. Indeed, Das Gupta and Katzer (1983) demonstrate that changing query or document representation in a search yields sets of relevant documents in the various searches which are almost disjoint. This makes one suspect that such estimates of numbers of relevant documents in an operational service are likely always to be low.

The second problem is that it is difficult to take account of interactive searching procedures using the usual retrieval effectiveness measures of recall and precision (proportion of relevant documents retrieved). In an online environment, users see documents (or at least document surrogates) one at a time, rather than all together, and their queries are often modified through interaction. In such cases, it is difficult to see how a recall measure can be applied. Furthermore, such interaction also implies stopping points, which may not be related to either recall or precision at all. Although some attempts have been made to adapt retrieval effectiveness measures to this dynamic situation, such as relevance feedback (e.g. Robertson and Sparck Jones, 1976), this problem still remains a serious objection to the use of retrieval effectiveness for evaluation of operational information systems.

Cleverdon (1974) noted that retrieval effectiveness as we have described it was designed to evaluate and test individual components of the IR system, from the point of view of managers of such systems. That is, the goal was to improve various such components, rather than to relate their performance to some idea of value of the system to the user. This seems an especially limiting factor given the importance of the user in the information interaction, as we have seen it in this review. Finally, although some suggestions have been made for a single measure of retrieval effectiveness (e.g. Van Rijsbergen, 1979), by and large two measures have been necessary for any evaluation, which trade off with one another. This is seen as a disadvantage,since there are no good rules for determining which measure has priority.

In general, there seems to be some disquiet in the information science community about the status of recall and precision as evaluative measures for information interaction (see, e.g. Oddy, 1977a,b; Belkin, 1981), or more broadly, about the use of this notion of retrieval effectiveness as an evaluative criterion. Indeed, Cooper (1973, 1976, 1979) has demonstrated that there appears to be a logical flaw in an evaluation schema for a system which depends upon things which the user never sees, and thus which presumably cannot affect the user (that is, unretrieved relevant documents). This has led Cooper to suggest utility as the criterion by which IR systems should be evaluated.

9.2.2 Utility

In response to the problems associated with the notion of retrieval effectiveness discussed above, and also on *a priori* grounds, some people have suggested that utility be the criterion of evaluation for IR systems. Cooper (1973, 1976, 1979) has been the strongest proponent of this position, but others (e.g. Cleverdon, 1974), while not necessarily embracing Cooper's specific methodology, begin with more or less the same assumptions. These assumptions, basically, are that an 'information system ought to be evaluated on the basis of how useful it is to its users' (Cooper, 1976, p 367), and that this is not equivalent to the system's having retrieved all and only the relevant documents in the collection. Having agreed this far, however, the approaches begin to divide.

Cooper goes on to specify quite precisely what he means by usefulness, that being utility in the utility-theoretic sense. He arrives at this suggestion by a second assumption, based on his first. This is that 'what must be measured is the utility to the user of the documents with which he is brought into contact by the system' (Cooper, 1976, p 367). Such utility, Cooper suggests, can be measured by using well-understood and well-developed concepts of utility theory. Very briefly, what this amounts to is asking the user of a system to put some utility value on each experience that user has had with each document presented by the system. This could be by asking people how much money they would have been willing to pay for the experience (or for avoiding the experience — negative utility), or how much effort they would have been willing to put into system operation, etc., in order to obtain the experience (in, say, person-hours). The point is to force a choice of value in some standard units. Then average utility can be computed for all the document experiences of all the users, to give a single value for the system, which could be compared with the utility value for another system.

The advantages to this approach over the traditional retrieval effectiveness approach, in terms of evaluation of information interaction, appear numerous. First, it provides a single measure for evaluation. Second, it reduces, if not eliminates, dependence on unretrieved relevant documents, since it is only concerned with retrieved documents. Third, it allows explicitly for the dynamic aspect of information interaction. And finally, it takes more account of the role of the user in information interaction than was possible in the retrieval effectiveness model. In particular, the *user* evaluates the system's performance.

There have been many objections to Cooper's proposals, which can be divided basically into two classes. Robertson's (1974) argument is on the logic and usefulness of the proposal; that is, that it is not sufficient to evaluate systems as black boxes, that in order to improve systems it is necessary to analyse them and that other measures than utility might be necessary for this; and that, in any event, relevance will be an important component of any utility estimate. Soergel (1976) objects on the ground that a system's not retrieving a particular document might in certain cases mean that it has performed very badly indeed (in the case of an existence search, for instance), and therefore utility cannot be an appropriate measure, since it only considers those documents which the user has actually seen. To such objections, however, Cooper has published responses which seem to take account of them. But perhaps the most serious objection is one he raises himself: the difficulty of actually implementing the evaluation, for we still have no test or experiment which has actually done so.

The major point of the utility approach is that there are many factors other than relevance which will affect the user's evaluation of the system's performance, and that it is up to the user to evaluate that performance in his or her own terms. Cooper has suggested what some of these factors might be, and how utility theory could deal with such a situation. Cleverdon (1974) presented another approach to this problem, by recognizing that in current systems traditional retrieval effectiveness measures are inappropriate, but suggesting ways in which they could be used in combination with more user-oriented measures, to produce an evaluation on roughly utility (but not utility-theoretic) grounds. He suggested that such factors as subjective satisfaction statements, search costs, time spent, person doing the search, and so on, could be related to nominal recall and precision values in such a way as to indicate how various parameters ought to be changed. Although he used a highly contrived example situation to demonstrate his idea, it appears that it might be possible to implement such an evaluation strategy.

The major limitations of the utility approach to evaluation of information interaction appear to be that it is extremely difficult to implement, and that in order to do something with it, it is necessary to break it down into its component parts, thus negating its advantage of simplicity. Also, in spite of its claim to be broad in what it evaluates, in terms of our view of the IR interaction, it seems strangely limited. Cooper's view of evaluation, for instance, seems very much limited to the user in interaction with the mechanism. For instance, he states '... it is feasible for an investigator to observe the actions of a patron throughout his entire experience with the system, including all his experience with the fruits of his search as he reads or examines the documents retrieved by the system' (Cooper, 1973, p 83); that is, as the user sits in the library. Cleverdon is also rather limited to the document situation, but at least some of his suggested factors include things that go beyond the direct user-document interaction; in this sense, his suggestions relate to those which consider *satisfaction* as the appropriate evaluation criterion.

9.2.3 Satisfaction

Satisfaction as a criterion for evaluation of information systems is a concept explicitly intended to extend the range of factors relevant to the evaluation. In particular, the intention is to move away from evaluation according to system performance, the basis of retrieval effectiveness, and toward an overall judgment based on user reaction to the system. The major distinctions between this approach and the utility approach discussed above are that satisfaction considers factors other than those associated with the user-document interaction, that it offers some directly applicable methodologies, and that, in general, it looks explicitly at multiple rather than single measures.

The rationale is not complex. Tagliacozzo (1977), e.g., in arguing for satisfaction measures based directly on user evaluation, says:

> Any method that tests how well the system is performing will tell much about the system but probably very little about the degree of satisfaction of the users. Especially when the system is based on technological innovation, the user's reaction and his degree of acceptance may be influenced by factors other than the performance of the system.

And further:

> From a practical point of view, 'users' acceptance' may be an adequate substitute for 'users' need satisfaction'. (Tagliacozzo, 1977, p 243.)

Similarly, Tessier, Atherton and Crouch, (1977, p 383) suggest that:

> When the user determines satisfaction with computer based retrieval situations, he focuses on four distinct aspects: the output, the interaction with the intermediary, the service policies and the library as a whole. Measuring satisfaction requires investigation of each aspect with appropriate techniques.

Although the idea behind satisfaction as a criterion is simple, it is obvious that actually measuring it is not, since it must be a multi-faceted variable. The issue of how to do this has been explored by a number of authors. Tessier, Atherton and Crouch (1977, p 386) specify three assumptions to this approach, which they claim imply how satisfaction should be measured:

1. User's satisfaction will be a function of how well the product fits his requirement.

2. User's state of satisfaction is experienced within the frame of his expectations.

3. People may seek a solution within an acceptable range instead of an ideal or perfect solution.

They also survey a number of methods which have been suggested or used for measuring satisfaction within this framework, including various methods for analysis of interpersonal communication, as well as the more traditional methods of performance evaluation and direct questioning. These ideas are extended and applied in detail in a large-scale study of satisfaction with the pre-search interview, reported by Tessier (1981).

Tagliacozzo (1977, pp 242-3), in discussing the utility of direct questioning of users as a means to measure satisfaction, says:

> ...one should be wary in taking the data of a single rating scale to assess the value that an information system has for its users. In

particular, if the rating scale measures a global judgment of the service ... rather than the appraisal of specific search results, a single response may be inadequate to assess the extent to which a user's information needs were satisfied by the search. A questionnaire ... should tap several aspects of the user's reaction to the outcome of his request for information.

Although she does not provide a theoretical justification for the factors she used, her results indicated that users' attitudes and perceptions, knowledge and expertise in the area of the search, previous acquaintance with the literature, and type of search, all influenced their degree of satisfaction, as indicated by a number of rating scales.

Price (1983), in a study of information interaction dialogues, developed an interview form which concentrated on satisfaction of both user and intermediary with the interactional, interpersonal and problem-solving components of the interview, in order to relate satisfaction or 'success' in the interview with the functional structure of the dialogue. And Auster and Lawton (1984) report on an extensive and detailed investigation of the relationships among interview techniques used by intermediaries, amount of information gained by the user, and the user's overall satisfaction with the quality of the items retrieved. Both these studies were able to demonstrate measurable effects of the variables investigated on satisfaction.

Thus, we see that satisfaction as an evaluative criterion appears to have some advantages over the other criteria we have investigated: namely, that it takes explicit account of the user; that it is operationalizable; that realistic measures can be obtained; and, that it appears to involve, at least in principle, most of the components of the IR interaction. It does not, however, seem to offer a means for comparison of systems overall, because there is no possibility for a single measure on which to do this. Satisfaction, as a global measure, is obviously inadequate. This is an interesting result, and certainly has strong implications for the validity of retrieval effectiveness or utility as sole criteria for evaluation. Perhaps the most interesting result of such work, however, is in its identification of factors which affect satisfaction, and which should be taken into account in evaluation of the information interaction.

9.2.4 Use

One factor of primary importance to the IR interaction has not been taken into account by any of the evaluative criteria discussed above.

This factor is the use to which the user puts the information gained from the interaction. If we recall our discussion in Chapter 2, we note that it seems agreed that people enter information systems in order, usually, to do something. Surely, in this case, it might make sense to investigate whether the result of the interaction actually helped the user to do what she or he wanted to do; that is, to investigate the use made of the results, and to use this as the criterion of evaluation. Unfortunately, although this approach has been suggested for some time (see Chapter 2, and, e.g., Soergel, 1976), there has been very little (practically no) actual evaluation work based on this criterion, and only a handful of suggestions as to how it might be operationalized.

Whittemore and Yovits (e.g. 1973) have suggested that the function of an information system is to provide data of value in decision making, and have proposed a system design (including evaluative feedback) based on this model. Although the calculus is developed in detail, the notion of use still seems rather narrow, and the framework seems not to have been applied as a strictly evaluative criterion.

The problem, of course, is that the actual use of information is remarkably difficult to investigate, especially since to do so requires first of all a concept of the problem which prompted the user to enter the system. Investigations such as those of Wilson and Streatfield (e.g. 1977) and Dervin *et al* (1976, 1977) are examples of the few studies where use of information was investigated. Unfortunately, no one appears to have been able to use the results of such large-scale investigations actually to evaluate the IR interaction.

So our conclusion on the use of use as an evaluative criterion for IR interaction is that, although it has long been suggested as the ultimate, most appropriate criterion, and although, in the context of our analysis of IR interaction, it is logically the best such criterion, the theoretical and practical difficulties of the concept are such that it is still a criterion for the future. Although there are some current research projects which attempt to approach this question (e.g. Belkin, proposal to the British Library Research and Development Department, 1982) we feel it safe to say that there are still no firm results.

9.3 Conclusions

Our discussion of the criteria which have been suggested for evaluation of IR interaction seems to us to imply the following conclusions. There is a definite progression in measures actually used for evaluating IR interaction, from a very simplistic concept of the functions and components of the IR system, to an ever more complex idea of this situation. Although the initial ideas about evaluation still have their place, it is clear that the concept of retrieval effectiveness alone is insufficient for evaluation of the IR interaction. In particular, the work on utility, and, even more strongly, on satisfaction, has indicated that any realistic evaluation of this situation must be multi-dimensional. This is not to imply that individual components of the system cannot be analysed and evaluated on their own, but rather to stress that they can never, as was once the case with retrieval effectiveness, be construed as being sole measures of the system's performance.

We have also seen a progression from evaluation by logic (e.g. Farradane, 1974) and by outside judges to evaluation by the users themselves, which has much in common with our description of the IR interaction. And, furthermore, we have seen a strong tendency away from single measures, and from evaluation of components having to do with the actual search and representation toward multiple measures, and toward evaluation of components having to do with interaction, and to some extent with integration of the results into the user's own life.

These progressions are not meant to imply, however, that all is well with evaluation. On the contrary, things in some ways look worse than ever. Although recall has its problems, and utility seems difficult to implement, they at least offered measures on which one could hope to compare system performance. The trends we have noted make this very difficult indeed. Also, no one has yet discovered retrieval effectiveness measures which are really applicable to the online IR interaction, although all agree that any evaluation must have retrieval effectiveness as a significant component. More positively, the progressions we note seem to coincide well with our interactive model of the IR situation. Although the question of use of information is still open as far as an evaluative criterion is concerned, other aspects of the interaction seem to be increasingly taken account of in the general trend of evaluation studies. We can only hope that this trend will soon, or eventually, lead to measures which will be able to account for all the facets of the IR interaction, within one framework. It is only when this happens that it will be possible to establish relations among all the components, which will be relevant to the system function as a whole.

References

ABELSON R P
Differences between belief and knowledge systems.
Cognitive Science, 3, 1979, pp 355-366

ABELSON R P, ARONSON E, McGUIRE W J, NEWCOMB T M,
ROSENBERG M J and TANNENBAUM P H
Theories of cognitive consistency: a sourcebook.
Rand McNally, Chicago, 1968, 901pp

ADAMS A L
Planning search strategies for maximum retrieval from bibliographic
databases.
Online Review, 3(4), December 1979, pp 373-379

AIKINS J S, KUNZ J C, SHORTLIFFE E H and FALLAT R J
PUFF: an expert system for interpretation of pulmonary function data.
Stanford University, Report No. STAN-CS-82-931, September 1982,
21pp

ALLEN T J
Managing the flow of scientific and technical communication.
MIT, Cambridge, Mass. Report No. PB-174440, 1966

ALLEN T J
Information needs and uses.
Annual review of information science and technology, 4, 1969, pp 3-31

AMAREL S
Problem solving and decision making by computer.
In: *Cognition: a multiple view,* Garvin P L, ed.
Spartan Books, 1970

AMAREL S
Representations and modelling of problems of program foundation.
In: *Machine Intelligence 6,* Meltzer B and Michie D, eds.
Edinburgh University Press, 1971

AMAREL S
Review of characteristics of current expert systems.
Rutgers University, State University of New Jersey, Report No. CBM-
TM-89, March 1981, 9pp

ANDERSON A R and BELNAP N D
The pure calculus of entailment.
Journal of Symbolic Logic, 27, 1965, pp 19-51

APTE C
Expert knowledge management for multi-level modelling with an application to well-log analysis. Thesis proposal.
Rutgers University, Technical Report LCSR-TR-41, December 1982

AQVIST L
A new approach to the logical theory of interrogatives.
University of Uppsala, Uppsala, 1965

ASSOCIATION OF COMPUTATIONAL LINGUISTICS
18th Annual Meeting. Proceedings.
ACL, Philadelphia, 1980

ATHERTON P and CROUCH W W
Presearch Interview Project Progress Report, covering May 1979 to January 1980.
School of Information Studies, Syracuse University, NY, February 1980, 49pp.
Report of the Presearch Interview Project. (Sponsor: National Library of Medicine, EDRS ED-205182)

AUSTER E
The development, implementation and evaluation of a training program for educational information consultants.
Paper presented at the Annual Meeting of the American Educational Research Association, Toronto, Canada, 27-31 March, 1978, 35 pp. (Sponsor: Ontario Department of Education, Toronto, EDRS ED-160130)

AUSTER E
User satisfaction with the online negotiation interview.
Reference Quarterly, 23, 1983, pp 47-59

AUSTER E and LAWTON S B
Meeting Ontario's need for educational information: an evaluation of the SDC ERIC online bibliographic search service.
Ontario Institute for Studies in Education, Toronto, March 1973, 92 pp (EDRS ED-077531)

AUSTER E and LAWTON S B
The Educational Information System for Ontario. Summary of final

report.
Ontario Institute for Studies in Education, Toronto, 1978, 26 pp
(EDRS ED-168500)

AUSTER E and LAWTON S B
Educational Information System for Ontario. Final Report.
March 1977 - April 1978
Ontario Institute for Studies in Education, Toronto, 1978, 223 pp
(EDRS ED-163969)

AUSTER E and LAWTON S B
Negotiation process in online bibliographic retrieval.
Canadian Journal of Information Science, 4, May 1980, pp 86-98

AUSTER E and LAWTON S B
Search interview techniques and information gain as antecedents of
user satisfaction with online bibliographic retrieval.
Journal of the American Society for Information Science, 35(2), 1984,
pp 90-103

AUSTIN J L
How to do things with words.
Oxford University Press, London, 1962

BADDELEY A D
The psychology of memory.
Harper and Row, New York, 1976

BALES R F
Interaction process analysis.
Addison-Wesley, Cambridge, Mass., 1950

BAR-HILLEL Y
Language and information.
Addison-Wesley Publishing Company, Inc., London, 1964

BAR-HILLEL Y and CARNAP R
Semantic information.
British Journal of Philosophy of Science, 4(14), August 1953, pp
147-157

BARNARD P and HAMMOND N
Cognitive contexts and interactive communication.
Hursley Human Factors Laboratory Report No. HF070. Cambridge,
HHFL, 1982

BARR A
Artificial intelligence: cognition as computation.
Department of Computing Science, Stanford University, 1982

BARR A, BENNETT J and CLANCEY W
Transfer of expertise: a theme for AI research.
Report No. HPP-79-11. Heuristic Programming Project, Computer
Science Department, Stanford University, 1979

BARR A and FEIGENBAUM E A
The handbook of artificial intelligence (Vol.1-3).
Kaufmann, Los Altos, Ca, 1981

BATES M J
Information search tactics.
Journal of the American Society for Information Science, 30(4), July
1979, pp 205-214 (a)

BATES M J
Idea tactics.
Journal of the American Society for Information Science, 30(5),
September 1979, pp 280-289 (b)

BATES M J
Search techniques.
Annual review of information science and technology, 16, 1981,
pp 139-169

BAYER A E and JAHODA G
Online searches: characteristics of users and uses in one academic and
one industrial organization.
In: *The information age in perspective: proceedings of the 41st Annual
Meeting ASIS, New York, 1978,* Brenner E H, ed.
Knowledge Industry Publications, White Plains, NY, 1978, pp 165-167

BAYER A E and JAHODA G
Background characteristics of industrial and academic users and
nonusers of online bibliographic search services.
Online Review, 3(1), 1979, pp 95-105

BELKIN N J
A concept of information for information science.
PhD thesis, University of London, 1977

BELKIN N J
Anomalous states of knowledge as a basis for information retrieval.
Canadian Journal of Information Science, 5, 1980, pp 133-143

BELKIN N J
Models of dialogue for information retrieval.
In: *Proceedings of the 4th International Research Forum in Information Science, IRFIS4,* August 1981

BELKIN N J
Cognitive models and information transfer.
Social Science Information Studies, 4, 1984, pp 111-129

BELKIN N J
Representation and matching of anomalous states of knowledge and document texts.
Grant proposal to the BLRDD, London, The City University, 1982

BELKIN N J, BROOKS H and ODDY R N
Representation and classification of anomalous states of knowledge and information for use in interactive information retrieval.
In: *Proceedings of the 3rd International Research Forum in Information Science, IRFIS3,* Oslo, 1979

BELKIN N J, BROOKS H and ODDY R N
Representing and classifying anomalous states of knowledge.
In: *Informatics 5. The analysis of meaning, March 25-28, 1979, Oxford,* Gray K I and MacCafferty M, eds.
Aslib, London, 1979, pp 227-238

BELKIN N J, HENNINGS R D and SEEGER T
Simulation of a distributed expert-based information provision mechanism.
Information Technology Research and Development, 3, 1984. In press

BELKIN N J, ODDY R N, and BROOKS H M
ASK for information retrieval, Parts I and II.
Journal of Documentation, 38, 1982, pp 61-71, 145-164

BELKIN N J, SEEGER T and WERSIG G
Distributed expert problem treatment as a model for information system analysis and design.
Journal of Information Science, 5(5), February 1983, pp 153-168

BELKIN N J and WINDEL G
Using MONSTRAT for the analysis of information interaction.
In: *Representation and exchange of knowledge as a basis of information processes. Proceedings of the 5th International Research Forum in Information Science, IRFIS 5,* Dietschmann H, ed.
North-Holland, Amsterdam, 1984, pp 359-384

BELL A and QUILLIAN M R
Capturing concepts in a semantic net.
In: *Associative information techniques,* Jachs E L, ed.
Elsevier, New York, 1971

BELL M
Questioning.
Philosophical Quarterly, 25, 1975, pp 193-212

BELNAP N D and STEEL T B
The logic of questions and answers.
Yale University Press, New Haven, 1976, 209 pp

BENNETT J L
The user interface in interactive systems.
Annual review of information science and technology, 7, 1972, pp 159-196

BENNETT J S
On the structure of the acquisition process for rule-based systems.
Machine Intelligence (Infotech State of the Art Report Series 9, No.3), 1980

BENNETT J S and GOLDMAN D
CLOT: a knowledge-based consultant for bleeding disorders.
Department of Computing Science, Stanford University, Memo PP-80-7, 1980

BENNETT S W and SCOTT A C
Computer-assisted customized antimicrobial dosages.
American Journal of Hospital Pharmacy, 37, 1980, pp 513-530

BENSON J and MALONEY R K
Principles of searching.
Reference Quarterly, 14(4), Summer 1975, pp 316-320

BERLYNE D E
Conflict, arousal and curiosity.
McGraw-Hill, New York, 1960

BERLYNE D E
Structure and direction in thinking.
J Wiley, New York, 1965, 378 pp

BISS K, CHIEN R T, STAHL F and WEISSMAN S J
Semantic modeling for deductive question-answering.
IEEE Transactions on Computers, C-25(4), April 1976, pp 358-365

BIVINS-NOERR K T and NOERR P L
The display device: a user-oriented intelligent terminal.
In: *6th International Online Information Meeting, London, 1982.*
Learned Information, Oxford, 1982, pp 373-378

BLAIR D C
Searching biases in large interactive document retrieval systems.
Journal of the American Society for Information Science, 31, 1980.
pp 271-277

BOBROW D G
Natural language input for a computer problem-solving system.
PhD thesis, MIT Project MAC, 1964

BOBROW D G
A question-answering system for high school algebra word problems.
Proceedings Fall Joint Computer Conference, 26, 1964, pp 591-614

BOBROW D G
Natural language input for a computer problem-solving system.
In: *Semantic information processing,* Minsky M, ed.
MIT Press, Cambridge, Mass., 1968

BOCK G
Soziologie und Bibliothek: zur theoretischen Bestimmung des
Begriffs, 'Soziologische Benutzerforschung'.
Nachrichten für Dokumentation, 22, 1971, pp 231-236

BODEN M A
Artificial intelligence and natural man.
Basic Books, New York, 1977

BOOKSTEIN A
The perils of merging Boolean and weighted retrieval systems.
Journal of the American Society for Information Science, 29(3), 1978, pp 156-157

BOOKSTEIN A
Fuzzy requests: an approach to weighted Boolean searches.
Journal of the American Society for Information Science, July 1980, pp 240-247

BOOKSTEIN A
Explanation and generalization of vector models in information retrieval.
In: *SIGIR/ACM, Research and Development in Information Retrieval, Berlin, May 1982.*
Springer-Verlag, Berlin, Heidelberg, New York, 1983, pp 118-131

BOOKSTEIN A and SWANSON D R
A decision basis for the use of co-occurrence data in information retrieval.
Journal of Documentation, 33(2), 1977, pp 106-119

BORGIDA A, COHEN P, MYLOPOULOS J, ROUSSOPOULOS N, TSOTOS J and WONG H
TORUS: a step towards bridging the gap between databases and the casual user.
Information Systems (GB), 2(2), 1976, pp 49-64

BORODIN A, KERR L and LEWIS F
Query splitting in relevance feedback systems.
Department of Computer Science, Cornell University, Report ISR-14, 1968

BOUCHER V
Nonverbal communication and the library reference interview.
Reference Quarterly, 16, 1976, pp 27-32

BRACHMANN R J and SMITH B C
Special issue on knowledge representation.
SIGART Newsletter, 70, 1980

BRENNER L P, HUSTON-MIYAMOTO M, SELF D A, SELF P C and SMITH L C
User-computer interface designs for information systems: a review.
Library Research, 2(1), Spring 1981, pp 63-73

206

BRIGGS R B
The user interface for bibliographic search services.
In: *The use of computers in literature searching and related reference activities in libraries. Proceedings 1975 Clinic on Library Applications of Data Processing, April 27-30, 1975,* Lancaster F W, ed.
University of Illinois, Urbana-Champaign, 1976, pp 56-77

BRITTAIN J M
Information and its users.
Bath University Press, Bath, 1970

BROADBENT D E
A mechanical model for human attention and immediate memory.
Psychological Review, 64(3), 1957

BROOKS H M
Information retrieval and expert systems: approaches and methods of development.
In: *Informatics 7. Intelligent information retrieval,* Jones K, ed.
Aslib, London, 1984

BROOKS H M and BELKIN N J
Using discourse analysis for the design of information retrieval interaction mechanism.
In: *SIGIR/ACM, Research and Development in Information Retrieval, 6th International Conference Washington DC, 1983,* Kuehn J J, ed.
ACM, New York, 1983, pp 31-47

BROWN G and YULE G
Discourse analysis.
Cambridge University Press, Cambridge, 1983

BRUNER J S, GOODNOW J J and AUSTIN G A
A study of thinking.
J Wiley, New York, 1962

BUCHANAN B G and FEIGENBAUM E A
DENDRAL and Meta-DENDRAL: their applications dimension.
Artificial Intelligence, 11, 1978, pp 5-24

CARD S K, MORAN T P and NEWELL A
The psychology of human-computer interaction.
Erlbaum, Hillsdale, NJ, 1983

CARHART R E
CONGEN: An expert system aiding the structural chemist.
In: *Expert system in the micro-electronic age,* Michie D, ed.
Edinburgh University Press, 1979

CARLSON L
Dialogue games.
Reidel, Dordrecht, Boston, 1982

CARMON J L
Model of the user interface for a multidisciplinary bibliographic information network.
University of Georgia, Office of Computing Activities, 1975

CARMON J L and PARK M K
User assessment of computer-based bibliographic retrieval services.
Journal of Chemical Documentation, 13(1), 1973, pp 24-27

CERRI S and BREUKER J
A rather intelligent language teacher.
In: *Proceedings of the AISB-80 Conference on Artificial Intelligence, Amsterdam, 1-4 July, 1980.*
The Society for the Study of Artificial Intelligence and Simulation of Behaviour, 1981

CHAFE W L
Discourse structure and human knowledge.
In: *Language comprehension and the acquisition of knowledge.*
Winston, Washington, 1972

CHAFE W L
Meaning and the structure of language.
University of Chicago Press, 1972

CHAFE W L
The recall and verbalization of past experience.
In: *Current issues in linguistic theory.* Cole R W, ed.
Indiana University Press, Bloomington, 1977

CHAFE W L
The flow of thought and the flow of language.
In: *Syntax and semantics,* V12, Givon T, ed.
Academic Press, New York, 1978

CHAPMAN J L
A state transition analysis of online information-seeking behaviour.
Journal of the American Society for Information Science, 32(5), 1981,
pp 324-333

CHOMSKY N
Syntactic structures.
Mouton, The Hague, 1957

CHOMSKY N
Studies on semantics in generative grammar.
Mouton, The Hague, 1972

CLEVERDON C W
User evaluation of information retrieval systems.
Journal of Documentation, 30(2), June 1974, pp 170-179

COCHRANE P
Study of events and tasks in pre-search interviews before online
searching.
In: *Proceedings of the 2nd National Online Meeting, March 24-26, 1981,
New York*, Williams M E, and Hogan T H, eds.
Learned Information Inc., Medford, N J, 1981, pp 133-147

COHEN P R, PERRAULT C P and ALLEN J F
Beyond question answering.
Bolt Beranek Newman, Cambridge, Mass., 1981

COLLINGWOOD R G
Autobiography.
Oxford University Press, Oxford, 1939

COLLINS A M and QUILLIAN M R
Retrieval time from semantic memory.
Journal of Verbal Learning and Verbal Behavior, 8, 1969, pp 240-247

COOPER W S
A definition of relevance for information retrieval.
Information Processing and Management, 7, 1971, pp 19-37

COOPER W S
On selecting a measure of retrieval effectiveness. Part 1.
Journal of the American Society for Information Science, 24(2),
March-April 1973, pp 87-100

COOPER W S
On selecting a measure of retrieval effectiveness. Part 2.
Implementation of the philosophy.
Journal of the American Society for Information Science, 24(6),
November-December 1973, pp 413-424

COOPER W S
The paradoxical role of unexamined documents in the evaluation of
retrieval effectiveness.
Information Processing and Management, 12(6), 1976, pp 367-375

COOPER W S
A perspective on the measurement of retrieval effectiveness.
Drexel Library Quarterly, 1979, pp 25-39

COULTHARD M
An introduction to discourse analysis.
Longmans, London, 1977, 195 pp

CROUCH W W
Verbal behaviours of librarians in presearch interviews.
School of Information Studies, Syracuse University, NY, April 1981,
94 pp.
Report of the Presearch Interview Project. (Sponsor: National Library
of Medicine) (EDRS ED-205187)

CROUCH W W and LUCIA J
*Analysis of verbal behaviours in the presearch interview: codebook
with instructions for transcribing interviews.*
School of Information Studies, Syracuse University, NY, July 1980,
81 pp.
Report of the Presearch Interview Project. (Sponsor: National Library
of Medicine, ERDS ED-205184)

CULLINGFORD R E
Script application: computer understanding of newspaper stories.
Department of Computer Science, Yale University, Research report
116, 1978

CULNAN M and JAHODA G
Unanswered science and technology reference questions.
American Documentation, January 1968, pp 95-100

DAMERAU F J
The transformational question answering (TQA) system: operational statistics.
Report No. RC-7739, Computer Science Department, Thomas J Watson Research Center, IBM, Yorktown Heights, NY, 1978

DAS GUPTA P and KATZER J
A study of the overlap among document representations.
In: *SIGIR/ACM, Research and Development in Information Retrieval, 6th International Conference, Washington DC,* Kuehn J J, ed.
ACM, New York, 1983

DAVIS E A
The form and function of children's questions.
Child Development, 3, 1932, pp 51-74

DAVIS R
Interactive transfer of expertise: acquisition of new inference rules.
Artificial Intelligence, 12, 1979, pp 121-157

DE KLEER J, DOYLE J, STEELE G L and SUSSMAN G J
Explicit control of reasoning.
In: *Artificial intelligence: an MIT perspective,* Winston P J and Brown R H, eds.
MIT Press, Cambridge, Mass., 1979, pp 93-116

De MEY M
The cognitive viewpoint: its development and its scope.
In: *International Workshop on Cognitive Viewpoint, 24-26 March 1977, University of Ghent,* De Mey M, ed.
University of Ghent, 1977

De MEY M
The relevance of the cognitive paradigm for information science.
In: *Theory and application of information research. Proceedings of the 2nd International Research Forum in Information Science, IRFIS2, Copenhagen, Aug. 3-6, 1977,* Harbo O and Kajberg L, eds.
Mansell, London, 1980

DERVIN B
Information as a user construct: the relevance of perceived information needs to synthesis and interpretation.
In: *Knowledge structure and use: perspectives on synthesis and interpretation,* Ward S and Reed L, eds.

Report prepared for Research and Educational Practice Unit, National Institute of Education and Cemrel Inc., St Louis, Miss., March 1980, 40 pp

DERVIN B, *et al*
The development of strategies for dealing with the information needs of urban residents: Phase I - citizen study. ED 125 640.
University of Washington, Seattle, 1976

DERVIN B, *et al*
The development of strategies for dealing with the information needs of urban residents: Phase 2 — information practitioner study. ED 136 791.
University of Washington, Seattle, 1977

DIJKSTRA E W
A note on the two problems in connection with graph.
Numerische Mathematik, 1, 1959, pp 269-271

DIJKSTRA E W
Guarded commands, nondeterminacy and formal derivation of programs.
Communications of the Association For Computing Machinery, 18 (8), 1975, pp 453-457

DOYLE L B
Semantic roadmaps for literature searchers.
Journal of the Association for Computing Machinery, 8, 1961, pp 553-578

DOYLE L B
Information retrieval and processing.
Melville Publishing Company, Los Angeles, 1975

EASON K D
Dialogue design implications of task allocation between man and computer.
Ergonomics, 23(9), September 1980, pp 881-891

EDMONDSON N
Spoken discourse.
Longmans, London, New York, 1981

ELLIS A B and TEIDEMAN D V
Can a machine counsel? Information system for vocational decisions.

212

Project Report No. 17, CEEB-SSRC Conference on Computer based Instruction, Learning, Testing and Guidance, Austin, Texas, 21-22 October 1968, 41pp

FARRADANE J
The evaluation of information retrieval systems
Journal of Documentation, 30, 1974, pp 195-209

FEIGENBAUM E A, BUCHANAN B G and LEDERBERG J
On generality and problem solving: a case study using the DENDRAL program.
In: *Machine Intelligence 6*, Meltzer B and Michie D, eds.
Edinburgh University Press, 1971

FEIGENBAUM E A, ENGELMORE R S and JOHNSON C K
A correlation between crystallographic computing and artificial intelligence research.
Acta Crystallographica, A33, 1977, p 13

FENICHEL C H
The process of searching online bibliographic databases: a review of research.
Library Research, 2(2), Summer 1980, pp 107-127

FENICHEL C H
An examination of the relationship between searching behaviour and searcher background.
Online Review, 4(4), 1980, pp 341-347

FENICHEL C H
Methodologies available for studying the man-machine interaction in online systems.
In: *Proceedings 1st National Online Information Meeting, New York, March 25-27 1980*

FENICHEL C H
Intermediary searchers' satisfaction with the results of their searches.
In: *Communicating information. Proceedings of the 43rd Annual Meeting ASIS, Anaheim, Ca., 1980*, Benefeld A R and Kazlauskas E J, eds.
Knowledge Industry Publications, White Plains, NY, 1980, pp 58-60

FENICHEL C H
Online searching: measures that discriminate among users with different types of experiences.

Journal of the American Society for Information Science, 32(1), 1981, pp 24-32

FENICHEL C H, ed
Changing patterns in information retrieval: 10th Annual National Information Retrieval Colloquium, Philadelphia, 1973.
American Society for Information Science, Washington, DC, 1974

FENICHEL C H and HOGAN T H
Online searching: a primer.
Learned Information Inc., New York, 1981, 160 pp

FIDEL R
Operationalist and conceptualist searcher: a case study based pattern model of online searching styles.
In: *The information community: an alliance for progress. Proceedings of the 44th Annual Meeting ASIS, Washington, DC, 1981,* Lunin L F *et al,* eds.
Knowledge Industry Publications, White Plains, NY, 1981, pp 68-70

FIDEL R and SOERGEL D
Factors affecting online bibliographic retrieval: a conceptual framework for research.
Journal of the American Society for Information Science, 34(3),1983, pp 163-180

FILLENBAUM S
Recall for answers to 'conductive' questions.
Language and Speech, 11, 1968, pp 46-53

FILLENBAUM S
Processing and recall of compatible and incompatible question and answer pairs.
Language and Speech, 14, 1971, pp 256-265

FRANCILLON M
Information retrieval: a view from the reference desk.
Journal of Documentation, 15 (4), 1959, p 187

FRANCOZ M J
The logic of question and answer: writing as inquiry.
College English, 41(3), November 1979, pp 336-339

FURAKAWA K
A deductive question answering system on relational databases.
IJCAI, 5*, 1977, pp 59-66

GAGNE R M
Conditions of learning.
Holt, Rinehart and Winston, New York, 1970

GAINES B R
From ergonomics to the Fifth Generation: 30 years of human-computer interaction studies.
In: *INTERACT '84, Proceedings of the 1st IFIP Conference on Human Computer Interaction.*
IFIP/Elsevier, Amsterdam, 1984

GALLAIRE H and MINKER J, eds.
Logic and databases.
Plenum, New York, 1978

GARNER W R
Uncertainty and structure as psychological concepts.
J Wiley, New York, 1962

GASCHNIG J
Preliminary performance analysis of the PROSPECTOR consultant system for mineral exploration.
In: *Proceedings of the 6th International Joint Conference on Artificial Intelligence, Tokyo, 1979.*
IJCAI, 1979, pp 308-310

GASCHNIG J
An application of the PROSPECTOR system to DOE's national uranium resource evaluation.
In: *Proceedings of the First Annual National Conference on Artificial Intelligence, Stanford, 1980.*
AAAI,1980, pp 295-297

GAVRYCK J
Applying task group research to the information retrieval interview.
Behaviour and Social Science Librarian, 2, Spring 1982, pp 31-38

*Proceedings of the 5th International Joint Conference on Artificial Intelligence.

GAVRYCK J and HAMMER M M
The theoretical views of the online reference interview. Part 1. Search analysts as successful librarians. Part 2. Applying task group research to the information retrieval interview.
Behaviour and Social Science Librarian, 1982, 2(2-3), pp 21-29 and 31-37

GOFFMAN E
Frame analysis.
Harper and Row, New York, 1974

GOFFMAN W
An indirect method of information retrieval.
Information Storage and Retrieval, 4(4), 1969, pp 361-373

GORDON D and LAKOFF G
Conversational postulates.
In: *Papers from the 7th Regional Meeting of the Chicago Linguistic Society, Chicago, 1971.*
Reprinted in: *Syntax and semantics 3: Speech acts,* Cole P and Morgan J L, eds.
Academic Press, New York, 1975, pp 83-106

GORRY G A, SILVERMAN H and PAUKER S G
Capturing clinical expertise: a computer program that considers clinical responses to digitalis.
American Journal of Medicine, 64, 1978, pp 452-460

GOTHBERG H M
Communication patterns in library reference and information services.
Reference Quarterly, 13, 1973, pp 7-13

GOTHBERG H M
User satisfaction with a librarian's immediate and non-immediate verbal-nonverbal communication.
Doctoral dissertation, University of Denver, 1974

GOTHBERG H M
Immediacy: a study of communication effect on the reference process.
Journal of Academic Librarianship, 2, 1976, pp 126-129

GOWER J C
Maximal predictive classification.
Biometrics, 30, 1974, pp 643-654

216

GREEN B F, WOLF A R, CHOMSKY C and LAUGHERY K
BASEBALL: an automatic question answerer.
In: *Computers and thought,* Feigenbaum E A and Feldman J, eds.
McGraw-Hill, New York, 1963

GREEN C
Theorem proving by resolution as a basis of question-answering
systems.
In: *Machine Intelligence 4,* Meltzer B and Michie D, eds.
Edinburgh University Press 1969, pp 183-205

GRICE H P
Logic and conversation.
In: *Syntax and semantics 3: Speech acts,* Cole P and Morgan J L, eds.
Academic Press, New York, 1975, pp 41-51

GROSZ B J
The representation and use of focus in dialogue understanding.
PhD thesis, University of California, Berkeley, 1977

GROSZ B J
Discourse knowledge.
In: *Understanding spoken language,* Walker D E, ed.
North-Holland, Amsterdam, 1978, pp 229-346

HAAS N and HENDRIX G G
An approach to acquiring and applying knowledge.
In: *Proceedings of the First Annual National Conference on Artificial
Intelligence, Stanford, 1980.*
AAAI, 1980, pp 235-239

HAMBLIN C L
Questions.
In: *Encyclopedia of philosophy,* Vol.7, Edwards P, ed.
Macmillan, New York, 1967, pp 49-53

HAMBLIN C L
Mathematical models of dialogue.
Theoria, 37, 1971, pp 130-155

HAMMER M M
Search analysts as successful reference librarians.
Behaviour and Social Science Librarian, 2, Spring 1982, pp 21-30

HARPER D and VAN RIJSBERGEN C J
An evaluation of feedback in document retrieval using co-occurrence data.
Journal of Documentation, 34(3), September 1978, pp 189-216

HARRAH D
A logic of questions and answers.
Philosophy of Science, 28, 1961, pp 40-46

HARRAH D
Communication: a logical model.
MIT Press, Cambridge, Mass., 1963

HARRAH D
The logic of questions and its relevance to instructional science.
Instructional Science, 1, 1973, pp 447-467

HARRIS L R
ROBOT: a high performance natural language processor for database query,
SIGART Newsletter, 61, 1977, pp 39-40

HART P E
What's preventing the widespread use of expert systems?
In: *Proceedings of the 1st Expert Systems Workshop, San Diego, 1980*

HAWES L C
The effects of interview style on patterns of dyadic communication.
Speech Monographs, 34, 1972, pp 114-123

HAYES P
Expanding the horizons of natural language. Parasession on topics in interactive discourse.
In: *Proceedings of the Association of Computational Linguistics,* 1980, pp 71-74

HAYES P and REDDY R
An anatomy of graceful interaction in spoken and written man-machine communication
Carnegie-Mellon University Report No. CMU-CS-79-144, September 1979

HEISER J F, BROOKS R E and BALLARD J P
A computerized psychopharmacology advisor. Progress report.

In: *Proceedings of the 11th Collegium Internationale Neuro-Psychopharmacologicum, Vienna, 1978*

HENDRIX G G
The LIFER manual: a guide to building practical natural language interfaces.
SRI International, AI Center, Technical Note No.138, 1977

HICK W E
On the rate of gain in information.
Quarterly Journal of Experimental Psychology, 4, 1952, pp 11-26

HILTZ S R, JOHNSON K and RABKE A M
The process of communication in face-to-face vs computerized conferences: a controlled experiment using Bales interaction process analysis. Parasession on topics in interactive discourse.
In: *Proceedings of the Association of Computational Linguistics,* 1980, pp 75-79

HINTIKKA K J J
Logic, language-games and information.
Clarendon Press, Oxford, 1973

HITCHINGHAM E E
Online literature searching.
Special Libraries, 64(12), 1973, pp 6A-9A

HITCHINGHAM E E
Selecting measures applicable to evaluation of online literature searching.
Drexel Library Quarterly, 13(3), 1977, pp 52-67

HITCHINGHAM E E
User evaluation of online searching: categorization of elements in user evaluation forms.
Mid-Year Conference, ASIS, Rice University, Houston, Tx, 1978, 22 pp

HITCHINGHAM E E
A study of the relationship between the search interview of the intermediary searcher and the online system user, and the assessment of search results as judged by the user. Final report.
Bureau of School Systems, Washington, DC, Office of Libraries and Learning Resources, (EDRS ED-180478), August 1979, 107 pp (a)

HITCHINGHAM E E
Online interviews: charting user and searcher interaction patterns.
In: *Information choices and policies. Proceedings of the 42nd Annual Meeting ASIS, Minneapolis, 1979, New York,* Tally R D and Dueltgen R R, eds.
Knowledge Industry Publications, White Plains, NY, 1979, pp 66-74
(b)

HOLLNAGEL E
Qualitative aspects of man-machine communication.
RISO National Laboratory, RISO-M-2114, Electronics Department, June 1978

HOLLNAGEL E
The relation between intention, meaning and action.
In: *Informatics 5. The analysis of meaning, March 25-28, 1979, Oxford,* Gray K I and MacCafferty M, eds.
Aslib, London, 1979, pp 135-147

HOLLNAGEL E and WOODS D D
Cognitive systems engineering: new wine in new bottles.
International Journal of Man-Machine Studies, 18, 1983, pp 583-600

HORN R
Why they don't ask questions.
Reference Quarterly, 13(3), Spring 1974, pp 125-133

HORNE E E
Question and communication.
In: *Communicating information. Proceedings of the 43rd Annual Meeting ASIS,* Anaheim. Ca., 1980, Benenfeld A R and Kazlauskas E, eds., pp 143-145

HOVLAND C I
A 'communication analysis' of concept learning.
Psychological Review, 59, 1952, pp 461-472

HUTCHINS M
Introduction to reference work.
American Library Association, Chicago, 1944

HYMES D
Models of the interaction of language and social life.
In: *Directions in sociolinguistics,* Gumperz J and Hymes D, eds.
Holt, Rinehart and Winston, New York, 1972, pp 35-71

IDE E
New experiments in relevance feedback.
In: *The SMART retrieval system — experiments in automatic document processing,* Salton G, ed.
Prentice-Hall, Englewood Cliffs, NJ, 1971, pp 337-354

IDE E and SALTON G
Interactive search strategies and dynamic file organization.
In: *The SMART retrieval system — experiments in automatic document processing,* pp 373-393

INGWERSEN P
Search analysed from the cognitive point of view.
Journal of Documentation, 38(3), 1982, pp 165-191

INGWERSEN P and KAAE S
User-librarian negotiations and information search procedures in public libraries: analysis of verbal protocols. Final research report.
Research Report, Copenhagen, Royal School of Librarianship, 1980, 117 pp, (EDRS ED-211051)

JAHODA G
Reference question analysis and search strategy development by man and machine.
Journal of the American Society for Information Science, 25(3), May 1974, pp 139-144

JAHODA G
Instruction in negotiating the reference query.
Florida State University, School of Library Science Report, 25 August, 1975, 17 pp (Sponsor: Office of Education), (EDRS ED-111421)

JAHODA G
The process of answering reference questions: a test of a descriptive model.
US Department of Health, Education and Welfare, 1977

JAHODA G and BRAUNAGEL J S
The libraries and reference queries.
Academic Press, New York, 1980

JAHODA G and OLSON P E
Analyzing the reference process.
Reference Quarterly, 12(2), 1972, pp 148-156

JAMIESON S H
The economic implementation of experimental retrieval techniques on
a very large scale using an intelligent terminal.
In: *SIGIR/ACM 2nd International Conference Information Storage
and Retrieval,* Dallas, Texas, 27-28 September 1979

JAMIESON S H and ODDY R N
Implementation and evaluation of interactive retrieval through an
intelligent terminal.
Project proposal to BLRDD, University of Aston in Birmingham,
June 1979, 24 pp

JEFFERSON G
Side sequences.
In: *Studies in social interaction,* Sudnow D, ed.
The Free Press, New York, 1972, pp 294-338

JOSEL N A
Ten reference commandments.
Reference Quarterly, 11(2), 1971, pp 146-147

KATZ H A, WARRICK P and GREENBERG M H
Introductory psychology through science fiction.
Rand McNally, Chicago, 1974

KATZ J J and POSTAL P M
An integrated theory of linguistic universals.
MIT Press, Cambridge, Mass., 1964

KATZ W A
*Introduction to reference work. 3rd ed. Vol.2: Reference services and
reference processes.*
McGraw Hill, New York, 1978, 288pp

KAY M and SPARCK JONES K
Automated language processing.
Annual review of information science and technology, 6, 1971,
pp 141-166

KAZLAUSKAS E
An exploration study: a kinesic analysis of academic
library public service points.
Journal of Academic Librarianship, 2, 1976, pp 130-134

KEARSLEY G P
Question asking as cognitive modelling.
Center for Advanced Study in Theoretical Psychology, Progress Paper
250A, 1975

KEARSLEY G P
Questions and question-asking in verbal discourse: a cross-disciplinary
review.
Journal of Psychological Research, 5(4), 1976, pp 355-375

KELLOGG C H, KLAHR P and TRAVIS L
Deductive planning and pathfinding for relational databases.
In: *Logic and databases,* Gallaire H and Minker J, eds.
Plenum, New York, 1978

KEMENY J G
A logical measure function.
Journal of Symbolic Logic, 18, 1953, pp 289-308

KEMP D A
Relevance, pertinence and information-system development.
Information Storage and Retrieval, 10, 1974, pp 37-47

KING D W, ed.
Key papers in the design and evaluation of information systems.
Knowledge Industry Publications, White Plains, NY, 1978

KING D W and PALMOUR V E
User behaviour.
In: *Changing patterns in information retrieval: 10th Annual National
Information Retrieval Colloquium, Philadephia, 1973.*
ASIS, Washington, DC, 1974, pp 7-33

KING G B
The reference interview.
Reference Quarterly, 12(2), 1972, pp 157-160

KING J I
Query optimization by semantic reasoning.
PhD thesis, Report No.CS-81-857, Computer Science Department,
Stanford University, 1981

KINTSCH W
Memory and cognition.
J Wiley, New York, 1978

KIRSCH R A
Computer interpretation of English text and picture patterns.
IEEE Transactions on Electronic Computers, EC-13, 4, 1957, pp 363-376

KIRSCH R A, CAHN A, RAY C and URBAN G H
Experiments in processing pictorial information with a digital computer.
In: *Proceedings of the Eastern Joint Computer Conferences,* 1957, pp 221-229

KNAPP S D
The reference interview in the computer-based setting.
Reference Quarterly, 17(4), 1978, pp 320-324

KOCHEN M and BADRE A N
Questions and shifts of representation in problem-solving.
American Journal of Psychology, 87(3), September 1974, pp 369-383

KRAFT D H and BOOKSTEIN A
Evaluation of information retrieval systems: a decision theory approach.
Journal of the American Society for Information Science, 21, 1978, pp 31-40

KRAFT D H and WALLER W G
A Bayesian approach to user stopping rules for information retrieval systems.
Information Processing and Management, 17, 1981, pp 349-361

KUBINSKI T
Essay in the logic of questions.
In: *Atti del XII Congress Internazionale de Filosofia, Venezia 1958,* pp 315-322

KUBINSKI T
Wstep do logicznej teorii pytan.
Panstwowe Wydawnictwo Naukowe, Warsaw, 1970

KUNZ J C, FALLAT R J, McCLUNG D H, OSBORN J J, VOTERI B A, NII H P, ATKINS J S, FAGAN L and FEIGENBAUM E A
A physiological rule-based system for interpreting pulmonary function test results.
Report No.HHP-78-19, Heuristic Program Project, Computer Science Department, Stanford University, 1978

LABOV W
Rules for ritual insults.
In: *Studies in social interaction,* Sudnow D, ed.
The Free Press, New York, 1972, pp 120-169

LABOV W and FANSHEL D
Therapeutic discourse.
Academic Press, New York, 1977

LACHMAN R and LACHMAN J L
Cognitive psychology.
Erlbaum, Hillsdale, NJ, 1979

LANCASTER F W
MEDLARS — report on the evaluation of its operating efficiency.
American Documentation, 20, 1969, pp 119-142

LANG R
Questions: structure and semantic studies.
PhD thesis, Australian National University, 1970

LEDERBERG J
*DENDRAL-64: a system for computer construction, enumeration and
notation of organic molecules as tree structures and cyclic graphs. Part
1. Notation algorithm for tree structures.*
NASA, Report No.CR-57029, 1964

LEDERER K, ed. with GALTUNG J and ANTAL D
Human needs, a contribution to the current debate.
Oelgeschlagen, Gunn & Hain, Cambridge, Mass., 1980

LEHNERT W G
The process of question-answering.
PhD thesis, Yale University, 1977, 293 pp. Research Report No. 88
(Sponsored by Advanced Research Projects, Washington DC,
No.N00014-75-C-1111), (EDRS ED-150955)

LEHNERT W G
The process of question answering: a computer simulation of cognition
Erlbaum, Hillsdale, NJ, 1978

LEHNERT W G
Question answering in natural language processing.
In: *Natural language question-answering systems,* Bolc L, ed.
Carl Hanser Verlag, Munich, Macmillan, London, 1980, pp 9-72

LEHNERT W G
A computational theory of human question answering.
In: *Elements of discourse understanding.*
Cambridge University Press, Cambridge, 1981 pp 145-176

LIN N and GARVEY W D
Information needs and uses.
Annual review of information science and technology,
7, 1972, pp 5-37

LINDSAY P H and NORMAN D A
Memory processes.
In: *Human information processing. 2nd ed.*
Academic Press, New York, 1977

LINDSAY R, BUCHANAN R S, FEIGENBAUM E A and
LEDERBERG J
DENDRAL.
McGraw-Hill, New York, 1980

LINDSAY R K
A program for parsing sentences and making inferences about kinship
relations.
In: *Symposium on simulation models: methodology and applications
to the behavioral sciences.*
South-Western Publications, Cincinnati, 1963

LIPETZ B A
Information storage and retrieval.
Scientific American, 215, 1966, pp 19-26

LOFTUS G R and LOFTUS E F
Human memory.
Halsted Press, New York, 1976

LOTKA A J
Elements of physical biology.
William and Wilkins, Baltimore, 1924

LUK W S, SIU M K and YU C T
On models of information retrieval processes.
Information Systems, 4(3), 1979, pp 205-218

LYNCH M J
Reference interviews in public libraries.

Library Quarterly, 48, 1978, pp 119-142

McCORDUCK P
Machines who think: a personal inquiry into the history and prospects of artificial intelligence.
W H Freeman, San Francisco, 1979

MacKAY D M
The informational analysis of questions and commands.
In: *Proceedings of the 4th London Symposium on Information Theory, September 1960,* Cherry E C, ed.
Butterworths, London, 1961, pp 469-476

MAGUIRE M
An evaluation of published recommendations on the design of man-computer dialogues.
International Journal of Man-Machine Studies, 16, 1982, pp 236-261

MARCUS R S
Investigations of computer-aided document search strategies.
MIT Laboratory for Information and Decision Systems, Report LIDS-R-1333, September 1982 (a)

MARCUS R S
User assistance in bibliographic retrieval networks through a computer intermediary.
IEEE Transactions on Systems, Man, and Cybernetics, SCM-12(2), 1982, pp 116-133 (b)

MARKEY K
Levels of question formulation in negotiation of information need during the online pre-search interview: a proposed model.
Information Processing and Management, 17(5), 1981, pp 215-225

MARKEY K and ATHERTON P
ONTAP — online training and practice manual for Eric database searchers.
Eric Clearinghouse on Information Resources, New York, Report ED 160 109, 1979

MARON M E and KUHNS J L
On relevance, probabilistic indexing and information retrieval.
Journal of the Association for Computing Machinery, 7 (3), July 1960, pp 216-244

MARTYN J
Information needs and uses.
Annual review of information science and technology,
9, 1974, pp 3-23

MEADOW C T
Individualized instruction for data access.
Drexel University, Philadelphia, 1977

MEADOW C T
The computer as a search intermediary.
Online, 3(3), July 1979, pp 54-59

MEADOW C T and COCHRANE P
Basics of online searching.
J Wiley, New York, 1981, 245 pp

MEADOW C T, HEWITT T T and AVERSA E S
A computer intermediary for interactive database searching. Part I:
Design, Part II: Evaluation.
Journal of the American Society for Information Science 33, 1982,
pp 325-332, 357-364

MEYER W J and SHANE J
The form and function of children's questions.
Journal of Genetic Psychology, 123(1), 1973, pp 285-296

MICHIE D
The machine representation of knowledge.
Reidel, Dordrecht, Holland, 1976

MILLER R A, POPLE H E and MEYERS J D
INTERNIST-I: an experimental computer-based diagnostic
consultant for general internal medicine
New England Journal of Medicine, 307(8), 1982, pp 468-476

MINKER J
An experimental relational database system based on logic.
In: *Logic and databases,* Gallaire H and Minker J, eds.
Plenum, New York, 1978

MINSKY M, ed.
Semantic information processing.
MIT Press, Cambridge, Mass., 1968

MISHLER E G
Studies in dialogue and discourse: II. Types of discourse initiated by
and sustained through questioning.
Journal of Psycholinguistic Research, 4(2), 1975, pp 99-121

MORAN T P
Guest editor's introduction: an applied psychology of the user. (Special
issue on: The psychology of human-computer interaction.)
ACM Computing Surveys, 13(1), 1981, pp 1-11

MORROW D I
A generalized flowchart for the use of ORBIT.
Information Storage and Retrieval, 27, 1976, pp 57-62

MUECKSTEIN E M M
Q-TRANS: Query translation into English
In: *Proceedings of the 8th International Joint Conference on Artificial
Intelligence, Karlsruhe, 8-12 August 1983.*
IJCAI, 1983, pp 660-662

MUNOZ J L
The significance of nonverbal communication in the reference
interview.
Reference Quarterly, 16, 1977, pp 220-234

MYLOPOULOS J, BERNSTEIN P A and WONG H K T
A language facility for designing database-intensive applications.
Association for Computing Machinery, 5, 1980, pp 185-207

NEILL S D
Problem-solving and the reference process.
Reference Quarterly, 14(4), 1975, pp 310-315

NEUMANN J von
The computer and the brain.
Yale University Press, 1958

NEWELL A, SHAW J C and SIMON H A
Chess-playing programs and the problem of complexity.
IBM Journal of Research and Development, 2, 1958, pp 320-355

NEWELL A and SIMON H A
*Human problem solving: a new approach to psychology of human
problem solving based on detailed analyses of human behaviour and*

basic studies of the information processing systems.
Prentice Hall, Englewood Cliffs, NJ, 1972

NEWELL A and SIMON H A
Computer science as empirical inquiry: symbols and search.
Communications of the Association for Computing Machinery, 19(3),
March 1976, pp 113-126

NILSSON N J
Learning machines: foundations of trainable pattern-classifying
systems.
McGraw-Hill, New York, 1965

NILSSON N J
Principles of artificial intelligence.
Tioga Publishing Company, Palo Alto, Ca., 1980

NOREALT T, KOLL M and McGILL M
Automatic ranked input from Boolean searches in SIRE.
Journal of the American Society for Information Science, 28(6), 1977,
pp 333-341

NORMAN D A
Steps towards cognitive engineering: design rules based on analyses
of human error.
In: *Proceedings of the Human Factors in Computer Systems*
Conference, New York.
ACM, New York, March 1982

ODDY R N
Reference retrieval based on user-induced dynamic clustering.
PhD thesis, University of Newcastle upon Tyne, 1975

ODDY R N
Information retrieval through man-machine dialogue.
Journal of Documentation, 33(1), March 1977, pp 1-14 (a)

ODDY R N
Retrieving references by dialogue rather than by query formulation.
Journal of Informatics, 1(1), April 1977, pp 37-53 (b)

ORGASS R J
Logic and question answering.
IBM Thomas Watson Research Center, Yorktown Heights, 1970

PAISLEY W J
Information needs and uses.
Annual review of information science and technology, 3, 1968, pp 1-30

PARSONS T
Societies: evolutionary and comparative perspectives.
Prentice-Hall, Englewood Cliffs, NJ, 1966

PATIL R S, SZOLOVITS P and SCHWARTZ W B
Information acquisition in diagnosis.
In: *Proceedings AAA1-82,* pp 345-348

PAUKER S, GORRY G A, KASSIRER J and SCHWARTZ W
Towards the simulation of clinical cognition.
American Journal of Medicine, 60, 1976, pp 981-996

PECK T
Counseling skills applied to reference services.
Reference Quarterly, 14, 1975, pp 233-235

PEJTERSEN A M
Design of a classification scheme for fiction.
In: *Theory and application of information research. Proceedings of the 2nd International Research Forum in Information Science, IRFIS 2,* Copenhagen, 3-6 August, 1977, Harbo O and Kajberg L, eds. Mansell, London, 1980

PHILLIPS A V
A question-answering routine.
Memo 16, AI Project, MIT, Cambridge, Mass., May 1960

PIAGET J
The language and thought of the child.
Routledge and Kegan Paul Ltd., London, 1926, 288pp

PIERCE W
Anxiety about the act of communicating and perceived empathy.
Psychotherapy: Theory, Research and Practice, 8, 1971, pp 120-123

PITTS W and McCULLOCH W S
A logical calculus of the ideas imminent in nervous activity.
Bulletin of Mathematical Biophysics, 5, 1943, p 115 on

PLAGEMANN S and WINDEL G
Beschreibung von Untersuchungen der Benutzerforschung.

Freie Universität Berlin, Dept. Commun. Report MIB.PI 7/81, 1981

POLLITT A S
End user touch searching for cancer therapy literature: rule based approach.
In: *SIGIR/ACM, Research and Development in Information Retrieval, 6th International Conference, Washington DC, 1983,* Kuehn J J, ed.
ACM, New York, 1983, pp 136-145

POLYA G
Mathematical discovery.
J Wiley, New York, 1962

PREECE S E
Clustering as an output option.
In: *Innovative developments in information systems. Proceedings of the 36th Annual Meeting of ASIS, Los Angeles 1973,* Waldron H J and Long F R, eds.
American Society for Information Science, Washington DC, 1973, pp 189-190

PREECE S E
An online associative query modification methodology.
Online Review, 4(4), 1980, pp 375-382

PRICE L E T
Functional and satisfaction analysis of information interaction dialogues.
MSc thesis, Department of Information Science, The City University, London, 1983

PRIOR M and PRIOR A
Erotetic logic.
Philosophical Review, 64, 1955, p 43

QUILLIAN M R
Semantic memory.
In: *Semantic information processing,* Minsky M, ed.
MIT Press, Cambridge, Mass., 1968, pp 216-270

QUILLIAN M R
The teachable language comprehender: a simulation program and theory of language.
Communications of the Association for Computing Machinery, 12(8), 1969, pp 459-476

RAMSEY H R and GRIMES J D
Human factors in interactive computer dialogue.
Annual review of information science and technology, 18, 1983, pp 29-59

RAPHAEL B
A computer program for semantic information retrieval.
In: *Semantic information processing*, Minsky M, ed.
MIT Press, Cambridge, Mass., 1968

RAPHAEL B
The thinking computer: mind inside matter.
W H Freeman, San Francisco, 1976, 322 pp

REICHMAN-ADAR R
Extended person-machine interface.
Artificial Intelligence, 22, 1984, pp 157-218

REITER R
On reasoning by default.
TINLAP-2, 1978, pp 210-218

REITER R
On closed world data bases
In: *Readings in artificial intelligence*, Webber B L and Nilsson N J, eds.
Tioga Publishing Company, Palo Alto, Ca., 1981, pp 119-140

REITMAN W R
Heuristic decision procedures, open constraints, and the structure of ill-defined problems.
In: *Human judgments and optimality*, Shelley M W and Bryan G D, eds.
J Wiley, New York, 1964

RICH E
User modelling via stereotypes.
Cognitive Science, 3, 1979, pp 329-354

ROBERTSON S E
The parametric description of retrieval tests, parts 1 & 2.
Journal of Documentation, 25, 1969, pp 1-27, 93-107

ROBERTSON S E
Letter to the editor.

Journal of the American Society for Information Science, 25, 1974, pp 208-209

ROBERTSON S E
The probabilistic character of relevance.
Information Processing and Management, 13, 1977, pp 247-251 (a)

ROBERTSON S E
Theories and models in information retrieval.
Journal of Documentation, 33, 1977, pp 126-148 (b)

ROBERTSON S E and SPARCK JONES K
Relevance weighting of search terms.
Journal of the American Society for Information Science, 27(3), May 1976, pp 129-146

ROBINSON W P and RACKSTRAW S J
A question of answers.
Routledge and Kegan Paul, London, 1972

ROSENBERG R S
Artificial intelligence and linguistics: a brief history of a one-way relationship.
Paper presented at the 1st Annual Conference of the Berkeley Linguistic Society, Berkeley, Ca., February 1975, 15pp (EDRS ED-108511)

ROSENBERG R S
Approaching discourse computationally: a review.
In: *Representation and processing of natural language,* Bolc L, ed.
Carl Hansen Verlag, Munich, 1980, pp 11-83

ROUSE W B and ROUSE S H
Human information seeking and design of information systems.
Information Processing and Management, 20(1-2), 1984, pp 129-138

ROUSSOPOULOS N D
A semantic network model of databases.
Computer Science Department, University of Toronto, 1977

RUMELHART D E
An introduction to human information processing.
J Wiley, New York, 1977

SACERDOTTI E D
A structure for plans and behavior.
Elsevier, New York, 1977

SACKS H
An initial investigation of the usability of conversational data for
doing sociology.
In: *Studies in social interaction,* Sudnow D, ed.
The Free Press, New York, 1972, pp 31-74

SACKS H, SCHEGLOFF E A and JEFFERSON G
A simplest systematics for the organization of turn-taking for
conversation.
Language, 50, 1974, pp 696-735

SALTON G
Dynamic information and library processing.
Prentice-Hall, Englewood Cliffs, NJ, 1975

SARACEVIC T
*The effect of question analysis and searching strategy on performance
of retrieval systems; selected results from an experimental study.*
Case Western Reserve University, Center for Docum. Communication
Research Report No. CSL-TR-15, May, 1968, 12 pp (EDRS
ED-029652)

SARACEVIC T
*An inquiry into testing of information retrieval systems. Comparative
Systems Laboratory final technical report, Part II: analysis of results.*
Case Western Reserve University, Cleveland, Report No. CSL-TR-
FINAL-11 1968, 204 pp. (Sponsored by Public Health Service,
Washington, DC), (EDRS ED-027042)

SARACEVIC T
Comparative effects of titles, abstracts, and full texts on relevance
judgements.
In: *Cooperative information societies. Proceedings of the 32nd Annual
Meeting ASIS, San Francisco, 1969,* North J B, ed.
American Society for Information Science, Washington DC, 1969,
pp 293-299

SARACEVIC T
The concept of relevance in information science: a historical review.
In: *Introduction to information science.* Saracevic T, ed.
Bowker, 1970, pp 111-151

SARACEVIC T
Selected results from an inquiry into testing of information retrieval
systems.
In: *Introduction to information science,* Saracevic T, ed.
Bowker, 1970, pp 665-681

SARACEVIC T
Ten years of relevance experimentation. A summary and synthesis of
conclusions.
In: *The information conscious society. Proceedings of the 33rd Annual
Meeting ASIS, Philadelphia, 1970,* North J B, ed.
American Society for Information Science, Washington DC, 1970,
pp 33-36

SARACEVIC T
Relevance: a review of and a framework for the thinking on the notion
in information science.
Journal of the American Society for Information Science, 26(6),
November 1975, pp 321-343

SARACEVIC T
Intellectual organization of knowledge: the American contribution.
Bulletin of the American Society for Information Science, 2 (8), March
1976, pp 16-17

SARACEVIC T
Problems of question analysis in information retrieval.
In: *The information age in perspective. Proceedings of the 41st Annual
Meeting ASIS, New York, 1978,* Brenner E H, ed.
Knowledge Industry Publications, White Plains, NY, 1978, pp 281-283

SARACEVIC T
Classification and structure of questions in information retrieval.
Research proposal.
School of Library Science, Case Western Reserve University,
Cleveland, Ohio, February 1980, 23pp. (Research proposal to the
Division of Information Science & Technology, National Science
Foundation, Washington, DC)

SCHANK R C
SAM — a story understander.
Department of Computer Science, Yale University, Research Report
No.43, 1975

SCHANK R C
Interestingness: controlling interfaces.
Artificial Intelligence, 12, 1979, pp 273-297

SCHANK R C
Language and memory.
Cognitive Science, 4, 1980, pp 243-284

SCHANK R C and ABELSON R P
Scripts, plans, goals and understanding.
Erlbaum, Hillsdale, NJ, 1977

SCHANCK R C, GOLDMAN N, RIEGER C and RIESBECK C
MARGIE: Memory, analysis, response generation and inference in
English.
IJCAI, 3*, 1975, pp 255-261

SCHEGLOFF E A
What type of interaction is it to be? Parasession on topics in interactive
discourse.
Proceedings of the Association of Computational Linguistics, 1980,
pp 81-82

SCOTT A C, CLANCEY W J, DAVIS R and SHORTLIFFE E H
Explanation capabilities of knowledge-based systems.
American Journal of Computational Linguistics, Microfiche 62, 1977

SEARLE J R
Speech acts: an essay in the philosophy of language.
Cambridge University Press, Cambridge, 1969

SHANNON C E
Algebra for theoretical genetics.
PhD thesis, MIT, 1940

SHANNON C E
Communication in the presence of noise.
Proc. Inst. Radio Engr., 37, 1949, pp 10-21

SHANNON C E
Prediction and entropy of printed English.
Bell System Technical Journal, 30(1), 1951, pp 50-65

*Proceedings of the 3rd International Joint Conference on Artificial
Intelligence.

SHANNON C E and WEAVER W
The mathematical theory of communication.
Bell System Technical Journal, 27, 1948, pp 379-414

SHAW D E
Knowledge-based retrieval on a relational database machine.
Computer Science Department, Stanford University, Report No.
TR-823, 1980

SHERIF M and SHERIF C W
Social psychology.
Harper and Row, New York, 1969

SHERMAN H B
A comparative study of computer-aided clinical diagnosis of birth defects.
MSc thesis, Laboratory of Computer Science, MIT, 1981

SHNEIDERMAN B
Software psychology: human factors in computer and information systems.
Winthrop, Cambridge, Mass., 1980 (a)

SHNEIDERMAN B
Natural vs. precise concise languages for human operation of computers: research issues and experimental approaches. Parasession on topics in interactive discourse.
Proceedings of the Association of Computational Linguistics, 1980, pp 139-141 (b)

SHORTLIFFE E H
Computer-based medical consultations: MYCIN.
Elsevier, New York, 1976

SIDNER C
Discourse and reference components of PAL.
In: *Frame conceptions and text understanding,* Metzing D, ed.
Walter de Gruyter, Berlin, 1980, pp 120-133

SIDOROV I G
Similarities and differences in problems of associative retrieval and pattern recognition.
Automatic Documentation and Mathematical Linguistics, 3, 1969, pp 61-65

SIMMONS R F
Storage and retrieval of aspects of meaning in directed graph
structures.
Communications of the Association for Computing Machinery, 9,
1966, pp 211-215

SIMMONS R F
Answering English questions by computer: a survey.
In: *The growth of knowledge: readings on organization and retrieval
of information,* Kochen M, ed.
J Wiley, New York, 1967, pp 264-291

SIMMONS R F
Natural language question-answering systems.
Communications of the Association for Computing Machinery, 13(1),
January 1970, p 17

SINCLAIR J M C H and COULTHARD R M
Towards an analysis of discourse.
Oxford University Press, London, 1975

SMITH L C
Artificial intelligence in information retrieval systems.
Information Processing and Management, 12(3), 1976, pp 189-222 (a)

SMITH L C
Artificial intelligence in retrieval systems as an alternative to human
intermediaries.
In: *Proceedings of the 5th ASIS Mid-Year Meeting. Compendium of
presentations, May 20-22, 1976.*
American Society for Information Science, Washington, DC, 1976,
pp 51-57 (b)

SMITH L C
*Selected artificial intelligence techniques in information retrieval
systems research.*
PhD thesis, Information Transfer, Graduate School, Syracuse
University, April 1979, 318 pp

SMITH L C
Implications of artificial intelligence for end user use of online systems.
Online Review, 4(4), 1980, pp 383-391 (a)

SMITH L C
Artificial intelligence: applications in information systems.

Annual review of information science and technology, 15, 1980, pp 67-105 (b)

SMITH L C
Machine intelligence vs. machine-aided intelligence in information retrieval: a historical perspective.
In: *SIGIR/ACM, Research and Development in Information Retrieval,* Berlin, 1982.
Springer-Verlag, Berlin, Heidelberg, New York, 1983, pp 263-274

SOERGEL D
Is user satisfaction a hobgoblin?
Journal of the American Society for Information Science, 27(4), July 1976, pp 256-259

SOMERVILLE A N
The place of the reference interview in computer searching.
Online, 1, 1977, pp 14-23

SOWA J F
Conceptual graphs for a database interface.
IBM Journal of Research and Development, 20, 1976, pp 336-357

SPARCK JONES K
Index term weighting.
Information Storage and Retrieval, 9, 1973, pp 619-633

SPARCK JONES K
Does indexing exhaustivity matter?
Journal of the American Society for Information Science, 24, 1973, pp 313-316

SPARCK JONES K
Search term relevance weighting given little relevance information.
Journal of Documentation, 35(1), 1979, pp 39-48

SPARCK JONES K, ed.
Information retrieval experiment.
Butterworths, London, 1981

SPARCK JONES K and BATES R G
Research on automatic indexing 1974-1976.
British Library Research and Development Report 5464, London, 1977

SPARCK JONES K and VAN RIJSBERGEN C J
Information retrieval test collections.
Journal of Documentation, 32, 1976, pp 59-75

SPERANTIA E
Remarques sur les propositions interrogatives.
Actes du Congrès International de Philosophie Scientifique, 1936

SPERBER D and WILSON D
Mutual knowledge and relevance in theories of comprehension.
In: *Mutual knowledge,* Smith N V, ed.
Academic Press, London, 1982, pp 61-85

STACHOWIAK H
Denken und Erkennen in kybernetischen Modell.
Springer, Vienna, New York, 1965

STAHL G
La logica de las preguntas.
Anuales de la Universidad de Chile, 102, 1956, pp 71-75

STIBIC V
Influence of unlimited ranking on practical online search strategy.
Online Review, 4(3), September 1980, pp 273-279

STUBBS M
Discourse analysis: the sociolinguistic analysis of natural language.
Blackwell, Oxford, 1983

SWARTOUT W
A digitalis therapy advisor with explanations.
IJCAI, 5, 1977, pp 819-823

SZOLOVITS P, ed.
Artificial intelligence in medicine. AAAS Selected Symposium.
Westview Press, Inc., 1982, 226pp

SZOLOVITS P and PAUKER S
Categorical and probabilistic reasoning in medical diagnosis.
AI Journal, 11, 1978, pp 115-154

TAGLIACOZZO R
Estimating the satisfaction of information users.
Bulletin of the Medical Library Association, 65(2), April 1977,
pp 243-249

TAYLOR R S
Question-negotiation and information-seeking in libraries. Studies in the man-system interface in libraries. Report No.3.
Lehigh University, Bethlehem, Pa, July, 1967, 88 pp, Report No. AD-659-468,(EDRS ED-015764)

TAYLOR R S
Question negotiation and information-seeking in libraries.
College and Research Libraries, 29(3), May 1968, pp 178-194

TESSIER J A
Satisfaction measures in presearch interviews.
Syracuse University, NY, April 1981, 31 pp. Report of the Presearch Interview Project. (Sponsor: National Library of Medicine, EDRS ED-205186)

TESSIER J A, ATHERTON P, and CROUCH W W
New measures of user satisfaction with computer-based literature searches.
Special Libraries, 68(11), November 1977, pp 383-389

THOMPSON F
English for the computer.
In: *Proceedings of AFIPS Conference.*
Spartan Books, Washington, 1966

TRIGOBOFF M L
IRIS: a framework for the construction of clinical consultation systems.
PhD thesis, Rutgers University, 1978

TRIGOBOFF M L and KULIKOWSKI C
IRIS: a system for the propagation of inferences in a semantic net.
IJCAI, 5*, 1977, pp 274-280

VanderBRUG G J and MINKER J
State-space, problem reduction and theorem proving — some relationships.
Communications of the Association for Computing Machinery, 18(2), 1976, pp 107-115

*Proceedings of the 5th International Joint Conference on Artificial Intelligence.

VanderBRUG G J
Problem representations and formal properties of heuristic search.
Information Sciences, vol.2, 1976, pp 279-307

VAN DIJK T A
Text and context.
Longmans, London, 1977

VAN MELLE W
A domain-independent production-rule system for consultation programs.
In: *Proceedings of the 6th International Joint Conference on Artificial Intelligence, Tokyo, 1979*
IJCAI, 1979, pp 923-925

VAN MELLE W, SHORTLIFFE E H and BUCHANAN B G
EMYCIN: a domain-independent system that aids in constructing knowledge-based consultation programs.
Machine Intelligence (Infotech State of the Art Report Series 9, no.3), 1981

VAN RIJSBERGEN C J
Information retrieval. 2nd ed.
Butterworths, London, 1979

VAN RIJSBERGEN C J
Retrieval effectiveness.
In: *Information retrieval experiment,* Sparck Jones K, ed.
Butterworths, London, 1981, pp 32-43

VAN RIJSBERGEN C J and SPARCK JONES K
A test for the separation of relevant and non-relevant documents in experimental retrieval collection
Journal of Documentation, 29, 1973, pp 251-257

VERNIMB C
Automatic query adjustment in document retrieval.
Information Processing and Management, 13(6), November 1977, pp 339-353

WALLER W G and KRAFT D H
A mathematical model of the weighted Boolean retrieval system.
Information Processing and Management, 15(5), 1979, pp 235-245

WALTZ D L
An English language question answering system for a large relational database.
Communications of the Association for Computing Machinery, 21, 1978, pp 526-539

WARNER E *et al*
Information needs of urban residents.
Westat Research, Baltimore, 1973, EDRS Report No.088 464

WEAVER W
Translation.
In: *Machine translation of languages,* Locke W N and Booth A D, eds.
Technical Press of MIT and Wiley, 1955

WEISS S M and KULIKOWSKI C A
EXPERT: a system for developing consultation models.
In: *Proceedings of the 6th International Joint Conference on Artificial Intelligence, Tokyo, 1979.*
IJCAI, 1979, pp 942-947

WEISS S M, KULIKOWSKI C A and SAFIR A
A model-based consultation system for the long-term management of glaucoma.
In: *Proceedings of the 5th International Joint Conference on Artificial Intelligence, 1977.*
IJCAI, 1977

WEIZENBAUM J
ELIZA: a computer program for study of natural language communication between man and machine.
Communication of the Association for Computing Machinery, 9, 1966, pp 36-45

WERSIG G
Information — Kommunikation — Dokumentation.
Verlag Dokumentation, Pullach bei München, 1971

WERSIG G
The problematic situation as a basic concept of information science in the framework of social sciences: a reply to BELKIN N J. Theoretical problems of informatics: new trends in informatics and its terminology.
FID 568.
Moscow, VINITI, 1979

WERSIG G *et al*
Information und Handeln. FUB-IFB 7/82.
Freie Universität Berlin, Projekt INSTRAT, Berlin, 1982

WHITE M D
Dimensions of the reference interview.
Reference Quarterly, 20, 1981, pp 373-381

WHITTEMORE B J and YOVITS M C
A generalized conceptual development for the analysis and flow of
information.
Journal of the American Society for Information Science, 24, 1973,
pp 221-231

WIENER N
Cybernetics.
MIT Technology Press, New York, 1948

WILENSKY R
Meta-planning: representing and using knowledge about planning in
problem solving and natural language understanding.
Cognitive Science, 5, 1981, pp 197-233

WILLIAMS P W
Intelligent access to online systems.
In: *Fourth International Online Information Meeting, London, 1980.*
Learned Information, Oxford, 1980, pp 397-407

WILSON D and SPERBER D
On Grice's theory of conversation.
In: *Conversation and discourse: structure and interpretation,* Werth
P, ed.
Croom Helm, London, 1981, pp 155-178

WILSON P
Situational relevance.
Information Storage and Retrieval, 9, 1973, pp 457-471

WILSON T D
On user studies and information needs.
Journal of Documentation, 37(1), March 1981, pp 3-15

WILSON T D and STREATFIELD D
Information needs in local authority social services departments: an

interim report on Project INISS.
Journal of Documentation, 33, 1977, pp 277-293

WINDEL G
Theorie. MIB PI 2/80.
Freie Universität Berlin, Institut für Publizistik und Dokumentations-
wissenschaft, Berlin, 1980

WINOGRAD T
Understanding natural language.
Academic Press, New York, 1972

WINOGRAD T
What does it mean to understand language?
Cognitive Science, 4, 1980, pp 209-241

WOODS W A
The lunar sciences natural language information system.
Bolt Beranek Newman, Cambridge, Mass., 1972

WRIGHT P
Some observations on how people answer questions about sentences.
Journal of Verbal Learning and Verbal Behavior, 11, 1972, pp 188-195

WYNN E
What discourse features aren't needed in online dialog. Parasession
on topics in interactive discourse.
Proceedings of the Association of Computational Linguistics, 1980,
pp 87-90

YOUNG J Z
Programs of the brain.
Oxford University Press, Oxford, 1978

YU C T and LUK W S
Analysis of effectiveness of retrieval in clustered files.
Journal of the Association for Computing Machinery, 24, 1977,
pp 607-622

ZADEH L A
Fuzzy sets.
Information and Control, 8, 1965, pp 338-353

Other reports

Library and Information Research (LIR) Reports may be purchased from Publications Sales Unit, British Library Lending Division, Boston Spa, Wetherby, West Yorkshire, LS23 7BQ, UK. Details of some other LIR Reports are given below.

LIR Report 20. Flowerdew, A D J, Oldman, C M and Whitehead, C M E. *The pricing and provision of information: some recent official reports.* August 1984, pp viii + 96. ISBN 0 7123 3029 1.

The purpose of this report is to examine the economic principles relevant to the issues raised in some recent reports considering the production and dissemination of information in electronic form. It also seeks to compare these principles with those stated or implied in the text of the reports and to draw any justifiable policy conclusions. Since the production and dissemination of information have some characteristics which resemble those of the production and dissemination of ordinary economic goods and services, some which resemble more closely those of other types of economic activity such as transport, and some features which can be considered unique, the authors examine whether this was being taken into account in these reports. They also try to establish whether new theoretical results were being used or new empirical evidence cited, which would have implications elsewhere.

LIR Report 23. *Information demand and supply in British industry 1977-1983.* October 1983. pp xxii+ 118. ISBN 0 7123 3033 X.

Between November 1982 and April 1983 a study was conducted into the effects of the current recession on the supply of technical and commercial information services in British industry. The purpose was to see how industrial information services have adjusted and to investigate how information providers outside industry have reacted to any changes in demand from industry. Questionnaires were distributed among 238 library and information service units in industry, and among 305 external information providers of various kinds. More than half of these provided responses that were analysed. There is evidence that the pattern of demand for, and supply of, information in British industry has changed substantially, and possibly permanently, since 1977.

LIR Report 24. Rudduck, J and Hopkins, D. *The sixth form and libraries: problems of access to knowledge.* July 1984. pp xii + 126. ISBN 0 7123 3034 8.

The concern of the project can be summarised in a statement by its director:

> It is about the transition of pupils to studentship ... moves from dependence on instruction to capacity for independent study — that kind of move depends on a change in the epistemology of the learner ... there must be a point when the person discovers something of the problematic nature of knowledge. Most people don't do that lower down [the school].

The project was designed as a multi-site case study programme involving teachers, students and librarians in 24 institutions covering a range of sixth form settings. The selection of institutions took account of the need to have access to different environmental and social settings and different levels of library provision. Interviews were the main method of data gathering, and they focused on a core of interrelated topics: academic study in the sixth form, pedagogy, books, libraries and the idea of independent learning.

LIR Report 25. Ratcliffe, F W with the assistance of Patterson, D. *Preservation policies and conservation in British libraries: report of the Cambridge University Library Conservation Project.* February 1984. pp xii + 134. ISBN 0 7123 3035 6.

The Cambridge Conservation Project had two immediate objectives: to establish the facts about preservation policies and practices in libraries in the UK and to identify the educational and training facilities available to librarians and practitioners. Nationwide surveys by questionnaires, interviews and seminars were among the methods used. The report makes recommendations for action in two areas, first within individual libraries, involving little or no additional expenditure and immediately applicable, secondly at a national level. Among the latter, the twin neeeds for cooperative action, for which no mechanism exists at present, and for a focal point for preservation,some sort of National Advisory and Research Çentre, are of prime importance. The status, funding and location of the latter need further clarification but involvement of the British Library in any such undertaking seems essential to its success.

LIR Report 26. Teskey, F N. *Information retrieval systems for the future.* October 1984. pp viii + 72. ISBN 0 7123 3037 2.

In the first part of the report, the author describes those functions of free-text information systems regarded as fundamental by a number of users. He then goes on to look at some existing and proposed hardware and software methods for implementing such systems. Finally, he proposes a design for a new information retrieval system. Methods of implementing such a system are discussed and some possible applications are outlined.

LIR Report 27. Barrett, R. *Further developments in optical disc technology and applications.* July 1984, pp viii + 34. ISBN 0 7123 3038 0.

During a visit to the USA in April 1983, the author updated information on current developments in optical disc technology and applications. He looked at developments in both the optical video disc and the digital optical recording disc. The data presented in the report are based on information given in the form of discussions and technical papers by staff of the Library of Congress, the National Library of Medicine and BRS Medical.

LIR Report 28. Templeton, R and Witten, A. *Study of cataloguing computer software: applying* AACR2 *to microcomputer programs.* August 1984. pp viii + 77. ISBN 0 7123 3041 0.

Using education as an example, this project established and tested some guidelines for the cataloguing of microcomputer software, based on an examination of Chapter 9 of *AACR2*. Over 200 programs were catalogued, in three stages, two interpretive and one of application. The results of the project include recommendations for bibliographic control, including guidelines for publishers, and for cataloguing standards, and a brief manual of practice for cataloguers.

LIR Report 29. Shackel, B and Pullinger, D J. *BLEND-1: background and developments.* December 1984. pp xiv + 155, ISBN 0 7123 3042 9.

The report describes a four-year experimental programme jointly organized by two universities and called the Birmingham and Loughborough Electronic Network Development (BLEND). The aims are to assess the cost, efficiency and subjective impact of an electronic communication system, and to explore and evaluate alternative forms of user communication through an electronic journal and information network.

LIR Report 30. Gadsden, S R and Adams, R J. *The administration of interlending by microcomputer.* December 1984, pp viii + 58. ISBN 0 7123 3044 5.

A systems analysis of some interlending departments was carried out and a questionnaire survey sent to a sample of British Library Lending Division users. From this a system specification was created and a number of software packages tested against this and other criteria. The selected package was tested against an experimental database, and a demonstration system set up.

LIR Report 31. Wilson, T D. *Office automation and information services: final report on a study of current developments.* March 1985. pp vi + 75 ISBN 0 7123 3045 3.

The report reviews the current developments in office automation and gives an impression of their impact on, and relevance to, information systems and services. The author conducted interviews with the managers of a number of the Department of Trade and Industry Office Automation test sites as well as in sites in the private sector.

LIR Report 32. Katzen, M. *Technology and communication in the humanities: training and services in universities and polytechnics in the UK.* March 1985. pp x + 121. ISBN 0 7123 3046 1.

A survey investigated the training provided for humanities students in locating reference sources; the extent of online searching for humanities users; the provision of instruction on techniques of oral and written presentation; and the availability and use of computers in the humanities.